Caretaking a New Soul

Writings on Parenting from
Thich Nhat Hanh to Z. Budapest

by
Anne Carson

THE CROSSING PRESS
FREEDOM, CALIFORNIA

Dedication

*To the memory of Katherine Griffin Carson (1914-1999),
and to David Price (1940-1999).*

For information on bulk purchases or group discounts for this and other Crossing Press titles, please contact our Special Sales Manager at 800/777-1048.
www.crossingpress.com

Library of Congress Cataloging-in-Publication Data

Spiritual parenting in the New Age
    Caretaking a new soul : writing on parenting from Thich Nhat Hanh to Z Budapest / [edited by] Anne Carson.
        p. cm.
    Originally published : c 1989.
    Includes index.
    ISBN 1-58091-018-1
    1. Parenting—Religious aspects. 2. Children—Religious life. 3. New Age movement. I. Carson, Anne, 1950 Dec. 16-
    [BL625.8.S65 1999]   98-55282
    291.4'41—dc21   CIP

Acknowledgments

"Suffering is Not Enough" from *Being Peace* by Thich Nhat Hanh, Copyright © 1987, reprinted by permission of Parallax Press; "The Education of the Buddhist Child" by Rev. Jiyu Kennett Roshi, Copyright © 1974, originally appeared in *Sufi Wings*, reprinted from *The Journal of the Zen Mission Society* by permission of the author; "How Parents Can Help a Child's Understanding of Spirituality" by John Ambarisa Mendell Shields appeared in a slightly different form in *Spiritual Mothering Journal*, reprinted by permission of the author and publisher; "Welcoming the New Mother" and "Self Dedication for Young Men" from *The Holy Book of Women's Mysteries, Part II* by Z Budapest, Copyright © 1980 by Zsuzsanna Emese Budapest, reprinted by permission of the author and Wingbow Press; "The Nursing Mother and Feminine Metaphysics" from *Listening to Our Bodies* by Stephanie Demetrakopoulos, Copyright © 1983 by Stephanie Demetrakopoulos, reprinted by permission of Beacon Press; "Brit Kedusha: a home ceremony for the birth of a daughter" by Ellen and Dana Charry, from *Sistercelebrations: Nine Worship Experiences*, ed. Arlene Swidler, Copyright © 1974, reprinted by permission of Fortress Press; "Turning Toward the Morning" by Rene Knight-Weiler, "Call It Something Else" and "Children and Angels" by Karey Solomon, all reprinted from *Spiritual Mothering Journal* by permission of the authors and publisher; "A Child Plants a Seed" by Joel Copenhagen originally appeared in the *Christian Science Monitor*, reprinted by permission of the author; "How to Be an Effective Nature Guide" from *Sharing Nature With Children* by Joseph Bharat Cornell, Copyright © 1979, reprinted by permission of Dawn Publications; excerpts from *Meditating With Children* by Deborah Rozman, Copyright © 1975, reprinted by permission of the author and the publisher, University of the

Table of Contents

Introduction to the Second Edition
by Anne Carson

Twelve years have passed since I was first handed my perfect, surprised-looking baby. The round little toddler of the book I called *Spiritual Parenting in the New Age* is now a willowy preteen nearly as tall as I am, running off to the school bus each morning with her jaunty hat and bouncing backpack. I have learned a great deal about spiritual life in the intervening years, as well as about parenting, although I still have a lot to learn about spiritual parenting.

To an even greater degree than when this book first appeared, spirituality is acknowledged as a vital force in American life—not just as the external practice of "religion," but as the true ground of all relations between people and the world. Catholic and mainline Christians by the thousands are rediscovering the practice of contemplative prayer and monastic forms of spiritual life; Buddhism continues to provide the basis of spiritual practice for many Americans; the mystical heritage of Judaism is studied by Jews and Gentiles alike; and the visibility of American Muslim, Hindu, and Sikh youth has prodded parents and educators to consider issues of religious and cultural diversity. The Goddess/Pagan movement has become both more visible as a distinct spiritual philosophy, and more integrated into traditional forms of practice. Many people incorporate forms of so-called New Age and/or Native American spirituality into their religious and political lives without explicitly identifying themselves as dedicated to those paths.

In her spiritual life (which ideally is the soup-stock of all life), much of my daughter's experience has been influenced by the community in which we live. Ithaca is a college town in the heart of the rural Finger Lakes region of upstate New York, and home to some 25,000 university students. Professors and scholars come to Ithaca from all over the world; many residents, however, are here simply because they came to visit friends and found it too congenial to leave. The *Utne Reader* named Ithaca "The Most Enlightened Community in America," an accolade that has made many a local lip curl, and my home town is notorious as a refuge for Birkenstock-wearing granola addicts. Yes, it's true—many of our children wear tie-dye, are vegetarian, and as likely as not have "weird parents" who take them along to meditation/prayer sessions, political action meetings, or on trips to Nepal. My daughter's elementary school even had a group for children of gay and lesbian parents. The Ithaca area supports Montessori and Waldorf schools, as well as an alternative middle/high school which is part of the public school system, and several Christian schools. Dozens of children are taught at home, by aging hippies as well as by conservatives.

As I observed when I first produced this book, children have their own agendas and cunningly resist being lumps of clay to be molded according to their parents' desires. My daughter Catherine is not particularly mystical, but she is a healthy, talented, bright, and loving girl whose sense of self-worth is entirely independent of the approval of boys. Her own spiritual forays have included the folklore of fairies (especially the Flower Fairy books by Cicely Mary Barnes), a collection of Catholic holy card images, the Touched by an Angel television series, and, unexpectedly, ancient Egypt. On her own she has become best friends with Kirsten, whose mother already had a copy of the first edition of this anthology, and Hannah, who was educated at the Waldorf School. Their mothers are devotees of Satya Sai Baba—so the girls know all about "weird parents."

In my enthusiasm as a new mother, I could hardly wait to try out my own (and others') good advice. Some of the activities contained in this guide have worked well with Catherine. On days off from school we sometimes had "Pagan School," in which I taught her subjects like spelling and social studies using Goddess literature. Children tend to think concretely, and thus respond more readily to the cultural artifacts of religion and folklore rather than to abstract concepts. The activity books by Amber K ("How a Pagan Priestess Parents Children") have been successful resources in this regard. Together we watch *Xena, Warrior Princess* and *Hercules*, and I provide low-key instruction in the historic and mythic themes portrayed, which often means correcting the inaccurate ways the ancient deities are depicted.

For some time we have been constructing little scenes for each pagan holyday, similar to Naomi Strichartz's "Shadow Boxes"—a farm/harvest scene for Lammas, flower fairies for May Day and Midsummer, "Mrs. Thaw" assuming control over the earth at Candlemas (Groundhog Day) as King Frost retreats into his crystal cave and the Root Children emerge from their homes beneath the ground. If Catherine doesn't grow up to be an architect, chef, or criminal mastermind, she has a great future as a set designer.

Perhaps the most successful implementation of the suggestions in this book has been in the area of nature awareness. In our community, environmental education is taken very seriously, and Catherine has attended summer camp offered by a local nature center where she is taught ecology and the principles of earth stewardship, and looks after goats and baby chicks. Since the age of six she has received a full dose of the natural world during family canoe trips in northern Quebec, where we sometimes go five or six days without seeing another person and are completely at the mercy of the Great Mother's wind and water, as well as our own wits. My husband David Price ("Growing with Plants") is an accomplished forager of wild foods and participates in an annual mushroom foray for amateur and professional mycologists. When Catherine was ten, she joined her dad for a weekend spent gathering, identifying, and tabulating the foray's haul of fungi, and brought home a toy gnome whose yarn garments had been colored with mushroom dyes. He now presides over the Nature Corner along with a pointy-hatted wise woman doll.

In the realm of healing, my daughter has found bodywork to be particularly helpful for emotional distress; she has received treatments from a practitioner of foot reflexology and acupressure, as well as from a Trager practitioner (who told me that her aura was full of holes and she needed more orange food). Rescue Remedy, flower essences, and the use of a special stone to "absorb" pain, as suggested by Diane Mariechild, have been helpful allies. In the past decade alternative and complementary medicine have come to be used by the majority of Americans, and even popular magazines like *Martha Stewart Living* and *Country Living* print articles promoting homeopathic remedies for minor illnesses. But Catherine has also received conventional medical care, including a visit to a neurologist during a period when she was seriously dysfunctional in school. He assured me with a smile, "It's all right, she's not a witch." Catherine almost retorted, "I am so!"

Of all the subjects discussed in these essays, the one which has ceased to be an abstract for our family is death, since as I write this, Catherine's father is living with advanced cancer. We do not know whether he will be alive to see the new edition of this book. All along we have informed our daughter of David's condition; the only thing we have not talked about is when he will die, for that is something we do not yet know, and children find it difficult to imagine past next week. But we have discussed the disposition of his body, and Catherine has developed strong opinions about where he should be buried, and will have contributions to make towards the rituals around his death.

Her first personal experience with death, apart from the passing of my cat, came not from the loss of an elderly relative but from the death of the eight-year-old son of a close friend of her father's, a boy just a few months older than she was. Peter was a happy, energetic, loving, and imaginative child who made the decision to be confirmed as a Roman Catholic when he was only in the second grade. Not long afterwards, he developed a lung infection from which he never recovered. At the funeral Catherine could barely comprehend that the small casket held Peter's body; she cried because everyone in the packed church was weeping. The impending loss of her father has given us an opportunity to discuss what happens after death, and she has even posed questions like, "What happens to mentally ill people when they die?" Our family's future is both certain and uncertain; I hope that I will have the spiritual resources to carry us through.

Since publishing *Spiritual Parenting in the New Age* I wrote a biography of the British teenage-novelist-turned-nun Caroline Glyn, whom I describe in the essay "The Magical Worldview: Can It Survive?" In trying to comprehend Caroline's spirituality I, too, began investigating the contemplative way, which in my usual eclectic style included participation in prayer/meditation groups inspired by the teachings of the Buddhist monk Thich Nhat Hanh ("Suffering Is Not Enough") and by the ecumenical monastic community in Taizé, France. Occasional attendance at the Episcopal church started out as research into the Anglican tradition but developed into meaningful religious expression. I have also been an ardent member of a women's meditation group which meets around the New Moons and the Pagan holy-days, and have added belly dancing to my spiritual practice.

But spiritual life is more than just returning to church or joining a group: the contributors to this anthology are people whose spirituality is an evolving organism. Some are travelling new paths: Wiccan priestess Margot Adler ("May Day") has found a comfortable framework in the Unitarian Church (a Pagan-friendly place); Diane Mariechild ("Sharing a Spiritual Path with Adolescents"), one of the foremothers of feminist spirituality, is deeply involved in Buddhist practice. In Ithaca there have been several attempts to form a permanent, inclusive women's spirituality circle, the upshot of which is that there are numerous small, overlapping groups rather than one quasi-institution. During one of these movements I met another "womanspirit" named Anne, who lived down the street from me and was homeschooling her three daughters. While Catherine was in kindergarten we attended a monthly New Moon circle for mothers and young daughters, at which the other Anne led singing and simple craft-making geared towards feminist pagan principles. Anne later conducted the "Cakes for the Queen of Heaven" programs on feminist spirituality at the local Unitarian church. Imagine my mild surprise when, several years later, I recognized her and her three daughters in the choir at the Episcopal church. I might have asked Anne, "What are you doing here?" but of course she would have replied, "The same thing you are."

The text of this edition of *Caretaking a New Soul* is as it stands in the first edition. In some ways it is of its time, the 1980s—before the "New Age" (a term which was actually coined decades ago) became dismissed by mainstream culture as a passing fad. The political climate has changed in some respects: the likelihood of nuclear war between superpowers has been replaced by the threat of bombings by domestic and foreign terrorists; journalists and scholars continue to warn about the depletion of the earth's resources; the fragility of the global web of life becomes manifest in violent storms and economic downturns. Interests change and evolve: for instance, the use of crystals for healing has diminished and is being replaced, or supplemented, by homeopathy and many forms of bodywork, such as aromatherapy and Reiki.

For this edition the original bibliography has been retained, although many of the books listed were published by small presses and are likely to be out of print, they are still available via interlibrary loan through your public library. I have appended an updated bibliography of like-minded parenting books published since the first edition. There is some wonderful material out there, including three other books entitled *Spiritual Parenting*.

To new parents: After a million years of human parenting, one would suppose that there would be a simple set of instructions for raising good children, as there should be for building a bridge or making bread. Yet humans have a thousand ways to build bridges or make bread, and as long as each child is a unique being, never before seen on the face of the earth, there will be a thousand ways to bring up children. Whatever you read in this or any other book, your child will find a way around it. As a new mother I wanted everything to be perfect, and the more imperfect things were, the unhappier I became, until I was willing to settle for "just regular." Seek the ideal, but don't insist on it. Diaper rash is only the beginning.

To parents of young children: Accept that no matter what religious/spiritual education you give your child, you are laying a trip on them, as we said in the Sixties. This used to be considered a bad thing. Actually, it's okay because the trip will evolve. We can examine our own upbringing and try to avoid the mistakes our parents made, even while we make new mistakes, but sometimes "Because I said so" sounds like a pretty good reason after all.

To parents of school-age children: "Being in the world" for your child also means "being in the world" as a parent, as you learn to deal with educational institutions and authorities. As with pregnancy and birth, no matter where you live or what your circumstances are, you and your child have options. These days both public and private schools find themselves so strapped for resources that they usually welcome the active input and involvement of parents. If you are concerned about the values and culture your children are exposed to at school—from peers as well as educators—you have every right to offer another way.

To the parents of preteens and adolescents: This may be the most important time for mothers to share the Divine Feminine with their daughters, as girls begin the transition from child to woman. They may actually find this an easier time to join their mothers in woman-centered gatherings. And don't overlook secular mother-daughter retreats such as those offered by Planned Parenthood. I leave it to fathers to find the most effective ways to nurture their sons into responsible manhood. Be prepared for adolescents to reject your ways and choose their own. That, too, is as it should be, as long as his or her basic interactions with others are caring and responsible. I have known some terrific teenagers with funky parents. They may roll their eyes at you, but they still love and need you. You are their rock—even if they think you're cracked.

Hopi women potters pray to the spirit of the pot before they begin to work with the clay, to call out the form that the pot spirit wishes to take. Sometimes our creations come out a bit lop-sided, or manifest forms we never intended. Still, babies continue to come into the world, and parents keep hoping to do it right this time. I have known parents who were deeply moral, kind, and wise people, who managed to convey values of strength and love without practicing any religion at all. They were not vocal atheists; they simply told their children, "Some people go to church, but we don't." And their children are compassionate, successful, and interesting people, all with a strong sense of who they are.

We and our children are now at the threshold of a real new age as the third millennium begins, and the lives that our children lead are, and will be, very different from the childhoods their parents experienced in the Sixties, Fifties, or Forties. To bear children is to manifest hope in the world. Help is there when you need it; you can learn from other parents even if you don't think they share your values. We may sow many spiritual seeds, but only a few take root. Have faith in those seeds.

Introduction to the First Edition
by Anne Carson

When I became a mother, the world instantly looked different. Like the fairy-tale king who ate of the white snake and at once understood the speech of the animals, within days of my daughter's birth I began to experience powerful reactions to the tragedies shown on the evening news. Reports of pit-bull attacks, the angry recounting by an old Chinese peasant woman of how desperate poverty had driven her to kill her own baby some forty years back, left me tormented and unable to sleep. Suddenly the full horror of child abduction or abuse came home to me. I saw a Mozambique child vainly trying to suck milk from breasts that were mere empty flaps, and I looked down to see my own fat infant drinking from my full breast. I became stunningly aware that I held the future in my arms.

As parents we are called to recreate the world with each new generation, and at this time in history, few of us hold comfortable assumptions about what the future will bring. Some are frightened, but others find the uncertainty exciting and inspiring.

A widespread reawakening of the human spirit is taking place all over the world. The arid materialism of the mid-twentieth century has collapsed in the aftermath of the sixties, and people on many continents are responding to a hunger for spiritual sustenance. Some have turned back to the traditional world religions with renewed fervor, and the vigor of fundamentalist movements in Christianity, Islam, and Judaism has made them a force to be reckoned with. But others of us have gone off in new directions, exploring a host of possible spiritual alternatives. We do not say passively, "Yes, I believe in God, but I don't go to church." We are sincere and adventurous people who have become disillusioned with the traditional religions, who are actively searching for something closer to our sense of what a religion ought to be. Thousands of us—perhaps millions—practice some form of non-church-oriented spirituality regularly. Some follow a specific path such as yoga, Zen, feminist Goddess religion, or the wisdom of one of the great modern teachers, while many combine practices and spiritual ideas from different traditions into an eclectic and highly personalized blend.

Who are we, whose path may have no name? We are a diverse group, willing to use any set of symbols that speaks to us. We might be powerfully drawn to Native American shamanism, as well as the philosophy of Gurdjieff, the use of crystals as healing tools, and woman-centered Goddess religion. In other countries this eclecticism is not at all unusual. In Japan no one thinks it odd to be a practicing Buddhist, observe the important Shinto holidays, and be married in a Western-style Christian wedding ceremony. In Brazil, many people attend the Catholic church on major Christian feasts while employing a spiritualist to intercede with African gods in the hopes of getting a better job or securing the affections of a lover.

People inclined to what is popularly termed New Age spirituality tend to think of God less as the great father in the sky and more as a loving mother, the creative life-force, or the prime mover of the universe. We almost certainly practice some form of meditation, sporadically or on a regular daily basis—yoga, Zen, Tantrism, or some individually defined mode of quiet contemplation.

Rather than rejecting science, we tend to feel that our spiritual views are validated and justified by the discoveries of modern physics, such as the concept that creation is not made up of discrete objects but is, in reality, a shimmering, humming web of energy—that in a certain sense there is no boundary between me and Thee. On reading Fritjof Capra's *The Tao of Physics*, which maintains that the ancient cosmologies of Hinduism, Buddhism, and Taoism may actually be attested to in the laboratory, some people murmur, with a kind of reverse creationism, "You see! That's what I've been saying all along!"

People of the New Age have a reverence for life while recognizing that Nature demands limits on life, and we consider the interrelationship of all living beings as one of the great and profound mysteries of the universe. We feel a keen concern for the environment, and may be found crusading against toxic waste, the loss of the world's rain forests, and nuclear power plants—or quietly cultivating our own gardens, taking nature walks, and living organically and in voluntary simplicity.

This individualistic approach to religion means that there is no single, clearly defined tradition to pass on to one's children. Yet parents who value the spiritual dimension in their own lives are eager to pass on an appreciation for spirituality, a sense of the divine, and a basis for ethical behavior. Within organized religion it is fairly simple to give one's children a religious upbringing: take them to services, send them to Sunday school, and make sure they are confirmed, add water and stir. But "Sunday school" is no simple matter for a parent who practices yoga regularly, observes the pre-Christian seasonal festivals of May Day and the Winter Solstice (while still putting up a Christmas tree), reads Zen poetry and the works of mediaeval women mystics such as Hildegard von Bingen—and whose spouse follows an entirely different path, or none at all.

We who are seekers after truth, and proudly non-dogmatic, must find ways to deal with our children's demand for certainty. What do you say when your child asks, "What happens when you die?" How do you deal with the questions, "Do animals have souls?" "Who is this person called Jesus?" "What happens if you don't believe in God?" How do you meet the challenges: "Billy says only Christians go to heaven"; "My teacher says there's no such thing as reincarnation"? Is "Well, dear, I'm not too sure myself" an adequate response? There may not be any easy answers to these questions, but at least we can face up to them.

Thousands of parents are struggling to impart to their children the values they consider most essential. And imparting a system of life-affirming ethics is now more critical than ever, as we live under the shadow of seemingly perpetual war, economic disaster, nuclear threat, and destruction of the environment. Moreover, any strong ethical sense must be linked to and supported by a coherent worldview, else our children will grow up spiritually impoverished when spirituality should be as natural to them as play.

When I was a freshman in college, my psychology class read *Summerhill* by A.S. Neill, who warned against the propensity of some parents to instill in their children their own likes, dislikes, and prejudices. The subject of religion came up, and most of us eighteen-year-olds grandly declared that when the time came we would introduce our children to different denominations and let them make up their own minds. One student stoutly insisted that he did not want to incline his child about religion in any way and that he would never take his child to church.

"What if he wants to go?" we asked.

"He can go if he wants to. I'll tell him I think it's stupid, but he can go."

"That's not influencing him?" we wondered. For it became clear that purposefully denying one's children a religious education was sending a very clear message about spirituality.

People who have suffered too strong a dose of Sunday school can feel that almost any directed religious education is an imposition. Often when a Sunday school-educated person leaves home, the pendulum swings the other way and they lose all interest in spirituality, believing perhaps that they are now grown up and don't need that stuff anymore. Conversely, people who never had much spirituality in their lives before sometimes redis-cover religion with a vengeance, falling prey to groups and gurus who tell you what to do and when to do it.

Because of this, progressive-minded parents may half-seriously consider raising their children in some repressive fundamentalist sect, so that when the kids rebel they will do so by leaving a stulti-fying religion, rather than joining one. But this is only wishful thinking, for religious educators of all faiths stress that religious training has no effect unless the parents are committed to it them-selves. In researching this book, I found this message repeated over and over. Children know a sham when they see one. Their honesty forces us to confront the question of whether we bring children into the world in order to create new, loving beings, or in order to reproduce carbon copies of ourselves. Whether the parent's worldview is grounded in traditional Judaism, Buddhism, or rad-ical eco-feminism is less important than whether it is a living ele-ment in daily life.

My own spiritual development is probably fairly typical of the journeys made by many of my contemporaries. I was raised a Roman Catholic in the pre-Ecumenical 1950s, when the Mass was in Latin, the congregation sat through the service in virtual silence, and a "mixed marriage" was between a Catholic and a Protestant. This was not the florid, melodramatic Catholicism of media stereotypes, but what might be termed white-bread Catholicism, the religion of upwardly mobile suburbanites who had long since left their ethnic communities and the ways of the old country. Our Lady of Mount Carmel may have been the largest church in town, but there were no processions through the streets on saints' days, no holy-water receptacles in my fam-ily's house, no pictures of Jesus pointing to his Sacred Heart. My father was a convert from the Episcopal Church, so none of the practices of Catholic culture were in his heritage; my Irish-Catholic mother had been on her own since the age of eighteen and was too cosmopolitan (and as a working mother, too busy) for emotional religious displays. Nevertheless my brother and I received a thorough grounding in Catholicism—what an Italian-American psychotherapist later called "a small but lethal dose." For the first six months of kindergarten I did attend parochial school (about five memories of St. Cecelia's remain, all bad), until we moved to another town, where the Catholic school was brimming over with fifty students to a classroom. This my schoolteacher father would not countenance, so I was sent to public school. By the time my brother was school-age my mother thought there was no point in having us attend two different schools, so that was the end of that.

In other respects our religious education was rigorous: we had to go to Mass whether we liked it or not (many were the times that my family stayed overnight with friends on a Saturday and got up and went to Mass in the nearest Catholic church the next day); we had to go to Sunday school whether we liked it or not (I envied my Protestant friends' option to attend or not to attend); we had to be confirmed whether we liked it or not (and I growled that the Church made sure children were confirmed at the age of twelve before they learned to think for themselves). My father sang in the choir; my brother was an altar boy; I attended Sunday school, and later evening CCD (Confraternity of Christian Doctrine) classes until I was eighteen, when I successfully petitioned my mother to allow me to quit.

Amid all of this, as a Catholic, you knew where you were. "Of course you can't skip Mass," my mother would insist briskly, "it's a sin." She didn't warn me about hellfire or my mortal soul: not going to church was a sin, and that was that. Churchgoing became so ingrained in me that when, at the age of eight, I met a girl who said, "We don't go to church," I was as shocked as if she had said, "I don't go to school." And years later when I was on a tour in Britain with a teenage group, I was genuinely surprised when we had to get up early on a Sunday to continue our itinerary with no provision for church.

Two important influences entered my life when I was six or seven: Grimm's fairy tales and the novels of the turn-of the century English writer E. Nesbit—*The Five Children and It, The Phoenix and the Carpet*, and *The Story of the Amulet*. Together they guided my interests for years to come. From Grimm I became devoted to myth, fantasy, folklore, and the Middle Ages; and from Nesbit I learned to regard magic as something as close as a gravel pit or a pet store. Nesbit's books, from which I practically learned to read, also made me a passionate Anglophile, and by extension sparked an interest in the Celtic realms, which was fueled by my Irish heritage. Thus my early twenties found me learning the Gaelic language while pursuing a graduate degree in mediaeval history.

As a child I also learned the Classical myths, and at ten drew a series of portraits of the Greek and Roman goddesses: Juno with her peacock, Ceres with her horn of plenty, Iris and her rainbow, and the others. At fifteen the Beatle movie *Help!*, with its thinly veiled parody of the goddess Kali (called "Kaili" in the film) provided an unlikely introduction to Hinduism and the possibility of a divine force that was female, passionate, and aggressive. My girlfriends and I, at first half-jokingly, then more seriously, composed litanies to Kali, styled ourselves High Priestesses of Kali, and rose at dawn to "sacrifice" straw images of our "enemies." This sort of thing is usually dismissed as schoolgirl giddiness, although boys, too, have had their secret societies with special passwords and symbolism. Without realizing it we were participating in a home-grown version of female mysteries. This was not exactly a spiritual quest—I was not rejecting the divinity of Christ and my understanding of

Hinduism was very limited. But it was an example of the adolescent's desire to make the world anew.

Currently my spiritual path is cobbled with stones of many colors. I read everything I can get my hands on in the area of feminist spirituality; for the past few years my psychic work has been with the Tarot; on and off I practice Kundalini yoga (after six years of intensive karate practice); on full moons, new moons, and the old Celtic holidays I perform private rituals; and one of my most profound spiritual experiences recently has been reading the works of Thich Nhat Hanh, a Vietnamese Buddhist monk who lives in France. My husband David Price, an anthropologist, has taught me about shamanism and Afro-Brazilian religion. During my pregnancy, when I was worried about high blood pressure, I derived comfort and healing from yoga and biofeedback, from reading Janwillem van de Wetering's books on his experiences with Zen meditation, and from reciting the Twenty-third Psalm before bed and sleeping with a crystal under my pillow.

Skeptics may throw up their hands in dismay, and exclaim that people with such a diversity of beliefs and practices could not possibly provide a meaningful introduction to the spiritual life for their children. Yet a similar spiritual eclecticism is shared by many other parents; only the details are different. Precisely because I find spiritual value in so many different directions, I felt the need for some kind of structure in my daughter's spiritual upbringing, while still allowing for freedom and experimentation. This book is the result.

Parents can learn a great deal from each other. (I use the term "parents" throughout this book, but recognize that children live in many different kinds of households, and may be raised by single parents, two women, two men, or in collectives). The contributors are mothers and fathers, teachers, co-parents. I relate my own story as a child growing up, and that of my daughter—the birth-story that every mother knows so well. Other contributors share their stories of nursing babies, teaching meditation, praying with children at night, introducing them to gardening, helping them discover the world of nature, dealing with death, making pagan holiday decorations, discovering the Tarot (that other Sacred Book), growing with teenagers, welcoming daughters and sons into adulthood, and celebrating the ancient rites at May Day and the Winter Solstice as family festivals. There are meditations to share with your children, guides to observing the seasonal stations of the year, rites to honor conception, pregnancy, birth, the vicissitudes of childhood, and puberty.

Some contributors are Buddhist, others Jewish, or Baha'i. Some are members of the International Society for Krishna Consciousness or the Wiccan/Goddess religions, while the spirituality of the rest is multi-dimensional, informed by Christianity, New Age spirituality, the teachings of Krishnamurti, Rudolf Steiner, and the great book of nature.

In this anthology we follow the child from before birth, engage in rituals with and for children, discover the beauty and terrors of parenthood. We learn to share our spirituality with other family members, and most importantly, we learn ways of including our children in what we find most meaningful, even when they are very little. A spiritual education begins early; it cannot be put off until the child attains some arbitrary age. As the Zen saying goes, not only is there no time like the present, there is no time *but* the present.

PART I

Parents as Guides

Whatever spiritual path is chosen, a child's first teachers are its parents. Educators from all traditions emphasize that the child's true attitude toward the role of spirituality in life, as well as her understanding of what it means to be a good and moral person, will ultimately derive not from teachers but from parents. If a parent has a serious, sincere, and humble attitude towards the spiritual life, the child will grow up with a respect and appreciation for religion, even if she does not share the parents' beliefs.

Thomas Armstrong stresses in *The Radiant Child*, "The important question is not 'Should I send my child to church?' but 'What is my own attitude towards life's great mysteries and how do I want to communicate with my child about these things?'"[1]

We, too, were children once, and when we look back upon our own upbringing it is not Sunday school we recall so much as the daily, weekly, and yearly round of spirituality within our families, which may have included daily prayers, attending services together, celebrating major holidays with community gatherings and special family customs, and having intense discussions with our parents and friends about God and heaven and ethical behavior. It is the philosophy we learn at home that sets the stage for our future spiritual journey.

In the essays which begin this book, we encounter several different approaches to sharing spirituality with children. Zen teacher Thich Nhat Hanh calls every parent to be a beacon of peace, love, and light, reminding us of that very difficult dictum that without peace in our hearts and our homes, we cannot hope to establish peace among nations. Just as martial artists teach that the karate match is decided even before the opponents bow to each other, Nhat Hanh teaches us that the relationship between parent and child begins before conception. We must prepare the way even while the baby is "a gleam in the parent's eye."

The Buddhist philosophy of education is described more fully by Rev. Jiyu Kennett, abbess of Mt. Shasta Monastery, who explains that all knowledge is already contained within us and need only be nurtured in order to grow and flower. While children may not always be little angels, neither are they little savages who need to be pushed in God's direction; rather, every child already bears within her a spark of the Buddha Nature.

From Buddhism we turn to the very different spiritual tradition of Wicca or Neo-Paganism, based on the pre-Christian traditions of Western Europe with influences from other ancient peoples. In her essay, priestess Amber K describes her religion's insistence on self-reliance and responsible, ethical behavior, for Wicca teaches that divinity resides inside each person—indeed, in all creation—not out there in some remote heaven.

Moving from the general to the specific, Gail Fairfield shows us how to tap into the child's imagination through the use of the symbol system of the Tarot card deck. Not every family is interested in this particular set of spiritual symbols, but Gail shows us that from young childhood to adolescence, these ancient images can foster greater knowledge of the budding Self. There probably are parents who work with other systems such as astrology, numerology, or the I Ching. The Tarot is included in part because it crosses cultural boundaries. It is a flexible system that is constantly being recreated, a Sacred Book with chapters continually being added. Because it is pictorial, children can come to it intuitively, while their intuition is still intact. For many in our society, religion, like old-fashioned hospital births of a decade ago, has become a sterile practice of the Law, but with symbol systems such as the Tarot or the I Ching, young hearts and intellects can work together.

Trained in psychology, John Shields discusses the basic principles involved in sharing spirituality with children, stressing the importance of gearing such training to the child's age and abilities. As the child matures and its thinking develops, spirituality can be introduced on varying levels.

From the outset it is important to define just what your goals are in spiritual education. In essence a parent's goals are to let the child know that she is loved and nurtured by her immediate environment as well as by the unseen forces of the cosmos, to convey to her that the world is basically a good place, and that we have a responsibility to our neighbors and to the Earth which nourishes us. It's as simple as that.

Suffering Is Not Enough

Thich Nhat Hanh

Life is filled with suffering, but it is also filled with many wonders, like the blue sky, the sunshine, the eyes of a baby. To suffer is not enough. We must also be in touch with the wonders of life. They are within us and all around us, everywhere, any time.

If we are not happy, if we are not peaceful, we cannot share peace and happiness with others, even those we love, those who live under the same roof. If we are peaceful, if we are happy, we can smile and blossom like a flower, and everyone in our family, our entire society, will benefit from our peace. Do we need to make a special effort to enjoy the beauty of the blue sky? Do we have to practice to be able to enjoy it? No, we just enjoy it. Wherever we are, any time, we have the capacity to enjoy the sunshine, the presence of each other, even the sensation of our breathing. We don't need to go to China to enjoy the blue sky. We don't have to travel into the future to enjoy our breathing. We can be in touch with these things right now. It would be a pity if we are only aware of suffering.

We are so busy we hardly have time to look at the people we love, even in our own household, and to look at ourselves. Society is organized in a way that even when we have some leisure time, we don't know how to use it to get back in touch with ourselves. We have millions of ways to lose this precious time—we turn on the TV or pick up the telephone, or start the car and go somewhere. We are not used to being with ourselves, and we act as if we don't like ourselves and are trying to escape from ourselves.

Meditation is to be aware of what is going on—in our bodies, in our feelings, in our minds, and in the world. Each day 40,000 children die of hunger. The superpowers now have more than 50,000 nuclear warheads, enough to destroy our planet many times. Yet the sunrise is beautiful, and the rose that bloomed this morning along the wall is a miracle. Life is both dreadful and wonderful. To practice meditation is to be in touch with both aspects. Please do not think we must be solemn in order to meditate. In fact, to meditate well, we have to smile a lot.

Recently I was sitting with a group of children, and a boy named Tim was smiling beautifully. I said, "Tim, you have a very beautiful smile," and he said, "Thank you." I told him, "You don't have to thank me, I have to thank you. Because of your smile, you make life more beautiful. Instead of saying, 'Thank you,' you should say 'You're welcome.'"

If a child smiles, if an adult smiles, that is very important. If in our daily life we can smile, if we can be peaceful and happy, not only we, but everyone will profit from it. This is the most basic kind of peace work. When I see Tim smiling, I am so happy. If he is aware that he is making other people happy, he can say, "You're welcome."

From time to time, to remind ourselves to relax, to be peaceful, we may wish to set aside some time for a retreat, a day of mindfulness, when we can walk slowly, smile, drink tea with a friend, enjoy being together as if we are the happiest people on Earth. This is not a retreat, it is a treat. During walking meditation, during kitchen and garden work, during sitting meditation, all day long, we can practice smiling. At first you may find it difficult to smile, and we have to think about why. Smiling means that we are ourselves, that we have sovereignty over ourselves, that we are not drowned into forgetfulness. This kind of smile can be seen on the faces of Buddhas and Bodhisattvas.

I would like to offer one short poem you can recite from time to time, while breathing and smiling.

Breathing in, I calm body and mind.
Breathing out, I smile.
Dwelling in the present moment
I know this is the only moment.

"Breathing in, I calm body and mind." This line is like drinking a glass of ice water—you feel the cold, the freshness, permeate your body. When I breathe in and recite this line, I actually feel the breathing calming my body, calming my mind.

"Breathing out, I smile," You know the effect of a smile. A smile can relax hundreds of muscles in your face, and relax your nervous system. That is why the Buddhas and Bodhisattvas are always smiling. When you smile, you realize the wonder of the smile.

"Dwelling in the present moment." While I sit here, I don't think of somewhere else, of the future or the past. I sit here, and I know where I am. This is very important. We tend to be alive in the future, not now. We say, "Wait until I finish school and get my Ph.D. degree, and then I will be *really* alive." When we have it, and it's not easy to get, we say to ourselves, "I have to wait until I have a job in order to be really alive." And then after the job, a car. After the car, a house. We are not capable of being alive in the present moment. We tend to postpone being alive to the future, the distant future, we don't know when. Now is not the moment to be alive. We may never be alive at all in our entire life. Therefore, the technique, if we have to speak of a technique, is to be in the present moment, to be aware that we are here and now, and the only moment to be alive is the present moment.

"I know this is the only moment." This is the only moment that is real. To be here and now, and enjoy the present moment is our most important task. "Calming, Smiling, Present moment, Only moment." I hope you will try it.

Even though life is hard, even though it is sometimes difficult to smile, we have to try. Just as when we wish each other, "Good morning," it must be a real "Good morning." Recently, one friend asked me, "How can I force myself to smile when I am filled with sorrow? It isn't natural." I told her she must be able to smile to her sorrow, because we are more than our sorrow. A human being is like a television set with millions of channels. If we turn the Buddha on, we are the Buddha. If we turn sorrow on, we are sorrow. If we turn a smile on, we really are the smile. We cannot let just one channel dominate us. We have the seed of everything in us, and we have to seize the situation in our hand, to recover our own sovereignty.

When we sit down peacefully, breathing and smiling, with awareness, we are our true selves, we have sovereignty over ourselves. When we open ourselves up to a TV program, we let ourselves be invaded by the program. Sometimes it is a good program, but often it is just noisy. Because we want to have something other than ourselves enter us, we sit there and let a noisy television program invade us, assail us, destroy us. Even if our nervous system suffers, we don't have the courage to stand up and turn it off, because if we do that, we will have to return to our self.

Meditation is the opposite. It helps us return to our true self. Practicing meditation in this kind of society is very difficult. Everything seems to work in concert to try to take us away from our true self. We have thousands of things, like video tapes and music, which help us be away from ourselves. Practicing meditation is to be aware, to smile, breathe. These are on the opposite side. We go back to ourselves in order to see what is going on, because to meditate means to be aware of what is going on. What is going on is very important.

Suppose you are expecting a child. You need to breathe and smile for him or her. Please don't wait until your baby is born before beginning to take care of him or her. You can take care of your baby right now, or even sooner. If you cannot smile, that is very serious. You might think, "I am too sad. Smiling is just not the correct thing to do." Maybe crying or shouting would be correct, but your baby will get it—anything you are, anything you do, is for your baby.

Even if you do not have a baby in your womb, the seed is already there. Even if you are not married, even if you are a man, you should be aware that a baby is already there, the seeds of future generations are already there. Please don't wait until the doctors tell you that you are going to have a baby to begin to take care of it. It is already there. Whatever you are, whatever you do, your baby will get it. Anything you eat, any worries that are on your mind will be for him or her. Can you tell me that you cannot smile? Think of the baby, and smile for him, for her, for the future generations. Please don't tell me that a smile and your sorrow just don't go together. It's your sorrow, but what about your baby? It's not his sorrow, it's not her sorrow.

Children understand very well that in each woman, in each man, there is a capacity of waking up, of understanding, and of loving. Many children have told me that they cannot show me anyone who does not have this capacity. Some people allow it to develop, and some do not, but everyone has it. This capacity of waking up, of being aware of what is going on in your feelings, is called Buddha Nature, the capacity of understanding and loving. Since the baby of that Buddha is in us, we should give him or her a chance. Smiling is very important. If we are not able to smile, then the world will not have peace. It is not by going out for a demonstration against nuclear missiles that we can bring about peace. It is with our capacity of smiling, breathing, and being peace that we can make peace.

The Education of the Buddhist Child

Rev. Jiyu Kennett, Roshi

With young Buddhists growing up around us by the score and more and more members of the Society* marrying and having their own children, not to mention interest in the education of the young on the part of the Sufis and other friendly religious organizations, I have been asked to discuss, or rather delineate, the usual method of education of the Buddhist child throughout the east. There are certain differences with regard to the approach to the education of Buddhists as opposed to members of other religions and I think these are basic to a Buddhist education anywhere, whether it is in the east or west. So, first and foremost, I would like to point out what is probably obvious to most of you, but which is certainly not obvious to the average parent in England, for example, where I myself was brought up; and that is that the child must be cherished—not merely looked after or even loved but cherished. However foolish its comments, however childish, however silly, however babyish, the child is trying to express itself and must never be thought of as something that is *needing* to be educated but rather as that which has within itself all the knowledge that matters that ever was. And it is our duty as educators to unlock the doors of that knowledge so that the child may *experience* and *express* what it already knows.

Buddhism, unlike some other religions, does not believe in original sin. Therefore it places no guilt on the child from the moment it is conceived. Instead, it says that we are simply born and later, as a result of what we do with ourselves, of what happens to us and as a result of our going into dual thinking—right and wrong—"this is right, that is wrong; this is good, that is bad"—we educate ourselves out of our original oneness of mind into a duality which, at a later date, we have to transcend if we are to be able to do anything whatsoever to overcome the spiritual illnesses our education has generated.

The average child going to school in the west is taught from the moment it enters, "Now, you are a child and I am *the* teacher. *You* do *not* know and I *do* know." I can certainly remember, and I am sure most of my readers can remember also, the moment when something inside us was almost killed or, at least, shut off by a watertight door. We were perfectly all right until the moment when it was made quite clear to us that we did not know and that the teacher *did*. For this was the moment when doubt entered our minds—and fear entered them because we had been told that we were inadequate—and we were already in the toils of duality.

Buddhist education does not do this. The Buddhist teacher, if he is a real teacher, says, "This child knows all, as indeed I know all, but he cannot yet express it and I can only express it partially. Therefore he and I are on the same road. I have been going along for it for a little longer than he has and I will try to go at the same speed he is going at so that he may catch up with me and, perhaps, be able to surpass me—who knows?" So it is the duty of the Buddhist teacher to get his egocentric self out of the way to a very, very great extent so that the education of the child may be a free and beautiful thing, untrammeled by "Look at what I have achieved in *my* educating of this child!" It is the child that does the educating of itself by using its experiences to fall back on later; the child that makes the running; and the child that matters—we are all children in the Buddha Nature. When we say, as teachers, "*I* know and *you* do not," we are really saying, "*Our* Buddha Nature is better than *your* Buddha Nature;" thus is set up duality, self, fear and inadequacy. If, on the other hand, we say, "Your Buddha Nature and our Buddha Nature are one but there is a difference between us because you are smaller than us and we are older than you; therefore we have run a little farther but we will come back to help you run as far," the difference in our attitude of mind, the difference in the attitude of the child to learning, is phenomenal.

I am often asked, "How do you teach meditation to a child and what is the best age to start at?" In the east the average child is taught to meditate as soon as it is possible for it to sit upright; i.e. around one or two years old. No doctrine is put into the child's head. The mother and father, and the rest of the family, will sit quietly in front of the family altar; the child, without being restrained, will either sit on the floor for a few moments or roll around on the floor with the parents taking no notice. The parents thus express their knowledge of the child's latent understanding and do not treat it as less than themselves. In a very short time the child wants to sit like the parents, as does, interestingly enough, the dog and cat. I have sat down to meditate and my cat has come up, looked at the wall and then sat down to look at it with me. Thus, if the parents meditate, the child will meditate too. I have seen children at the age of two and a half doing formal meditation in the laymen's meditation hall in Sojiji—and doing a wonderful job. I have photographs of them. These children do a meditation so pure and exquisite it is unbelievable to watch; but they would not be able to discuss the Buddha Nature with you, nor would they be able to put into words the doctrine of the Trikaya**—nor would they be able to explain the "all is one" and the "all is different"—they will express the Buddha Nature for they have learned to meditate with their whole being untrammeled by duality. They are indeed *whole* creatures and can teach us much.

The education of the child starts prior to birth, on the very night of its conception. The attitude of mind of the parents—whether they are in a selfish mood, simply wish to gratify their own pleasure, or whether they are wishing to produce a child which both of them will love—will affect the child at a later date. The Buddha Nature, which is within all of us, knows what is happening to itself, and the future child is conditioned by the attitudes of mind of the parents at conception. Therefore, education does not even begin at the first look that passes between the mother and the child; it begins with the look in the eyes of the two parents, whether they be full of lust or whether they be full of self-less love. There used to be an old saying that there was such a thing as a "love child" in existence. It is unfortunate that it became a derogatory term, pertaining to a child born out of wedlock.

From what I have said, therefore, in a very real sense, "The sins of the fathers are visited upon the children," and the children are born carrying the karmic load which the parents have put upon them; their teachers later force them to continue to carry it. This is indeed a great grief. Parents should know well what it is they do on the night of conception and make no mistakes. They should also know well why it is that a child may ask, at a later date, with genuine grief in his heart, the old Zen koan, "Why did you beget me? Why was I born? Before my parents conceived me, what was my original face?" These koans can be taken on many levels and can be understood by many, many means. The next step is for the parent to cherish the child, not merely love it; the parents must always be open to the child, never sneering at, or belittling its efforts, never looking down upon it, from first seeing it at birth until it becomes an adult.

Those of you who have read my diary will remember certain incidents in my own childhood: for instance when I came running home to my family, longing to tell them what I had learned, and the supercilious laughter when I explained, as best I could, what my lessons had been. "Oh, how clever you are," I was told, and something snapped shut inside me. This would never happen in a Buddhist family or school that is properly run. However childish the remarks, however silly even, the child will always be treated as if it is a serious human being. As the child gets steadily older the strictness with which it is treated by the teachers increases gradually, but it is never a strictness that is, in any way, derogatory of the child's ability. Even the stupidest child is fully accepted as having the Buddha Nature; it is embraced within the Buddha Mind and never made to feel inferior. "There are some Buddhas that are tall, some short, some fat, some thin, some bright, some stupid," say the scriptures. Unless you can see the Buddha in the little child who comes to you with his "silly" story, as we *great* grown-ups consider it; unless you can see the Buddha in the little boy with his hand in the cookie jar and unless you can see the Buddha when you spank him—and spank him with love and cherish him in your heart whilst doing it—you will not be able to educate the Buddhist child.

Formal education starts the moment the child is first held in his mother's arms. The openness within her heart and within her eyes are the beginning of that formal education. That openness must remain; the full acceptance of the oneness of the mother and child must also be the full acceptance of the oneness of the teacher and pupil. My advice to those who educate anyone is, "Remember, there is no difference between you and the pupil other than that of age. Neither of you possess more than the other; there is only the illusion of knowledge. Unless you understand that mental knowledge is an illusion in the religious sense you will never be able to impart anything whatsoever of real value."

We need to remember that age barriers are created by pride—"I am older than you, therefore I know more than you;" to which the young reply with the words, "We are younger than you and we don't care whether you know more than we do or not because we are younger than you and have more time to learn." So, by being proud, the old are despised, and so is their knowledge; and, by despising the old, the young are deprived of the passed-down practical wisdom of the ages. If, from the very beginning, education is understood as starting with unselfish conception and then the loving and the cherishing, not only of the child when it is your own, but when it is your pupil, there is no danger whatsoever of there ever being an age barrier and education is seen to be a means of growing together within the Spirit of the Buddhas.

---

*   The Zen Mission Society, centered at Mt. Shasta Abbey in California.
** Trikaya is a Mahayana Buddhist doctrine on the triform nature of the Buddha—Ed.

How a Priestess Parents Pagan Children

Amber K

Several days ago, I arose in the chill darkness before the Wisconsin dawn, helped pack four sleeping children (ages two, five, eight, and eleven) into the big red van we call the Fox Box, and took off for a 1300-mile journey to New Mexico. For most of the trip, there were two adults in the van to drive and take care of the kids; for much of the trip, I would not have minded having half-a-dozen nannies on hand to help with the young ones. For parts of the trip, I enjoyed the children thoroughly. For other parts, I would cheerfully have sold them to pirates if any had been around to make an offer. (Not really, but the fantasy crossed my mind.)

But those 1300 miles in the Fox Box taught me a few more things about parenting, and about how I parent. There is nothing like intensive contact in a confined space to bring out the best and worst in people.

Now, kids are kids the world over, no matter their culture or religion, and I believe that there are some rock-bottom essentials of good parenting anywhere. A good parent strives to keep her children healthy with good food, clean air and water, plenty of rest, appropriate clothes for the climate, and lots of sunlight and exercise. A good parent expresses her love for her children with hugs, smiles, warm words, and occasionally her *complete* attention. A good parent is consistent, but not harsh, about rules and discipline. A good parent teaches her kids how to survive and thrive in the world, or finds teachers who can do the job.

Beyond such basics, there are some parenting styles and goals which are specific to particular cultures or faiths. As a priestess deeply involved in the Wiccan faith—a nature-oriented religion with roots in ancient Europe—naturally I work to parent in a way which is consistent with my religious beliefs. Here are some things I teach the children in my family:

"Thou art God/dess." Deity is not some bearded old man up in the sky that we never hear from, S/he is an energy inside you and everyone else and the Earth and the wild creatures and the clouds and trees and stones...This has a lot of implications for the way we live.

First, we are each responsible for our lives and what we make of them. Having that Divine spark within us means that we have the power and ability to choose; we are never victims or pawns unless we allow ourselves to be. I focus a great deal on teaching kids to be resourceful, independent-thinking, and self-reliant. If something "bad" happens to a Pagan kid in my care, I may comfort them but I will also immediately help them figure out how to take charge of the event and turn it into a positive experience. I try not to demand a level of strength or maturity greater than they can give, but I will encourage them to stretch themselves and give their very best to the situation.

Because we are all intimately connected, all part of the same Divine family, anything we do to others affects us. If we hurt someone else, we hurt ourselves. If we help or heal or teach or bless someone else, the positive energy flows right back to us. This is the concept behind what we call The Law of Return: "Whatever you send out comes back to you threefold (magnified)." So we teach children to be very careful about what they send out, in their interactions with people and all other beings.

Reinforcing this law is our major ethical guideline, "An ye harm none, do as ye will." An approximate translation of the rather archaic language would be, "As long as you don't hurt anyone else, follow the Spirit within you (your 'true will')." This puts a lot of responsibility on each individual to decide what constitutes "harm" to another, and much of our ethical training focuses on making such decisions case by case.

Because the Earth and Her creatures are God/dess as much as we are, Pagan children are taught to respect and protect the environment and wildlife. My ten-year-old is very proud to belong to Greenpeace, and thinks that the people who block whaling ships in little rubber life-rafts are the greatest heroes in the world. Many Pagan families belong to organizations with a conservation or preservation ethic, such as the Sierra Club, Friends of the Earth, the Audubon Society, the International Wildlife Society, and so on. The Scouting program is a natural for people who revere nature, and many Pagan families participate.

God/dess expresses Herself in such a rich and colorful variety of ways, in all the peoples and customs of the world, as well as in green forests, rugged mountains, surging oceans, and sere deserts. She is in the tiniest wildflower underfoot, and in the candescent vastness of wheeling galaxies. By helping our children know and feel that they are part of it All, and that All is sacred, we help them learn to live in a sacred manner. After all, the very word "religion" means to "link" or "connect," and it is the opposite of alienation.

Yet our faith and our parenting would be incomplete if we focused only the beautiful and positive side of life. The Wiccan religion does not draw a line down the middle of the universe and label one half "good" and the other "evil," nor seek to become part of a mythical cosmic battle between the forces of light and darkness. The darkness, the cold, and even pain and anger and fear, are part of the real world, part of the Divine pattern, and not the malicious working of some "devil." We believe that it is a parent's responsibility to face the hard and negative parts of life head on, to work to understand their place in the pattern, to challenge and transform and heal, rather than to turn away, avoid, or escape. This includes facing, "owning," and working with the "dark places" in our own hearts, rather than repressing or denying our own pain, fear, and anger, or blaming them on some outside agency. We are creatures of both light and darkness, and must come to terms with that fact.

In helping our children face their own dark sides, we carefully avoid the concepts of sin and guilt. To us, our children are part of the God/dess, and not "born in sin" or inherently unworthy. They are good and beautiful and precious beings even if they get angry, break things, or forget and hurt others. Error is not sin. So if a child hits another, I don't yell, "Bad boy! You are so mean!" I say, "No hitting! That hurts! Hitting is wrong. You sit in that chair until you calm down, and then you can balance it." I make it clear that a mistake has been made and will not be overlooked, but I never suggest that the child himself is bad.

Balancing, as in balancing karma, is a key concept here. If a child (or adult) hurts someone or breaks or damages something, an apology is not sufficient ordinarily to set matters right (although if it is feelings alone that are hurt, a sincere "I'm sorry" might be enough). If someone is injured, they must be healed; if something is broken, it must be found or replaced. The emphasis is on action to restore the balance. This parallels the ethics of the traditional Hawaiian culture: if you steal a pig, all the remorse and repentance and apologies in the world don't rectify the situation: you have to give the pig back.

There is another difference between Wicca and mainstream religions, which is that we practice magick. Not stage tricks with rabbits and hats and colored scarves up the sleeve, but two kinds of spiritual techniques designed to help us grown and change, or to get through life safely and fairly comfortably. The first kind, magick for spiritual growth, is called "theurgy;" the bread-and-butter variety is called "thaumaturgy."

And of course our children grow up with a belief in, and understanding of, all kinds of magickal, psychic, and astral processes and phenomena. They speak with the plant devas before picking a flower (and if the flower says no, they don't pick). They call upon their totems or power animals for strength or help. They use simple divination to find a lost toy. (On a camping trip once, my ten-year-old lost a toy figure; no amount of searching would locate it until he began chanting "Pan, Pan, find my man." The toy turned up within seconds. Did Pan help, or did the chant help my child focus better... or both? In any case, it worked.) They learn to work *with* nature and energy currents seen and unseen, and I believe they grow up to be more sensitive, imaginative, and ultimately resourceful because of their experiences with magick. Not superstition, mind you: not archaic formulas that supposedly bring miraculous results if repeated in a certain way, not rings or talismans with amazing powers, or any of the other dramatic misconceptions of magick made popular in movies and comic books, but real magick, psychological and spiritual exercises that are hard work but can work subtle changes in conformity with natural law. Magick is not a quick and easy way to riches or anything else, and children soon learn this if their teachers know what they're doing.

Pagan children are also generally taught that all Gods and Goddesses are authentic facets or aspects of the Divine Source, and thus worthy of respect. Of course, some Deities, ancient and modern, seem destructive and/or negative; respecting Them does not mean one has to put prayer, energy or devotion into the Ones Which don't seem helpful. However, being polytheistic means having a wide range of Divine images to draw upon for strength, understanding, comfort, energy, or as role models. And if all Deities are true facets of Godhead, then all religious paths contain some measure of truth, and are appropriate for someone to follow. Paganism encourages tolerance of diversity and respect for others' spiritual choices, traits which can help Pagan children in their relationships with others.

One particular aspect of Pagan thealogy* which is unusual in Western culture is our love and respect for the Goddess. To people raised with the image of God-the-Father as bearded Patriarch (and bachelor), the image of God as Mother, Sister, or Daughter seems very strange. Yet these images come very naturally to children. To most little ones, the image and experience of "Mother" is more intimately connected with love, nurturing, warmth, and protection than "Father" (though this is changing a little, as more fathers discover that it's all right to be nurturing.) So at an age when Deity is understood mainly as a loving Heavenly Parent, it is very easy for kids to think about the Goddess as Divine Mother. Of course, this belief undermines the patriarchal notion that divinity and spirituality are exclusively male territory, and that is all to the good.

To sum up, because I care about my kids I work at keeping them healthy, helping them learn, and showing them that I love them. I feed them pretty carefully—no sugar or red meat, thanks—and make sure they bathe and brush their teeth. I teach them what I can, and tell them stories, and hug them a lot. I give each one special times and attention (though it never feels like enough). I insist they help around the house, and yell at them sometimes. I guess that's all part of parenting.

Because I'm a priestess of a Pagan faith as well, I also teach my kids that they are part of everything around them, and that Goddess and God are inside of us as well as all around. I teach them to care for the Earth and Her creatures, to love and heal and protect. And when they can't do that because they're mad or afraid or jealous or whatever, then I help them deal with those feelings and work them through. I teach them to work magick, and that magick is never enough—life requires hard and intelligent work too. I teach them that there is wonder and beauty and opportunity all around them, and that we have the power to make our lives very good indeed, especially when we work together. And by "we" I mean "WE"—all of us, Pagan and Christian and whoever, and animals and plants and stones and stars.

And I teach them to say "Blessed be," to themselves and all others. To you, too, who are reading this. Since the children aren't here right now, I'll offer it for them: Blessed be. Be strong. Be happy. Be loved. Help your kids do the same.

---

* "Thealogy" ("teachings about Goddess") is a term often used by feminists in place of "theology" ("teachings about God").—Ed.

Using the Tarot with Children

Gail Fairfield

The Tarot is a wonderful catalyst for enhancing intuition, encouraging inner awareness, and supporting intimate interaction. For adults, reading the cards encourages continual personal growth and psychic discovery. For children, the cards provide a framework for self-development as well as a foundation for future Taroting. Both adults and children can gain from the emotional and philosophical insights that the Tarot offers. Furthermore, the process of Taroting together allows people of all ages to pursue their spiritual development in a nurturing context.

In order to delve into this growth opportunity, adults may want to read some of the many books and resources available on the Tarot; or they may prefer to develop their talents along with their children. The cards can, of course, be explored intuitively. But it is also useful to combine the intuitive knowing with some conscious knowledge about the structure of the deck and its many applications. I intend that the following ideas and activities will provide a solid jumping off point for adults who want to go Taroting with kids. Incidentally, I only create Tarot experiences for a child if her parents or guardians have given approval. The non-parent Taroting adult will probably want to get permission before proceeding with Tarot-play.

For the adult who is approaching the Tarot for the first time, here's some information that's basic to an understanding of the cards. Most Tarot decks consist of a pack of seventy-eight cards which can be divided into two sections called the Major and Minor Arcana. The twenty-two Major Arcana cards symbolize key life events, lessons, or growth phases. They are labeled with such words as The Empress, The Tower, Strength, or Temperance. These cards are usually full of esoteric symbols which trigger intuitive responses. They also depict the images of people who are dressed and posed to represent what they mean. Most people, old or young, can look at the Major cards and sense what they symbolize by telling the stories that they imply.

The Minor Arcana is similar to a regular playing card deck because it consists of four suits (Wands, Cups, Swords, Pentacles) which range in number from Ace through King. Unlike playing cards, most Tarot decks include four Court cards (Page, Knight, Queen, King) instead of three. In some decks, the cards numbered Ace through Ten contain pictorial images of people engaged in a variety of activities. In others, these cards simply show the symbols and numbers of the suits: four Wands, three Swords, etc. The pictorial ones can be interpreted by storytelling while the plain cards present more of a challenge. For these cards, the symbolic meanings of the numbers and the suits serve as indicators of the cards' interpretations.

Once the adult has familiarized herself with the Tarot deck, she is already prepared to present it to a child. In fact, the novice will frequently allow the child more latitude and freedom in his growth and discovery. The experienced Tarotist has to remember not to present too much, too fast. When I introduce the Tarot to children, I try to maintain an open-minded perspective, allowing them to show me their next step, rather than forcing the pace. I like to answer their specific questions without rushing in to add a lecture. I trust that they will tell me or show me when they're ready for more. I consistently notice that children, when given an accepting environment, are incredibly attuned to their own intuitive perceptions. I am also aware that they, especially the young ones, are less able to deal in abstractions and applications. So I try to stay out of the way of the a child's intuition while providing a flexible but practical form for its use.

The first step in exploring the Tarot with children is choosing which set, or sets, of cards to use. I tend to use decks with pictorial number cards with kids because they provide more opportunities for storytelling and imagination. I prefer some of the more modern decks which have fewer frightening symbols but I also provide a choice of decks so that the child is using cards that she likes. I've had a seven-year-old tell me that a particular deck was too scary because it had black borders around the pictures. However, she didn't particularly object to images of stabbing swords. Some decks that appear somewhat gruesome to me could fit right into a child's cartoon-fantasy life. Physically, some of the smaller decks are easier for little ones to handle. Conversely, they enjoy looking at the larger decks because the illustrations are easier to see. Given a choice, children will demonstrate their preferences for certain decks of cards at an early age. As time goes on, they'll want to experiment with various decks as they explore expanded interpretations. For starters, the child might try out the Aquarian, Motherpeace, Sacred Rose, or Voyager Tarots.

I think it's practice and preferable to designate a particular deck of cards as the child's deck. The child who has her own deck will always feel that the Tarot is her personal, approachable friend, not an inaccessible mystery. The kid-deck can be stored in a box, a basket, or a drawer. It can even be secured with a rubber band! At the outset, I accept the fact that some of the cards will be lost, decorated, or destroyed, and that it's all part of the process. Older children, of course, can be expected to take care of their deck at least to the same degree as they care for their other possessions.

I want to emphasize here that the child will imitate the adults around him. If the adults utilize Tarot rituals such as storing their cards in silk, lighting candles before a reading, or shuffling and cutting a certain way, the child will want to try these things, too. He will probably try to light candles on his own! If the adults are playful, serious, social or private in their use of the cards, the child will tend to copy these attitudes. If the child hears that the Tarot is a tool for personal understanding, the word of God/dess, or a toy, she'll repeat what she's heard to her friends and neighbors. The little one may need to hear that it's not a religion and doesn't conflict with Christianity. It is one philosophical or spiritual choice among many. Generally, in presenting the Tarot to children, adults will want to be conscious of the precedents they're setting. For example, they may not choose candle-burning as a model for younger children. On the other hand, they may want to model a spiritual and meditative or practical and down-to-earth attitude. The adult's style and focus in approaching the Tarot will have as big an impact on the child as the cards themselves.

Once the cards have been opened, I find that it works well to have a child-oriented environment for Tarot activities. A carpeted floor, a bed, or a wide table can provide a flat, approachable surface for messing about with the cards. For younger kids, the child's attention span will dictate the frequency and length of time devoted to Taroting. The older ones may want to set aside a regular Tarot time. Otherwise, there is no substitute for spontaneous card-play.

After the environment is set, I create various structures for Taroting with children, depending on the developmental level of the child and her past experience with the cards. Often, making the cards available is the only structure that's needed. Sometimes children want more direction. The following ideas and activities are sequenced according to developmental stages but they are not limited to any particular age groups. In other words, use what's appropriate for this child, now, whatever his age.

Infants

Infants don't do much with Tarot cards except gum them. But once they can focus their attention, they do seem to enjoy grasping the cards and looking at the colors and pictures. Babies especially enjoy the images of people's faces. They may even demonstrate a preference for certain cards or symbols. At this stage, it seems most valuable to simply allow the child to destroy a few cards, see them in her environment, and notice the adults in her life playing with them. Additionally, adults can use the cards to discover something about the non-verbal infant's needs. On-going fussiness, for example, could indicate:

Wands—a movement toward greater independence and
    freedom; the drive for greater mobility
Cups—an emotional request for nurturance or touch; a
    request for the presence of a special person
Swords—a desire for visual or auditory stimulation; a
    response to a change in routine
Pentacles—a signal of physical discomfort or hunger; an
    indication of illness or "growing pains"

These are just examples, of course. The adults can use their own knowledge and intuition to expand the interpretation.

Toddlers

Toddlers will play with the cards, still mauling them, but also looking at them, arranging them, and stirring them around. At this stage, it seems to work best if the cards are just heaped up or spread around on the working surface. Trying to keep them in a neat stack or arrangement is close to impossible! Handling seventy-eight cards is also a big task so I suggest presenting a few cards at a time, maybe just the Major Arcana, to these young ones. Toddlers may tear or crumple some cards and carry others around. Cards that are singled out usually do indicate something about a child's state of being. The adult may want to talk about what the cards mean, remembering to use kid-centered words and simple concepts. Concrete examples and short sentences also help.

Toddlers can be asked to pick a card; they will probably pick two or three! These, too, will tell the adult something about how a child is feeling. Some toddlers enjoy picking out a special card or group of cards for each adult or child present. The more verbal ones will even talk about the cards, explaining who the people are and what they're doing. The adult can ask, "What's going on in this picture?" "How is this person feeling?" or even "Tell me about this card." At this stage, it's important for children just to become familiar with the cards, to experience choosing them, and to become exposed to the concept that they have meanings.

Young Children

Young children can move into Tarot activities that are a little most structured. They will probably begin to show pride in owning their own cards and may be less willing to share them with others. When adults are doing readings, they'll enjoy getting their cards and "playing" along. These kids will want feedback and ideas about their cards but they won't want long-winded explanations. Short, clear, child-oriented suggestions for techniques and interpretations will be most effective for them.

Storytelling is the best activity at this stage. Children can choose one card at a time and then talk about the pictures on them. Some kids may even be able to explain why the person is holding the round ball or where the group is going in the boat. There are no correct answers, of course. A child's comments simply show what's important to her at this time. After she is used to talking about individual cards, a child can be encouraged to choose two or three cards and lay them in a row. She might then talk about the cards as separate stories or she might be able to tie them together in a sequence. Prompts such as "and then what happened," or "what did he do here," can help them create connections between the cards. Some children will want to control the storytelling themselves; others will enjoy it when the adults add to or create the stories. Children at this age also love to know the principle characters in the story, enjoying it if the adults suggest that the people in the picture could represent familiar people—real or imaginary!

Naming the cards is fun for young children. Adults might simply refer to the cards by their proper titles without requiring that the children remember or repeat the names. They can also play games such as "Can you find the Empress?" or "Where is a Cups card?" Through these activities, they are familiarizing themselves with the deck and with the idea that the cards have specific names.

Sorting the cards is another great game for young children. They can make piles of Wands, Cups, Swords, and Pentacles. They can find all the Threes, all the Queens, or all the Major cards. Of course, a Major card with a sword in the image might get added to the Swords pile. Or the Emperor could show up with the Kings. Depending on the child's age and nature, the adult might choose to intervene and move the card to correct pile. I often don't. What's important is that the child is learning to recognize the significant symbols and to distinguish the differences and similarities among the cards.

Older Children
Older children can really begin to use the Tarot as a tool for insight and understanding. They are more likely to play with the cards independently or even use them with their friends. At this

stage, children may become aware that there are people in the world who do not use the Tarot cards; there are even people who think they're wrong or bad. This issue may never arise with some children but for most, at some stage, they'll encounter social prejudice. It makes sense to be ready with an understanding response. Talking with children about the use of these and other intuitive tools is always a valuable experience. The adult can explain that other people may have differing opinions and preferences and may utilize other kinds of tools in their lives. It seems important to me to emphasize that there's nothing "evil" about the cards—they are not a gate for the devil. The adult can emphasize that the Tarot will not trap or warp anyone's mind. On the other hand, the Tarot is a tool for self-understanding and insight, for growth and awareness. Older children can usually understand phrases such as:

> "The Tarot isn't bad and it won't hurt you or Johnny."
> "Some people don't like the cards because they're scared that you'll use them instead of (praying or) thinking for yourself."
> "You know that you use the cards to understand yourself better."
> "We use the cards to get new ideas about how to solve problems."
> "The Tarot is something we use in our family (home, daycare, etc.) to help us like ourselves and understand each other."

Whatever their experience with the outside world, these children will gain from having an understanding of the reasons for using the cards. At this time in their lives, they are learning that the Tarot is a useful and fascinating tool for self-discovery and life enhancement.

Storytelling is still a good activity for older children. They can create elaborate stories using five or ten cards with more complicated plots and characters. Historically, the Tarot has been seen as a book. This concept can be presented along with the idea that the story changes each time they mix up the cards. Every encounter with the cards becomes an opportunity for a new adventure. Older children may enjoy writing their stories down or dictating them to an adult. They could even record the cards in a notebook along with the stories. Eventually, they might get a whole anthology of Tarot tales.

Naming the cards becomes more specific at this stage. The older child will be able to read the names on most of the cards or at least recognize the pictures.

Interpretations start to have value now. The Minor Arcana meanings can be learned fairly easily if key phrases for the Suits and Numbers are repeated and emphasized. The child can separate out the Minor cards and, pulling them at random, explain that:

> "It's a Two so it's about making a choice."
> "It's a Wands card so it's about how I look or act."
> "It's a Page so it's about daring to do something, being brave."
> "It's a Pentacles card so it's about something I can touch."

They can go on to:

> "It's the Three of Swords so it's about planning what I want to say."
> "It's the Five of Pentacles so it's about rearranging something I can touch."
> "It's the Eight of Cups so it's about understanding people's feelings."

"It's the Knight of Wands so it's about focusing on
    myself."

The older child will enjoy applying the cards to situations in
his own life. "Rearranging what I can touch" might mean cleaning his room; "focusing on myself" might indicate minding his
own business about his sister's actions.

These children may or may not be ready for the subtlety of
reversed cards. If they are, the adult can suggest that "since it's
upside down, it means that it's happening inside you instead of
outside." With this added information, the Three of Swords
Reversed might mean "planning how I want to talk to myself,"
and the Eight of Cups might be "sorting out my own feelings."

The Major Arcana cards can be called teachers or guides,
individuals or forces that help in certain ways. When pulling
these cards, the child might say:

"It's the Emperor so it means that being responsible or
    talking to someone in charge will help."
"It's the Chariot so it means that being active or talking
    to someone who's very busy will help."
"It's the Wheel so it means that starting it or talking to
    whoever started it is important."
"It's the Hanged Man so it's better to wait for a good time
    or to talk to whoever's waiting."

As older children come to understand some Tarot interpretations, specific cards can be chosen to aid in interpersonal com-
munications. For example, the adult might refer to the High
Priestess to indicate that he needs alone-time. Or he might say,
"You're the Hermit, you already know the answer." If the child is
having difficulty describing her feelings, the adult might suggest
that she look through the cards until she finds one that really

expresses her emotional state. Often, with the Tarot card as a trigger, she'll be able to talk about what's bothering her.

Simple readings help these children understand how they feel, what they want, and what might happen in a given situation. This is the time to introduce the idea of asking a question of the cards. Single-card readings are most appropriate at the beginning. They might address such questions as:

Why is Billy mad at me?
How can I make friends with Rachel?
How can I concentrate better at school?
What am I scared about?

The degree of concreteness within the questions can be adjusted, depending on the child. The interpretive response, too, will vary according to the child's grasp of abstract concepts and applications. These older children will frequently find a very practical solution symbolized within the cards while the adult is merrily thinking of psychological processes!

Adults can encourage older children to create simple layout patterns that specifically suit their own needs and questions. The children may want to record these layouts and the cards that come up or they may not care. As they do these mini-readings, new questions will arise that can be addressed with new cards. At this stage, it's important to present the Tarot reading as an evolving process, not just a set format. The following examples are some ideas of simple layouts that children can use; they are, of course, only examples. They can be ignored or adapted.

Adolescents

Adolescents can truly utilize the Tarot independently and creatively. Some will keep the cards as a private interest and resist any efforts on the part of friends or adults to "read" for others.

Others will be delighted to give readings. A few will decide that they have more than a passing interest in the cards. They will want to read a variety of Tarot books, purchase several Tarot decks, and even attend classes. A few of those might even decide to design or create their own Tarot decks. Their ideas can be refined on index cards and then laminated or transferred to "blank" Tarot decks. They may want to collect their interpretations and layout ideas into a notebook. At this stage, the adult is supporting the adolescent to pursue the Tarot with as much, or as little, passion as she wants.

Like the older child, the teenager may need some feedback about how to handle social pressure or criticism. On the other hand, he may have friends who overwhelm him as they seek fortune-telling or emotional support. In an effort to please, the teenager may find herself trying to stretch beyond her abilities in order to play psychic or counselor. To avoid these difficulties, it's useful for the budding Tarotist to learn about setting boundaries and handling his "private practice." Teenagers are old enough to arrange trades with friends; they might exchange Tarot readings for a Saturday lunch or tickets to a game. Additionally, they can decide when and where they are comfortable doing readings and what kinds of questions they enjoy answering. Whatever, they arrange, it's important that they remember to value their time and talents.

The adult can actually help the teenager set up an environment that is conducive for her own Tarot explorations. He can help her plan how to organize her time and friends with regard to readings. He can do readings for her and request that she do readings for him. He can, above all, be available for feedback and advice about the meanings and uses of the cards. When the adult is uncertain about a particular Tarot application, he can participate in finding books and resources that will expand the adolescent's understanding. Depending on the adult's own

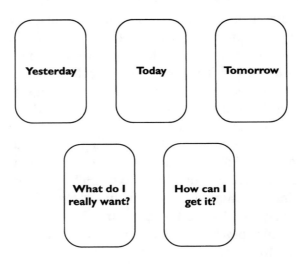

What will probably happen about:
What to do about:

What do I tell my parents?

knowledge of the cards, he'll be the teacher, the learning companion, or the client.

Moral support is, perhaps, the primary role of the adult with regard to Taroting with children of any age. Some kids will be deeply drawn to the cards. They may even demonstrate psychic insights early on. If this occurs, I treat their intuitive abilities as natural skills that have delightfully emerged. Ideally, these children can be encouraged to develop their talents without any accompanying fear or drama. Other children will maintain a light or intermittent interest in the cards. Whatever the child's level of involvement, adults can nurture a healthy, positive experience of the Tarot which will provide a foundation for all future Taroting.

Note: a wide selection of Tarot decks, including blank decks, is available through U.S. Games. Catalogs can be ordered from: U.S. Games Systems, Inc., 179 Ludlow Street, Stamford, Ct. 06902, (800) 544-2637. www.usgamesinc.com

How Parents Can Help a Child's Understanding of Spirituality

John-Ambarisa Mendell Shields

Modern society has advanced considerably in the area of mass education, but unfortunately, and ironically, more children and adolescents are subjected to drug abuse, delinquency, and suicide than ever before. Education has placed its emphasis on material advancement to the exclusion of the most important aspect of education: the spiritual aspect. The aim of education for children should be self-realization and the realization of spiritual values. So how is it that children learn about God and spiritual values? This is a question that has raised great concern among those parents who are cognizant of this aspect of learning as an integral part of their child's development.

The first question is not how a child learns about God, but rather from whom the child can learn about God. A good teacher will in fact admit that a child's parent is potentially the child's greatest teacher. The reason for this is that it is the parent who the child first learns to trust and to follow as a model for behaviors and for values. Parents certainly know more about their children than anyone else, and it is they who spend the most time with their children. Parents who are concerned about their children and want them to learn God consciousness must be willing to take the responsibility of imparting that knowledge themselves. Parents must be strong in their own spiritual convictions and practices, and at the same time be sensitive to the child's level of development and her physical, emotional, and environmental needs as well. That may initially sound like an insurmountable responsibility, but it is also a most joyous experience for a parent to watch his child grow in God consciousness.

I once read that a prospective parent becomes pregnant from the very moment that he or she imagines conceiving a child. At first that sounded a bit obscure, but over time it made better sense. With the first thought of bringing a new soul into the world, the parent assumes the responsibility of bearing and rearing that soul. God entrusts each parent with that responsibility, as the ultimate goal of parenting should always be to raise the God consciousness of their child such that the child may find self-realization, love of God, and peace in the world. So upon the first thought of conceiving a child, the pregnancy or the process of birth begins, both for the parent and for the child. At this stage the first question should be, "How will I raise the God consciousness of the soul that God has entrusted to me?"

If parents can adopt the mentality of modeling God consciousness from the child's very first breath, the process of the child's learning about God has already begun. Modeling God consciousness means providing the child with an environment where spiritual values and compassion are the rules and not the exceptions. Spiritual values and practices vary from family to family, but compassion always remains as the service to another spirit soul. Compassion can be thought of in this way because every soul is part and parcel of God, the original spiritual source and person. With this attitude, a parent is modeling compassion, and at the same time giving unconditional love and service to their child as a unique and special spirit soul.

When children are learning about God, it is important for their teachers to be aware of the development of the child's cognitive abilities and limitations at different ages. Children understand things differently than adults do. Hence adults must respect this difference and give children teachings that they can understand. For example, sometimes a parent might give a set of many successive directions to a young child, resulting in the child's failure at the task, whereas if the parent had given one direction at a time and waited until the child was successful before giving the next, the child would have felt a greater sense of achievement and consequently had her self-esteem enhanced. When a teacher or parent is not sensitive to the limits of cognitive development, the teaching process is not successful, and at best the child will be confused and misled.

Very young children from birth about eighteen months are of course just beginning to explore their world. They are identifying with those who care for them, bonding to primary caretakers, and finding that they are different from the external world around them. This is a time when parents can grow tremendously in their own appreciation for the child as developing soul. Parents can appreciate the beautiful gift of life that God has given to them, and meditate on the mercy of God so to give them strength in teaching their child.

The needs of the child at this stage are intimately connected to the child's later sense of security, trust, and overall adjustment to the world around her. Children at this age come to learn of the warm, intimate, and caring relationship that is so important as a precedent to later learning. This can be exemplified by the parent who spends those quiet, intimate moments with his infant and includes the infant in as many of his own spiritual practices as possible. In this way the parent is already modeling behaviors of spiritual practices and setting the tone for how they can be infinitely special.

From eighteen months to about seven years, numerous changes occur in the child's ability to understand and learn. The child is now able to represent something with something else, such as in her play and gestures, her speech, and in mental pictures. For example, play takes on the quality of pretend which allows the child to differentiate fantasy and reality. Language is a set of verbal representations, and gestures serve to have an implied meaning which is separate from the gestures themselves. The child at this stage is now more able to take the perspective of another person. This is also an age when children become most susceptible to modeling the behaviors of their parents. Children can be encourage to participate with parents in spiritual practices, and they can understand that these practices are special. Parents can help children to understand that these practices are special by having a special place in the house and even a time of day for the child to worship God.

This is also an age when children can learn more about God by exploring what God has created. God can be understood by the child to be the source of the things around her and as the creator of all things. It is important for children to learn about God through sharing these exploring opportunities with their parents. This can mean a quiet walk outdoors, sharing the scent of a newly blossomed rose, or touching the softness of a rabbit's fur. All of these represent to the child what God has created, and begin to develop an appreciation for God's unlimited diversity in the world around her. Since God is a concrete concept to a child of this stage, it is important that the child is not forced to adopt abstract interpretations of God. Young children are concrete in their thinking (unlike adults) and may be confused by abstract ideas about God. It may help if parents can provide in their place of worship a picture of the spiritual teacher or of the Deity so that the child can relate to what she is worshipping and learning about.

In the years from seven to eleven, children base their logic on objects and states that can be manipulated. For example, children can understand the sameness between materials that have been modified along previously similar dimensions, and they can now understand that objects can be classified along more than one dimension (as in the case of an orange which is a fruit as well as a round object). Again, understanding the child's predominantly concrete orientation is important, especially in the early years of this stage. Children should always be encouraged to take part in the worship of God through offering flowers, food, or incense to the pictures of the spiritual teacher or the Deity. This is a concrete activity by which children can appreciate the sincerity of the parent in his worship of God in this way. Children should be encouraged to join their parents in brief periods of meditation, chanting, singing, or prayer, as these are also ways by which the child can make an offering to God. Sitting quietly outdoors in a peaceful place with eyes closed and controlled breathing can help the child learn meditation as well as how to relax. Such meditation is an activity of worship and of learning about God's serenity, in which children can participate with their parents.

During the adolescent years, reasoning is now free from the concrete realm. Reason for the adolescent can be based on verbal or logical statements. Adolescents can construct belief systems, become actively engaged in the world of ideas, and reflect on their own thinking. This is the level of cognitive operations at which adults function, and will be easiest for parents to understand as it emerges in their child. At this stage the adolescent can formulate God as an abstract concept, and learn about God by abstract means. It is important, however, that parents encourage adolescents to continue participating in those practices which were established earlier. At this age, however, it is also important to allow the adolescent to formulate her own ideas, and to make her own judgments about how to apply them. If adolescents are forced against their own desires regarding spiritual practices, the result will often be rebellion. Instead, parents should try to be supportive and encouraging to the choices of their teenagers since adolescence brings so many difficult issues to cope with.

The importance of understanding the cognitive development schema of children is essential, especially when considering how a child learns about God. As the primary teachers of God consciousness for children, parents who are aware of their child's limitations and capabilities will be successful in their teachings. Also, the parent who develops an environment of worship within the home will increase his child's appreciation of God consciousness. The house should be thought of as a place for worship as well as a place to live. In such a place of worship, chores can be thought of as service to God, and relations among family members should always be in the consciousness of encouraging spiritual growth and enhancing self-esteem.

Knowledge of the all-pervading feature of God cannot be understood unless one is devoted to God. Understanding God as all-pervading is beyond our power of intelligence, mind, and sense. God must therefore be revealed to us, as we are limited in our understanding. This process takes place only through devoted service to worshipping God. Eastern scriptures teach that God exists everywhere, and everything exists within God, yet God is not visible everywhere. God is visible only through devotional service. This is a position that a child can understand, because the child is fully capable of making an offering to God as the supreme source of everything. For example, when preparing a meal, prepare it in order to make it an offering to God. As the foodstuffs are part of God's Divine creation, so they should first be offered back. Children can assist in the preparation of such offerings, and develop the consciousness that such offerings must be prepared with sincerity and devotion. The offering can then be placed on the altar in the home, and the child can recite her own offering prayer, or one that the parent uses in his devotional practice.

Since every one of God's energies, beauties, qualities, and opulence are unlimited, no one can understand God by his own power, but only by devotion. God is revealed to the parent and the child as a function of their desire to serve and as a function of their sincerity in devotion. This devotion can be modeled for the child by the parent. Again, since parents can be the best teachers, their example is the finest teaching tool. As the parent strives to increase his devotion, so will the child. As adults, we must strive to do so at every moment. In this way, we are by example setting the occasion for our children to also take up this process of increasing their devotion to God. As devotion increases, God is increasingly revealed to the student, no matter if the student is a small child or an adult.

Children, just as adults, learn about God through life experiences and through the wisdom of others. Children, however, need to have parents provide those life experiences which will allow them to have realizations about God and their spiritual life. For children, since they are under different cognitive and social constraints than adults, examples of God consciousness which are applicable to their own lives often set the occasion for an optimal learning experience. So on behalf of the world of children, I ask the parents of the world to meditate on being able to provide that ever-important element of their child's education.

PART II

The Spirituality of Motherhood

Two days before my daughter was born, I went shopping in the local whole foods co-op. At that point in my pregnancy strangers tended to smile at me and ask, "How are you feeling? When's the baby due?", eyeing me suspiciously as if it were about to happen on the spot, so I had taken to wearing a button that read "Just fine. June 1."

On that particular day a woman I had seen at the store a few times stopped me, and after we had exchanged the usual information, she said, "I hope that your birth experience will be as wonderful and beautiful and spiritual as mine was."

Spiritual it was, but not in the sense of being ecstatic, joyous, or even particularly beautiful. Rather, I knew myself to have been touched by the hands of the gods, blessed by them against all expectation: granted a rapid labor and delivery without drugs or incisions, and on top of it—the bonus prize behind door number three—gifted with a lusty daughter who was undeniably lovely and incontrovertibly my own.

For over twenty years I had looked forward to this greatest of life's passages, anticipated sharing in the experience of millions of women. So this is what labor pains are like; and yes, at the crowning you do feel you are being pulled apart (you're not), and yes, with each push you do feel sucked down into a pool of black water, and yes, Nature does as She wishes. Perhaps because I choose to envision the Divine as female and maternal, I can only stare mutely in awe of the tragedies She may decide to call forth upon our children—disease, deformity, retardation. One need not ask, as one might demand of the purportedly all-loving Father-God, Why me? Why my child? What did I do to deserve this? There is no punishment, only the inexorable forces of Divine Nature.

I know a man whose wife had a healthy pregnancy and a normal, home birth attended by an obstetrician, yet the child was ultimately found to be retarded. Now, at the age of sixteen, the daughter cannot walk or talk, care for herself or learn anything. No cause was ever found. Almost irreverently, one thinks of the commercial of some years back in which a pleasant, white-robed, matronly Mother Nature is fooled into believing a certain brand of margarine is butter. Her smile freezes. "It's not nice to fool Mother Nature," she warns, and in an instant the blooming forest is devastated by a winter storm. If you looked closely enough, surely you could just make out her fangs.

This is the terrible discovery one makes as a pregnant woman—that God has fangs.

It is easy to do as the Victorians and idealize (or idolize) children. "No thought of sin has ever crossed your brow!" cried Lewis Carroll, another old bachelor. Surely it is more comfortable to regard children as little angels or as special souls who have chosen their parents rather than as little demons. Life, in all its joyous, tragic, and obstinate forms, is indeed a miracle. My child has been transformed from a lumpy, invisible mass to a seemingly impossibly huge object to be expelled from my body, to a baby girl somehow deposited between my feet, arms outstretched, blue cord spiraling out between us. In these past months, no matter how many books and articles I read on infant development, those first sparks of intelligence remain wonderfully mysterious. If you look into a newborn baby's eyes, those cloudy orbs that search your face as if trying to recognize you, inevitably the question will arise: what is the origin of its spirit? A baby's eyes are a miracle that happens every day. Who can make an eye? Where her body came from is clear enough, but her little spirit—that invisible but no less real part of her being—where did that arise from? In the Book of Job we read: "Hath the rain a father? or who hath begotten the drops of dew? Out of whose womb came the ice?...Hast thou given the horse strength? hast thou clothed his neck with thunder?"

Is it true, as some of the world's peoples believe, that the laboring mother must descend into the underworld to fetch a new soul to inhabit her child? It was not until after Catherine was born that I read about this concept, yet it felt right. Those last ten or fifteen minutes, while I worked at pushing her out—each push was a plunge into black watery depths. The only way to get out of the depths was to dive back in. A few days afterwards my mother made a remark about my having just passed through the Valley of the Shadow of Death, which my brother found needlessly melodramatic. The fact was, however, that the Valley is precisely where I had been—for a blessedly brief time, it is true, but I instantly recognized her image. Giving birth, even with an easy delivery, is a descent into the depths. It is an act of extra-ordinary courage that is performed by women thousands of times a day.

In our zeal to make the world anew with each new life, we are prone to terrible guilt at any compromise or shortcoming. Our emotions during pregnancy will not always be serene; insisting upon a serene pregnancy is like expecting a calm demeanor from a soldier going to war. We need to remember that children are incredibly resilient—that even children who have grown up under the most terrible conditions of war, abject poverty, or abuse are nevertheless capable of becoming healthy, loving, and productive adults. Yet often we strive to have the perfect pregnancy, the perfect birth, the perfect baby, and all this perfection has to begin with the perfect frame of mind, doesn't it? But soon we find that it is no easy task to keep ourselves from being unduly influenced by all the prenatal and neonatal advice, warnings, and fears we are subjected to.

Despite all good intentions about keeping a good attitude and communing with the child within her, a woman may find herself tormented by fears and worries, if not about the impending birth itself then about the health of the baby and the skill and sensitivity of the birth attendants. At this time meditation, prayer, ritual, or all three are as vital to her well-being as milk and exercise. Fathers, too, need emotional care, for they tend to feel themselves even less in control of events than mothers-to-be, especially during a first pregnancy.

During pregnancy our spirits need to be specially nourished by those around us. It is a good thing for friends to gather together for a formal blessing of the pregnant woman at a time when she feels it is appropriate; such a blessing ritual is described later in this section. All too often an expectant mother or father is greeted with, "Boy, is your life going to change!" instead of, "How marvelous! Parenthood is a wonderful thing, it will make you so happy." And people who choose to become parents outside of a conventional heterosexual marriage may be subjected to such extreme negative emotions from family and acquaintances that some people will simply have to be excluded from your life during the pregnancy.

A lunar calendar is nice to have at this time, for the projected date of the birth is most correctly reckoned not as nine months but as forty weeks or ten lunar cycles. With a lunar calendar a woman can be aware of the possible influence of the full moon on conception and birth, since most women tend to be fertile around the full moon, which is also associated with births. I recount further along the story of a lovely conception ritual which might be performed at the full moon or when the woman to be blessed is in her fertile period. The moon can be honored throughout the pregnancy as well: as the child waxes within you, honor the Lady each month at the new moon or waxing crescent, giving thanks for the month that has just passed, and petition Her for a healthy and serene month to come.

For us, a home birth would have been possible, but David was nervous about the distance to the hospital in case of an emergency, and having attended two home births with doctors present, he preferred to have a physician at our birth, which made it mandatory for me to go to the hospital since in our community home births are attended by lay midwives but not doctors. One reason I did not press for a home birth is that I felt psychologically safest with my own physician, a woman my age who was not an obstetrician but a family practitioner. I was powerfully aware, too, of the very real bonding that a pregnant woman experiences with her birth attendant. Astronomer Carl Sagan claims that when dying people see a "being of light" approaching them at the end of a long tunnel, they are actually flashing back to their own births—the "being of light" is none other than the doctor. All the more reason, I thought, to make sure that the first face my baby sees is a special one.

Many progressive-minded people make the assumption that birthing in medical surroundings indicates some spiritual or moral failing on the part of the parents. One friend, on hearing me mention the hospital, said, "Oh, you didn't have a natural birth?" Feminists re-examining the birth experience as enacted in contemporary Western society have rightly criticized many aspects of it and warn that despite the movement towards midwifery, home birth, and natural methods, the true trend in

America today is towards an ever-more technologically managed conception, pregnancy, and delivery. While there is no disputing that historically hospitals have been dangerous and nasty places for women, it is also true that a birth experience there can be pleasant, supportive, and sacred. It depends on where you are and on being aware of the rules of sacrality: observing traditions of taboo and purification, the initiate (the mother) enters the House of Death, "dies," remains out of sight for three days, and finally re-emerges as/with a newly created being, for the birth of a child also signals the birth of a mother and a father.

The very use of the term "delivery" has been rejected by some women, as in "The doctor delivers the baby," i.e. frees it, liberates it from the confines of the woman's body, or "She is delivered of a son," i.e. the woman is freed from the fetters of pregnancy. Midwives and some doctors stress, "The *mother* delivers the child." I myself did not think of my doctor as delivering the baby, although she did indeed free her from the umbilical cord wrapped round her neck. Rather, she was one of my guides, at times acting as referee or traffic cop, since she had to shout to be heard through her mask and over the exhortations of David and our friend Ann Marie. "Put your foot there. Stop pushing. Don't breathe out."

The doctor, like the Greek childbirth goddess Eilithyia, approaches the birthing bed veiled head to foot. "I just dress this way so I won't get wet," she explains. While it is natural to want to protect one's clothes from the waters, the blood, and the wet infant, the true function of the green hospital clothes is that of ritual garb. Just as I wore a white lace gown at my wedding, lest I forget why I was in front of a homemade altar next to a horse pasture, the birth attendants wear their own form of ritual costume.

If an obstetrician from twenty years ago could have been transported in time to the hospital birthing room where

Catherine was born, he (even today the vast majority of obstetricians are male) would have been shocked at what he saw: the patient undrugged, unprepped, uncut, untrammeled and wearing unsterile kneesocks, two other non-medical personnel on either side of her, no one but the doctor wearing hats or masks, the father cutting the umbilical cord, the placenta and cord saved and put in the freezer.

If you discuss options with your childbirth educator, doctor or midwife, and friends who have given birth recently, you may discover possibilities you had never thought of. At one birth in our community a group of friends played guitars and sang to the laboring woman—the nurses would not permit candles for fear of fire, but they thought the music was a great idea. If you request it, the father may be allowed to receive the baby as it emerges or to cut the umbilical cord himself. I have heard of a father actually being permitted to lift the baby out of the mother's abdomen during a cesarean birth. Prospective parents tend to feel that they are simply at the mercy of the doctor and hospital, but this is not really the case. With a home birth, of course, you have much more leeway, but if the birth is going to take place in a hospital and there are non-traditional things you would like to do, ask. You may be surprised at the medical staff's flexibility.

When you go into the labor or birthing room, feel free to take possession of it by making it sacred space. Burning incense is not a good idea in a place where oxygen may be used, but by utilizing crystals, visualization, or simple prayer you can make the hospital room your own. Hanging up posters of birthing goddesses who are powerful and serene can give you more of a feeling of possession of the room. What better to focus on than matriarchal art? Besides, you may be there all night and into the morning, so you might as well have something pleasant to look at. In the section on "Resources" at the end of the book are listed some sources of birthing-goddess art, and later on in this chapter are described the sacred rites performed by Native American teacher OhShinnah Fastwolf and her family at the hospital birth of her grandchild.[2]

Lamaze instructors recommend the use of a "focus object", which may be anything from a photograph of a loved one to your left thumb, to which you direct your attention during a contraction. Here favorite sacred objects can be used, such as crystals, stones, pictures, herb bags, Tarot cards.

A propos of focus, many Eastern spiritual traditions emphasize focusing at a point near the womb or slightly below the navel during meditation or psychic work. In martial arts training we learn that this is one's power point, the source of the vital energy the Japanese call *ki* and the Chinese *ch'i*. During childbirth, however, maintaining focus is for the mind, not the body, for the secret of giving birth is that during labor you do not have to *do* anything: you allow the labor to do itself. The wisest and most experienced doctors, nurses, and midwives understand that the best births are the ones that are permitted to take place without interference, while bearing in mind that at times Nature might need a nudge. You don't give birth with your face, your arms and legs, or your hands, but with your womb, up to the final stage when the baby is being pushed out, when the entire body seems to suddenly go to work.

Prepared childbirth might be boiled down to two precepts: 1) Don't panic; 2) Keep your body relaxed. Granted, this is easier said than done when your belly is being gnawed and twisted, though every labor has its own character. After six years of karate and several years of yoga, relaxing certain parts of my body while other parts were tensed was more familiar to me than driving a car, yet I found I had to keep letting go of my limbs with a conscious effort. Rather than focusing on building power, it is more helpful to focus on opening the energy center, like a lotus unfolding, opening yourself up.

My doctor rolled her eyes but said nothing when we told her we wanted to keep the placenta and cord after our baby's birth. Keeping the birth material may never have come up at some hospitals, but there's no harm in asking. It is not clear whether the placenta and cord legally belong to the parents or to the hospital; usually the hospital lays claim to any organs, tissues, or body parts that have been removed, but recently some patients have sued hospitals to prevent body parts or substances being used without their knowledge or consent. In any case, if you don't make a point of asking to keep the placenta the hospital personnel almost certainly will discard it without mentioning it. It can be kept in a freezer container in the hospital until you leave.

In traditional Europe the placenta and cord were often buried under the doorstep. In the British film *The Wicker Man* a pagan community in modern Scotland planted trees for each child born, and hung the dried navel string from a branch.

I have read that the placenta can be cooked with onions and eaten (by the adventurous). It is recommended by some traditional healers that the mother eat a bit of the placenta, probably to restore some of the mother's estrogen, the level of which tends to plunge after a birth and can lead to post-partum depression.

Because I decided to stay in the hospital for an extra day after giving birth, we had very little time to dispose of the placenta before my parents were to arrive at our house. David cut a small chunk off the afterbirth which we kept in the freezer in case we wanted to fry it up with some liver, and the rest, along with the cord, was placed in a hole in the garden, over which a bleeding heart bush was to be planted.

I was amazed at the size of the afterbirth, as large as a hefty pot roast. No wonder my belly had gotten so huge! We had to work fast, lest my mother show up and wonder what we were doing. We had saved a bottle of red wine David had made in 1980—an excellent year for Chez Price—for just such a special occasion. The day was grey and damp, and I stood by the garden holding our new baby bundled up in a blanket—like most newborns, she slept through the rituals honoring her birth. We shared a chaliceful of the wine, giving thanks to the Goddess for coming through once again. To show the profound gratitude I felt for my birth experience—and the added gift of a daughter—I insisted that we pour all the rest of the wine into the ground with the placenta: a true and sincere sacrifice.

We never did eat the piece we saved. We kept looking at it, hemming and hawing, and finally, just before my mother came to visit a second time, David said, "We'd better get rid of this before she thinks it's a piece of liver." This time we buried it under the garlic. It had thawed slightly, and I felt awed by this seemingly alien hunk of tissue that had been a part of my body two months before.

If by any chance the baby is born with a caul, by all means save it. (The caul is simply a piece of the amniotic sac which has clung to the baby while it is being birthed.) Throughout Europe children born with cauls over their faces were believed to be special: psychic, especially lucky, or immune from drowning. Up through the nineteenth century the dried caul itself might be sold as a lucky charm, often to sailors.

A charming custom is planting a tree or bush near where you live in honor of the child so that the child can watch it grow and experience its power. Among Jewish people it has become a custom to have a tree planted in Israel in someone's honor, often at the birth of a child. From ancient times, Jews, like many other peoples, planted trees at the birth of a baby, the boughs being used years later for the bridal canopy or chuppah.

If planting a tree near the home is not practical, parents can have a tree planted in Israel or can make a donation in the child's name to some project that enhances the agriculture or environment of another country or another part of this country.

Most traditional cultures require a period of strict seclusion for mother and baby, often extending for several weeks. Even today a Chinese mother does not venture out of the house for six weeks following a birth. Hospitals, too, observe strict seclusion of the newborn, and for the same reason: to minimize the transmission of germs from visitors. Nowadays some parents are advising against taking the baby out in public right away (some babies are out and about only a few days after they are born), the reasoning being that the new little soul needs some time to accustom itself to our world and doesn't need more stimulation than its new life already provides. Customarily, two weeks is often the period adhered to; the first week after the birth is usually so hectic that the parents can't get it together enough to go anywhere anyway.

Parents can have an astrological chart done of the child, and you will find a number of books listed in the bibliography which outline the implications of a baby's chart. People who are skilled in astrology understand that the stars only show tendencies; they do not rigidly predict a person's future character.

The same caution should be given about doing numerology on the child's birthdate, i.e. adding up the digits to find the child's sacred number. A child born November 14, 1982, for example, has a sacred number of nine. It must be pointed out that, unlike the position of the planets at the moment of birth, which is verifiable for anyone born at a certain time and place, our months, days, and years are reckoned according to arbitrary custom. Is a Jewish child born in the year 5740, 1979 A.D., or 9979 A.D.A.? (A.D.A stands for "After the Development of

Agriculture," or 10,000 B.C., and is used by some spiritual feminists to reckon time by the religion of the Great Goddess.)

The number of letters in a name can be easily altered by changing the spelling, and this is often done when the individual starts to feel drawn to a different resonance and unconsciously tries to harmonize with this resonance by changing the letters in her or his name (viz. *Anne of Green Gables*, who insisted on being Anne with an E, and a host of subsequent Annes.)

It is not only the child who should be thought of at this time. Feminist witch Z Budapest, recognizing the new mother's powerful need for attention and affection after giving birth, shares a ceremony with us that celebrates the new status motherhood confers. Another important, yet generally neglected, event is the return of menstruation, which occurs when breast-feeding is lessened or ended. A ritual for this return of the blood cycle is included at the very end of this section, that we may acknowledge the closing of the sacred time of new motherhood.

After the birth of my daughter, the overriding emotions I experienced were first, relief—at a safe, easy delivery—and second, profound gratitude. I felt delivered indeed, saved, blessed, touched by the hand of God. In the following days and nights and weeks after a birth it can be difficult to maintain a sense of joy—when you roll out of bed at 4.30 a.m. for the fourth time since midnight, parenthood definitely loses some of its appeal. But when Uncle Wriggly turned into Mommy's Little Angel, dropping off to sleep in my arms after a nursing, I would gaze upon her pale, perfect skin and the gratitude would flow back into my heart. With all the difficulties of raising even a healthy, normal child, it is hard—maybe impossible, and perhaps rightly so—to maintain a sunny disposition and a song in your heart. But rather than gnashing our teeth at two a.m., we should be giving thanks to God for giving us these incredible lessons in love.

Instead of growling, "Rats! Won't that kid ever stay asleep?" we should rise up saying, "Thank you, God, for giving me the opportunity to get up in the night to care for a baby. And thank you for allowing me to sleep for two hours." And when our meditation, Tarot reading, or healing work is interrupted by the patter of tiny feet or the inevitable wail of an infant, we should take leave of our psychic work by saying, "And thank you for reminding me that I do not live for myself alone."

Conception Ritual

Anne Carson

Sometimes we feel that it is not enough to have a good mental attitude when we are seeking to become parents; we need to enlist the aid of the heavens. Women have been performing fertility rituals of one kind or another for thousands of years. Whether we offer flowers to Hera or burn a candle to Mary, the intent is the same: to obtain the assistance of the Great Mother of Life. During the months I was trying to conceive, in addition to seeking medical advice I kept images of fertility and good fortune on my desk/altar: Lakshmi, the Hindu goddess of abundance; a special rock from North Wales that has a small stone embedded in it, as if it were giving birth; from the Tarot deck, the Empress (symbolizing the feminine principle), the Queen of Pentacles (the body and the physical plane), the Queen of Cups (the emotional plane), the Nine of Pentacles (a well-to-do woman in her garden), and so forth. Some women may prefer to draw upon the good wishes of friends and relatives as they set forth on this new project, as in the following ritual which was described to me:

On a beautiful Saturday in October, at a cabin in upstate New York, a group of women held a fertility/conception ritual for a friend who was hoping to become pregnant. She had invited a small group of friends, all but one mothers themselves, asking each guest to bring something that reminded her of her own childhood or motherhood, as well as a baby picture of herself.

Since most of the women present had never participated in any kind of ritual before and were feeling rather awkward, one woman acted as facilitator of the ceremony, explaining to the group what the ceremony would entail and the importance of ritual itself. She explained that the ritual was simply a way to create a different sort of space and that no one had to feel that they were engaging in something dreadfully solemn or religious.

The women sat around an altar lit with candles, and using invocations from Starhawk's *The Spiral Dance*, the four cardinal directions were invoked. A cup of salt water was passed around, each woman sipping from it, and sage was burned, thus purifying the room and creating sacred space. A song by feminist musician Linda Tillery played on the tape recorder.

The woman for whom the ritual was being held shared the reasons she had invited these particular women to bless her fertility, for each of them bore some quality as mothers or as women which she wanted to pass on to her child.

The guests were given paper and pencil and asked to write down issues that they wanted to clear out from their lives, with the understanding that this would not necessarily be accomplished there and then. Each woman shared her issue, habit, or problem, and together the pieces of paper were burned in the woodstove. "That was the most intense part of the ritual," a participant recalled. "There was a lot of emotion and crying."

Then each woman showed what she had brought and explained its significance: one had brought her baby's gift book; another, an item she had been given when she was pregnant as well as something her child had been given as a baby; some women brought baby clothing; one woman brought a photograph of herself and her daughter. The woman for whom the ritual was being held had brought many things which she displayed and described, such as a shell contributed by her husband, for whom the beach and the ocean were of great importance.

At the close of the ritual, the four directions were thanked and taken leave of, and champagne was served.

Blessing of the Pregnant Woman

Anne Carson

One of the most thoughtful presents a pregnant woman's friends can give her is a blessing, either at the beginning of the pregnancy or near its conclusion. Simple blessings are often given spontaneously by people who do not ordinarily think of themselves as spiritual, but a ritualized blessing, especially when given by friends who are also mothers, is a beautiful, healing gift to the expectant mother, for in honoring one woman we honor all women. A blessing may be given as part of a baby shower, or it may be specially requested by the mother. If she is feeling particularly vulnerable psychically she may wish to include only her closest friends and relatives, and only those women who have had positive birth experiences. This will all depend upon the needs of the individual woman. If he wishes to participate, the father ought to be included too, for he will want to add his own blessings and perhaps speak of his own hopes and fears.

An ideal time and place would be outdoors on a sunny day, but in the winter a warm, firelit living room will serve just as well.

The participants are asked to bring prayers, songs, and presents, either gifts for the baby, such as a quilt made by the woman's friends or other practical items like clothing, or symbolic gifts such as flowers, special rocks, feathers, jewelry, beautiful pictures, or things that are interesting to touch. The mother can tuck these into her bag in preparation for the birth.

Friends and relatives may create a blessing book for the baby, with each page containing a blessing from a different person. (And let us bolt the door against the thirteenth, wicked fairy!)

Red candles, symbolizing the life-force, may be lit. For incense, burn sage, sandalwood, or Sophia (sacred to mothers and daughters).

The invocation is given:

"We call upon the Great Mother, Gaia, the Greek primordial Mother of All. She mothers children; more importantly, she mothers mothers. We are not called to be children in relation to her, but to be birthgivers ourselves."

The participants should sit or stand in a circle around the pregnant woman. With all holding hands, energy is raised by whatever means is appropriate to the group: breathing, singing, chanting, reciting prayers, or having each person speak her or his personal blessing.

A special song to sing is the Adi Shakti mantra from Kundalini yoga, which is a prayer to the Mother of the Universe:

Adi Shakti, Adi Shakti, Adi Shakti, Namo Namo.
Sarab Shakti, Sarab Shakti, Sarab Shakti, Namo Namo.
Pritum Bhagavate, Pritum Bhagavate, Pritum Bhagavate,
    Namo Namo.
Kundalini, Mat Shakti, Mat Shakti, Namo Namo.

(To the primal female power, I bow.
To the complete female power, I bow.
To the Mother of Creation, I bow.
To the Great Coil of Energy, the Mother Power, I bow.)

Repeat thirteen times, focusing on directing the energy towards the woman and her baby.

The woman may want to be touched and held during the blessing; her body, or just her feet, can be bathed in water infused with sweet-smelling herbs: rosebuds, lavender, rosemary. A pregnancy tea is prepared and drunk by all: raspberry leaves (to strengthen the womb), peppermint (to settle the stomach), and chamomile (for relaxation). Afterwards there can be a party for all, with food, advice, and laughter.

A Native American Birth Ritual

Anne Carson

At a workshop on the divine feminine energy, Native American teacher and healer OhShinnah Fastwolf described the birth of her daughter's child, which was attended by a physician in a hospital. "Make a friend of your birth attendant," she advised. "We used to have the doctor over for dinner, and by the time my grandchild was born he was ready to let us do anything." All or part of this ritualized birth may appeal to you, or you might prefer to make up your own ritual using traditions from Native American or other cultures.

Needed are: very small crystals, a feather (blue heron or water birds are best, don't use owl or buzzard), a piece of wood from a living tree that has been struck by lightning (symbolizing tenacity and the finitude of life), bee pollen (symbolizing food), and cedar or sage to serve as incense to smoke the area.

Four crystals are to be put under the bed, each pointing towards one of the cardinal directions. First the mother breathes a prayer into each one, starting with the direction of the season you are in (Spring-East, Summer-South, Autumn-West, Winter-North). If possible, the mother's feet should be pointing in that direction as well.

When the birth is near, the attendant or family member touches a crystal to the mother's sternum, her third eye, and then her crown chakra so that the body can open up. During each contraction the father takes the feather and waves it downward over the belly.

Just before the crowning, the attendant touches pollen to the mother's hands, solar plexus, soles of her feet, third eye, tongue, and crown chakra. At crowning the father touches the baby's head very lightly with the pollen, and rubs pollen on his hands so that he can receive the child as it is born.

After the child emerges it is brought at once to the mother's heart so that the heartbeat is the first sound it hears. The father whispers the baby's name into its ear so that it's the first person to hear it. The baby is blessed with pollen on the same spots as was the mother.

The placenta and umbilical cord are saved; the placenta is buried and a tree planted over it. This spot becomes a power place for the child. As for the cord, cut off about eight inches from the placenta end, milk it, put beads on it and knot the ends with white yarn. This will become the baby's teething ring. The rest of the cord is saved, along with a bit of cornmeal and tobacco, in a leather bag with a turtle on it. One of the birth crystals and a bit of the piece of wood from the lightning-struck tree are bound to the outside of the bag, which the baby will wear, minus the crystal, until it walks well. The feather is saved, and red yarn is wrapped around the base with a bit of tobacco inside.

After the birth the father goes outside and makes an offering of cornmeal or tobacco to the six directions (the four compass points plus sky and earth). (People who don't smoke can purchase loose tobacco at smoke shops.)

The parents should be on the lookout for an animal totem around the time of the birth, and when one is found, make up a song about the animal, which will be the child's totem until puberty.

Ten days after the birth, the naked baby, held in a cotton or wool blanket, is presented to earth and sky.

Welcoming a New Mother into the Circle of Mothers

Z Budapest

We have baby showers for expectant mothers, bridal showers for young brides, but once you become a mother, nobody cares a hoot. This must change. You, as a mother, now need attention and affection more than ever. You also need new clothes, new ideas, and new friends.

To give birth is as important as the greatest military victory, even more. To take life is easy. The American Indians believed that to go through labor, birthing, is to go down to hell to fetch a new spirit into the light. Society has decided to focus on your new baby more than you. You can change that by starting this new celebration of yourself.

The Ceremony

Time: After the woman has given birth and feels strong enough to do it. This should be the first thing the woman is participating in.

Invite: Women who have had babies, if you can. If not, invite all the   women whom you like and whose company you cherish.

This event should be planned by your friends. They should present you with three gifts of importance: 1) A new gown, or material for it. This can be any color, but green is preferred. A green-robed lady is the Goddess who gives birth, and then renews herself, becoming a virgin. 2) An herbal tea which is good for the womb, like raspberry. 3) Tickets to a cultural event that you have to go out for. It should be a treat with color and content.

The women establish a time when the new mother is to be in bed with her baby, resting. As a surprise, they enter her room. Three women representing the Fates—a Nymph, a Maiden, and a Crone—come bearing gifts. The women have branches of trees. Use whatever you can provide, but evergreen branches are best, as they are the symbols of rebirth. Do not use ivy, as it is sacred to death, along with being poisonous. Bring flowers too, whatever is in season, and some incense sticks. Sandalwood is best.

The first mother greets the new mothers, saying, "Blessed be thou...(insert the name of new mother). We heard in the air that you have returned to the world of mothers. Welcome to the company of creators of humanity!"

The second mother says: "Blessed be thou...(the new mother). We have brought you gifts that make you whole. This new gown was sent to you to clothe you with the beauty of your new life. Blessed be your body, that you will grow strong, to return you to your own after you were gone. Your body and soul fetched a new soul from the unborn." They kiss and exchange the gift informally.

The third mother says: "Blessed be thou...(the new mother). I give you an herb that is sweet to your womb. Drink it, and bless it. Be whole. Here are some theater tickets (invitation to a grand ball, a picnic, a hiking trip, tennis, a swimming party), to rekindle your spirits. You worked hard, and your spirit is tired. Come to this party, and we will all laugh and praise the Goddess!" They exchange the gift informally.

Then the new mother speaks to the three: "I am blessed today as a new mother, and welcomed into the circle of mothers."

The other three say: "We love you. It is done."

Conclude with a general party.

Ritual for the Return of the Blood Cycle After Birth

Anne Carson

The return of the monthly period after the cleansing post-partum bleeding is a signal that the everyday life of the body, alas, has returned to normal. Depending on frequency and duration of breast-feeding, the blood will re-appear when the baby no longer gets its primary nourishment from Mother, since with the lessening of nursing, the mother's body no longer needs to conserve its resources in order to provide food for the baby, and is ready to support another pregnancy. Now is the time to be vigilant about birth control, for the protective shield of lactation is no longer about you. It may have been a year and a half since the last period, and habits will have to be re-learned.

Now is the time, too, to recognize that the time of your sacred status as new mother has begun to come to a close. It will formally end when you wean your child, but for now you must accept that the rhythm of daily life is returning.

Sometimes as soon as the pregnancy becomes known we start wearing our hair in a new style, even if it is only parting it on the opposite side or using different ornaments, to maintain mindfulness of the changes occurring within us. If you have not yet done so, after the birth would also be an appropriate time to consider changing your appearance. Some new clothes will also be in order, since it may be many months before you can fit into your pre-pregnant clothes.

Life will never be "just like before," and from now on, when you look in the mirror, your altered body shape, new hairstyle, new clothes will remind you of the great transformation that has taken place.

Time: Full Moon (for fecundity), or Dark Moon (for end-
ings), or first night of the blood's return.

Wear clothes you owned before the pregnancy. If possible
wear your hair in the style you had *before* the baby.

Light a red candle.

Burn Sophia or sandalwood incense.

Sit alone, in a private place, as the women of old sat in their
moon-huts. Reflect on the changes and events that have occurred
since you became pregnant. Know that, yes, your life has altered
forever, and that it has changed for the good. You are on a great
adventure, a journey whose exact destination is unknown. Know
that the wisdom of the Mother, and of all the earthly mothers
who have gone before you, is always available. Feel the power of
the fire, the red power within you. Draw strength from the flame.
You will need it.

PART III

The Spirituality of Infants

The little one is in your arms and both of you are beginning to get to know each other. We read so much about the importance of bonding between parent (especially mother) and child, yet true bonding may take place gradually over several weeks, not just happen within an hour in the birthing room. Bonding between a particular mother and baby does not always flash into being but needs to unfold at its own natural pace. Nevertheless, the current can flow quite electrically. Some people who as children were aware of having psychic powers have told of sensing a telepathic bond between themselves and their mothers, the connection seeming to run more strongly from mother to child than from child to mother. Everyone has heard of a mother having "eyes in the back of her head," or knowing intuitively when her child has had an accident, even though they may be many miles apart. Since mother and child were for a time one flesh, this seems not unreasonable. Thousands of documented instances exist of mental telepathy or referred physical pain between identical twins, who also were one flesh originally, so however this mechanism works—and scientists can only attest to its existence, not explain it—it should come as no surprise that a kind of telepathy can operate between mother and child.

The physical bond between mother and child that exists before birth is well known, but the experience of sacred union does not end with the cutting of the umbilical cord. Many religious traditions teach that in the reality that lies behind form, all beings—human and other earthly creatures, even the rocks and the stars—are one. Spiritual seekers are ever in quest of this wisdom, but as mothers we are able to directly experience it. Perhaps for this reason men seem to pursue spiritual union with even more fervor than do women, because they start out one step farther from it.

After the bodily separation of mother and child at birth, their physical union takes on a psychic-spiritual character. Without being aware of this phenomenon, I experienced it myself within a few days after giving birth. Even before leaving the hospital, while my baby lay out of sight in the nursery (my roommate was extremely ill), I caught myself curling up in bed in positions similar to my daughter's, and I had the feeling that if I opened my eyes, the hands before my face would be hers, not mine. For several weeks this sensation that she was still a part of my body was very real to me. When a woman says that her child is her flesh and blood, this is no figure of speech, it is an actual physical sensation.

On the bodily level, the consciousness of unity is most strongly felt during breast-feeding, as nourishment flows directly from mother to child, now outside the womb, creating a new sort of mystical bond. My husband openly expressed a wistful envy at being unable to experience this kind of closeness with his child. In this section, Stephanie Demetrakopoulos explores in depth the spirituality and mystical character of nursing. The pregnant woman is God Incarnate, while as nursing mother, a woman becomes the image of the Goddess who "pours out Her gifts in abundance."

Breast-feeding is certainly the most efficient way to provide food for the baby—no bottles, no waiting, just aim the little mouth in the right direction and the baby takes it from there.

That fastening-on with its surprising force is the first real contact the child makes with the mother after birth. Yet nursing can also make a mother feel incapable of leaving the baby for longer than an hour, make her gnawed by guilt for every minute ticking by when she does so, and make both parents aggravated at the seemingly permanent interruption of sleep. I was convinced that no one who advocates breast-feeding on demand has ever actually had to do it themselves! And a mother may be irked at being forced to do "nothing" for half an hour, eight or ten times a day.

However, nursing may be the best illustration of the Zen adage, "Don't just do something, sit there!" It is not often that we have the opportunity to sit quietly many times a day, day after day. One might look upon these times as gifts from the Mother, who forces us to stop trying to carry on our pre-parental life but to sit and seemingly do "nothing." Nursing requires less conscious attention than giving a bottle: no need to be concerned over correct angle or spills. But we are not simply "doing nothing" when we breast-feed. We can read a good mystery, read all that baby literature we were given in the hospital. Or we can pray.

It is heartening to see that breast-feeding is once again receiving the honor it deserves, yet many mothers believe that after two or three months they needn't bother with it any more. Or their doctor may tell them that when the baby starts eating solid food, breast milk is no longer good enough for her or him. Of the four women who brought their five-month-old babies to the reunion of our childbirth class, only one was still breast-feeding. The assumption is often made that because a baby can take cow's milk that she should drink it, or because she can drink from a cup that suckling is no longer necessary. Certainly each mother will make her own decisions about breast-feeding and weaning, sometimes helped along by the baby's increased preference for food. Some babies lose interest in nursing altogether when they learn to eat food; others would seemingly nurse forever if their mothers let them. Women in many traditional cultures think nothing of nursing a three- or four-year-old; in this culture such mothers would be threatened by their pediatricians with all sorts of dire consequences for the child's psyche.

Still, to everything there is a season, and sooner or later nursing must come to an end. Bringing a child into the world causes us to see the sacredness present in even the most mundane details of life—not all rituals involve robes and bowing. Some parents have successfully accomplished weaning from the breast by means of a low-key sort of ritual that is not harmful to the child and at the same time deepens its relationship with the non-nursing parent: when definitive weaning is felt to be desirable, usually when the child is one-and-a-half to two years old and has learned to eat a variety of foods, the father or co- parent simply takes the child away from home on a trip of two to three days' duration, perhaps to visit friends or family so that the surroundings will not be too strange. The child learns to be comfortable away from the breast while still under the loving care of a parent, and by the time he returns home his interest in nursing is either extinguished or greatly diminished.

In her book *Truth or Dare: Encounters with Power, Authority, and Mystery,* feminist witch Starhawk relates the following weaning story: "Sophia created a ritual for her daughter Vanessa when she weaned her at the age of two. Sophia's mother had given Vanessa a special cup at her birth, in keeping with a long-standing family tradition. At weaning, Sophia gave the cup to Vanessa within a sacred circle. She poured dairy milk into the child's cup and her own ritual chalice, saying, "Now this will be your cup, and I will no longer be your cup. Now we can be sisters, and drink together."[3]

Babies are not normally thought of as having a spiritual life. Before the acquisition of language there is much that cannot be

conveyed to them. Yet babies and toddlers, like anyone else learning a language, can comprehend many things long before they
are able to actually articulate them. The first time you tell a one-
year-old to wipe his mouth or fetch his bear, he may surprise you
by doing just that. If he understands concrete commands, what
else is he aware of?

Unless you believe, as some people do, that babies remember
the heaven-world far more clearly than we do, there is not much
point in introducing any formalized spiritual concepts for the
first two or three years of life. In conventional religion, spiritual
education tends to be downplayed until formal Sunday School
begins at the age of six. Until that time the child is given a few
religious books, such as illustrated prayers and Bible stories,
taken to church or temple on the most important religious feasts,
or included in the Seder or the lighting of the Chanukah candles.

You cannot appeal to the intellect of the very young child,
because the intellect as such has barely begun to function. Don't
expect a three-year-old to understand the workings of karma!
This does not mean that you should not give way to your eager-
ness to share your spiritual life with your baby, it is just that spiritual education needs to be geared to the child's age. Just as we use
different ways to explain where babies come from to a three-year-
old, an eight-year old, and a twelve-year-old, you can expect to
use a variety of techniques in introducing spirituality to children.

For the first year or two, the child is reacting to her world not
with thoughts and ideas but through her senses and her experience of the environment, and thus it is to the senses that you
must appeal. Thinking of a kind does take place, of course: an
older baby who is quietly nursing in preparation for bed is certainly thinking—you can see it on his face. He may not be con-
templating Truth but he is very likely ruminating over the day's
events, imagining playing with his toys, and so forth. He may

suddenly stop nursing, raise his head and crow at you with a smile, as if to say, "Hey, you've got a really interesting nose!"

Instead of trying to reach a tiny mind it is more effective to stimulate the child's senses and to appeal to her inherent love of activity and play through songs, music, images, picture books, stories, dance, rhythm, and the experience of the natural world.

Some guidelines for sharing spirituality with babies (up to the age of one-and-a-half to two years):

• Babies of all ages respond to music. The first music they hear is generally a lullaby, and the father, with his deep, resonant voice, can sing to the baby while it is still in the womb. Singing what has become your own special song has been known to calm newborn infants in the delivery room. In addition to lullabies, many sacred songs that are making their way around the country via ritual circles lend themselves readily to bedtime. Most of them are by Anonymous and can be heard on a number of records and tapes (see the list of Resources at the end of the book). There is also a growing number of music tapes of a spiritual nature which are geared towards children.

The following song is sung at the end of my class in Kundalini yoga. Catherine heard it in the womb, and I sing it to her every night before putting her to bed:

You will certainly have favorite lullabies of your own. Make a point of getting the grandparents to teach them to you.

Some parents like to play a lot of classical music while the mother is pregnant (it has been demonstrated that plants do very well to classical music, tend to shrivel at loud rock, and do nothing at all to country music). At the age of nine months to a year babies start showing appreciation of rhythm and may enjoy rhythmic music or being danced with. In a ritual gathering they can be given their own drum or rattle.

• Nature walks can begin with rides in the baby carrier and stroller. From the age of one year, when children are usually walking on their own and can manipulate objects well, they can be set down to explore in the back yard or park. While preventing them from being destructive, recognize that they are intensely curious about their environment and will not hesitate to pick flowers and leaves and to tear them apart. Garden vegetables, too, will be at risk if they are within reach of little hands. At this age grabbing things and pulling them apart is a means of conducting scientific investigation, not malicious destructiveness, but of course children cannot be allowed to simply run wild. It can be surprisingly easy to teach toddlers that gardens are for walking around, not in, and that the red tomatoes are for picking, not the green ones. By using a baby's own gesture of pushing away rejected items you can quickly teach a child which berries may not be eaten and which plants are not to be touched.

• Let babies hold and play with crystals, special rocks, Tarot cards, but keep your own candles, incense, wands, etc. out of reach. Runestones must be left until the child is past the everything-goes-in-the-mouth stage. Tarot cards, as Gail Fairfield has shown us in her article in the first section of this book, can be introduced from birth: at first the scenes will probably appear only as intriguing images, but who can say for sure? Perhaps the better-designed decks contain primal images the child can recognize and respond to on some deep, buried level. When the baby is old enough to play with objects, she is likely to be interested in sorting the cards. The deck should be taken out only occasionally so that the cards don't get destroyed.

• Young children can be shown pictures and art with sacred or fantasy themes. Sometimes sacred art elicits strong reactions from children, so keep the images beautiful and gentle.

• My advice on including babies in rituals is that if the gathering is outdoors and attended by many people there will naturally be enough noise to accommodate a baby's occasional squeals and squawks. Very small babies will be either sleeping or crying, so you can judge what yours is likely to be doing by the time of day the gathering is held. Actually, most single people don't get to be around babies very often and are usually delighted to see them. Toddlers and active babies, of course, have to be watched, and when small gatherings are to be held in other people's homes it may be best to leave the child at home with a friend or relative. This is not unkind; many churchgoing couples take turns attending services while the other partner watches the baby.

Theosophist Thomas Armstrong offers the following three precepts:

• See the child as a being larger than its little ego.

• Keep in mind that the child's body may have come from you, but its spirit does not.

• The child has to make a transition from the astral plane to the material world, beginning before birth, and for some children this transition is more difficult than for others.

As an illustration of this last concept, in their book *Models of Love: the Parent-Child Journey*, Barry and Joyce Vissell mention that when their younger daughter was a tiny baby, she used to wake up not with a coo or a wail but a scream. They theorized that her little soul was not quite integrated into her body, so that she would suddenly incarnate in shock at being in this helpless, wet, hungry body. When I read this, I recognized that my daughter did the same thing for the first few weeks of her life—she didn't cry, she screamed—and like Catherine, the Vissells' daughter settled down somewhat after they performed a blessing ceremony for her when she was two months old.

Precisely because little babies cannot take the initiative in spiritual practice, we must assume the duty of calling upon the Higher Powers to bless and protect our children, just as we care for our babies' physical needs. Parents may find the two rites of blessing for a new baby which are included in this section to be helpful. The first, my husband and I performed for our daughter, based on the traditions of earth religion. The other is a variation on the ancient Jewish rite of *Brit Mila*, or dedication of the boy baby, adapted to honor the birth of a daughter—a very special ritual that comes truly from the heart while being rich in Jewish tradition.

The Nursing Mother and Feminine Metaphysics

Stephanie Demetrakopoulos

Not all women are mothers and not all mothers breast-feed, of course; but if a woman does nurse her baby, she can experience mystical and even metaphysical levels of her soul. If she is receptive to the knowledge that her body offers her, she can experience a revelation that has its own special grace.

It is well-known that breast-feeding has advantages for the infant and for the mother-infant bonding. It has also been established that women are rewarded for lactation in terms of their own health, and perhaps even erotically. I want to address the significance of breast-feeding as an aspect of women's religiousness, part of a feminine theology that women have lived without writing or speaking of it, keeping instead that feminine silence that is so ancient, deep, and fraught with knowledge.

Unity, Containment, and Transcending Downward

There is nothing like the monumental stasis of the filled, often dozing baby and the relief of the previously taut breast; being and becoming merge in a concrete way. As the mother lets go of her own ego, identifying instead with the baby's satisfaction, she may feel a sense of total unity with the child that is not unlike the more mystical moments of pregnancy. The gradual relaxation of the infant and mother until they have almost merged during a feeding is a form of *mysterium conjunctio*, both psychic and physical unification. Not only women have recognized this phenomenon; certain Renaissance artists who were particularly enamored of the feminine principle often painted Mary and the Christ Child tranquil and serene together after a nursing.

A nursing mother's sense of immersion in the body, the feeling of transcending downward through lactation, may even in fact be the most complete physical experience available to woman. The experience of nursing contains the mother and sets her apart not only from surrounding persons but from within, through her own body consciousness. Because tissue from the breast spreads around a woman's body, into her sides below the arms, the sensation of nursing surrounds the female body. Some women even sense the milk as being drawn from their backs, though the tissue is not there. This gives them a larger, more total sense of flowing out of self.

The flowing of the milk can be a holistic bodily metaphor for maternal *caritas*, an open, nurturing world love. Lactation may even provide the basis, the psychological ground, for future maternal feelings; a mother may relive her bodily response of joy as her child receives fulfillment from other life experiences. Women who force their children to eat, who stuff them with food instead of love, may be extending their lactation powers and fulfillment, forcing the children to act as replete and filled vessels of their gift of nourishment. This sort of mother may need weaning herself. Like everything, delight in the child as container can become pathological, but in normal proportions, maternal pride and joy in the child's feeding (its "containing" of maternal love) underlie an unselfish delight in the child's unique growth.

> Her future feeling for the child, when this close postpartum tie has been outgrown and it is a rambunctious toddler (indeed even later, when it is a pimply adolescent, or a greying eccentric), will always be flavored on some level—as it could not for a less intelligent mammal—with the memory of the passion which at this moment knots her belly and makes her nipples spurt.*

When I look at my oldest daughter, now twenty-five, I feel the oddest metaphysical start or shock to realize that this adult person is the same burrowing, suckling creature (the image of lovable larva comes to my mind) I nursed so many years ago. This gives me a special tenderness towards all adults, as I can psychically unpeel the layers of maturity and see the needy and vulnerable infant that all of the adult unfolding builds from and covers over. Perhaps women, through caring for infants and especially through the very concrete act of nursing, have a sense of the primordial seed in each person and of the mystery of human development which is often harder for men to come by.

Mother-Infant Sense of Reality

Physiological interaction between child and mother during the actual act of suckling clearly deepens their bond and their knowledge of each other. The infant learns to make the milk come; it learns patience with the irregularity of the flow of milk and of mother love itself, which in most cases is constant but inconsistent and varied. The bottle, in fact, seems an unfair image of biological or maternal reality for the infant; the bottle is always the same, and life is not like that. The mother's moods change her flow, and her diet changes the milk itself. The mother's body, both before and after birth, is the primary and first experience of the world for all infants. The occasional supplementary bottle can be viewed within this context as a lesson in the difference between mother and others and also as an assurance that world contains caring others.

The mother's nursing body also helps her learn to understand her child. The mother's whole body, not just her hearing, learns which tenor of cry is the hunger call; her milk surges forward or drops involuntarily as she awakens to the call at night. A mother learns to associate the infant's hunger with her own relief. Any sensitive and attentive mother also learns the differences among her infants' personalities through the way they feed and respond to her milk flow. One may be an intense and concentrating infant who grabs hold of the nipple and never slacks off until it is full; another may stop feeding to smile at its mother occasionally. Bottle-fed babies may do the same, but many infants fondle the breast or pat it playfully as they become older, and this may even presage the special affection the older child will give the mother.

Woman's milk can be seen as a kind of *agape* (a spiritual love that mingles nature and grace) that materializes to flow through the child and thence into the universe...Nursing can be among the deepest forms of communion, affording a grace that comes through an effortless participation and giving—a bonus, perhaps, for the often crushing arduousness of other facets of mothering, such as tending to indefatigable infants who are teething. The bluish, thin, translucent human milk even has a spiritual appearance. The way that one breast can leak while an infant suckles the other suggests an oddly communal quality even between the breasts, perhaps "sisters in charity." I am a thin and small-breasted woman and have always felt awe at this obvious surplus, a surfeit of nature with implications for the plenitude that the image of Goddess embodies.

Breast-feeding, then as well as other biological functions, connects women to a special kind of wisdom. Rather than separating woman from the spiritual realm, nature actually connects her more surely to cosmic principles, giving her direct access to metaphysical knowledge.

Some men, such as the sculptor Henry Moore or Leonardo da Vinci, have used woman's body to symbolize the transmutation of the physical world into culture and spirit; but women *live* this process. It is important to human religion that women write and speak of their bodily experience. Through women the body will once again become sacred as the conduit of grace and spiritual knowledge. The Western polarization of the body and the soul can be softened and modified, as women teach our species of the transformations possible through transcending downward. Even when women pass beyond this stage of life, the years of mothering, most women remember all their lives the lessons of universal process that their bodies have taught them. Feminine metaphysics takes as its bedrock a knowledge gleaned from women's concrete deeprootedness in the ground of being, which the female body at least equally well expresses and experiences as the so-called superior and more authentic copies of God, Adam, and his sons. The collective unconscious of women carries sacred images not available to men; and women understand from the depths of their unconscious that process, not absolutes, *is* Being.

---

* Dorothy Dinnerstein, *The Mermaid and the Minotaur: Sexual Arrangements and Human Malaise* (New York: Harper and Row, 1976), p. 79.

Blessing of the New Baby

Anne Carson

Calling upon the gods or the heavens to welcome and protect a new baby must be an act performed in all cultures. It can be as simple as pronouncing a prayer of thanksgiving (which every parent utters in his or her heart) or as elaborate and rich in tradition as a Jewish rite of circumcision. Newborn infants seem so fragile, their attachment to life so tenuous, that universally parents desire some seal or protection to be placed upon their little ones. Apart from enrolling the child in the religion of the parents' choice, rites of infant blessing or dedication serve other purposes—as a way of saying, "This one's going to live," or "See what I, with God's help, have made." There exists an instinctual desire to put some kind of stamp, a copyright or registration, on the child. And so we have birth certificates, baptisms, circumcision rites, and special baby scrapbooks, all to imprint the child's existence onto the world, to enroll him or her in the Book of Life.

Names are generally chosen before the baby is born, but sometimes the final decision takes a long time. I seriously considered naming my daughter Cerridwen, after the Welsh goddess of the cauldron, but realizing that nobody I knew could either spell or pronounce it, I settled on Catherine Clare. But there was another reason for my selecting a traditional name, which I was unable to articulate for some time: the truth was that I did not want to attract the attention of the gods, to tempt the hand of fate. In consciously not choosing an unusual name for what would very likely be my only daughter, I, an outwardly educated, sophisticated woman, was unconsciously striving to ward off the evil eye.

Many tribal peoples call their children by different names throughout their lives, changing the name as the child's personality or characteristics develop. Parents often find that the name that seemed to fit the tiny bundle in their arms becomes not quite right as the child grows. Unless you have given the child a convertible name like William or Elizabeth, you may be stuck, for our society does not generally allow choosing a completely different name every few years as the need arises. This is where middle names have come in so handy—they function as an alternate persona for many people. It might be worthwhile pairing an unusual or creative name with a more traditional one, so that the child can switch from one form of presentation of self to the other as he or she sees fit.

In Christian ritual the baby's name is formally bestowed at the rite of baptism. According to Christina Hole's *Folklore of England*, baptism, like so many other customs, was not original with Christianity but was adapted from pagan rituals. Both the Norse and the Celtic Druids had baptism-like water ceremonies.

Christian baptism serves three essential purposes: washing away original sin, protecting the child's soul from the devil, and enrolling it in the church of the parents. For some people, partaking in their family's heritage is a powerful act, but if you prefer to honor your child in a different way you can research rites performed by other couples, those conducted in other cultures, or make up your own. My husband and I don't believe in either original sin or the devil, nor did we feel justified in dedicating our daughter to a religion we did not identify with, so instead of a christening, we had a sort of rite of paganing—a ritual dedication of our baby to the forces of earth, water, sun, and sky. We used the traditional christening clothes both I and my brother had worn at our baptisms—a lace underdress handmade in the Philippines, white satin gown, coat, and bonnet—which my mother had carefully put away for her first grandchild, and we cautiously described the rite to my family as a "blessing."

This is the ritual David and I performed, drawn in part from rituals devised by Z Budapest and Pagan ritualist Ed Fitch. We performed this ritual on August 2, which is Lammas Day, the pre-Christian European harvest festival, at the eleventh annual South American Indian Conference at Bennington College, Vermont. I was a little nervous about how this ritual would be received by the anthropologists in attendance and their significant others, not knowing how any of them felt about alternative spirituality, but I needn't have worried, for most of them were quite familiar with ritual from their work with Indians. And in truth all twenty or so watched with delight and keen attention, several of them carefully photographing the proceedings and questioning me about the significance of the symbols, such as burying the garlic. Like many a native informant I had to admit, "I'm not too sure about the garlic…it's traditional, I guess."

The Ceremony

For this ritual you need: white candles, incense, flowers, a head of garlic, a bowl of corn, one of water, and one of salt. The baby is dressed in white, the mother in white or green. All stand in circle, preferably out of doors: the ceremony may take place in someone's backyard or field, or in a natural and private setting. The baby may be held by the mother or laid on a blanket on the ground, as it prefers.

One of the parents opens the ceremony, saying:

Christians have baptism, Jews have the rite of circumcision for sons—we welcome you to the dedication of our child to the powers of the Universe and a request for blessings of Mother Earth upon her. We call it a paganing.

The father sprinkles a bit of cornmeal in each of the four directions. He lights the incense and walks with it around the mother and child.

He then picks up the baby and presents her to the sky, saying:

> Behold this lovely child, (*Name*),
> Conceived and brought forth in love.
> Bless and protect her
> and grant her the gifts of wisdom, inspiration, and wonder.

He gives the baby to the mother, who says:

> Hail Earth, Mother of all,
> this is my infant, my love, and my jewel.
> Bless and protect her;
> Grant her your eternal strength.
> May she have a spirit that seeks the stars,
> and keeps its roots within your breast.

She replaces the baby on the ground and pours corn meal around it (or around herself if she is holding it):

> May she never know hunger of body, heart, or soul.

She sprinkles water over the baby:

> May she have the life force always strong within her.
> May she be infused with love for all living things.

She pours salt around the baby:

> Protect her and bless her with wisdom, courage, and a
> sense of humor.

Whisper the child's spirit name into her ear.

The father says:

> The atoms from which you are made
> were forged in the heart of vanished stars.
> Always remember this, and know
> how small you are, how fragile,
> and how short the sum of human years.

But stand in awe of life:
the wonder of its complexity,
the miracle that it exists,
and the remarkable human capacity
to contemplate its mysteries.

The eldest mother present says:

We welcome this child into our midst,
and welcome this mother into the company of
    mothers—emblems of the creative force in the universe,
givers of life and preservers of our species.

The new mother says:
I am blessed today with this child,
and take my place in the company of mothers.

Bury the garlic by a nearby tree or on the spot where the ritual took place and cover it with the leftover corn, salt, and water.

Brit Kedusha: a Home Ceremony Celebrating the Birth of a Daughter

Ellen and Dana Charry

In creating this ceremony, we have tried to supply something which we feel is missing in Jewish life. Our Law requires the formal induction of every male child into the Jewish people through the ritual *Brit Mila* (Circumcision), a distinctive ceremony. This ancient rite, dating from the time of Abraham, is performed on the eighth day after the baby boy in born, usually in the child's home. The simple operation is performed by a *mohel* (ritual circumciser), who leads the ceremony which includes the naming of the child and blessings for him and his parents. The ceremony is held with friends and relatives in attendance, but without the mother, who is usually "protected" from watching the circumcision of her son. The ceremony is usually followed by a celebration. Although one of our shortest rituals, the *Brit Mila* is certainly one of the most powerful and unforgettable.

Two other religious customs accompany the birth of a son in Jewish tradition. One is *Pidyon ha-Ben* (Redemption of the Firstborn), and the other is *Ben Zacher* (literally, Male Child). *Pidyon ha-Ben* is a brief ceremony reenacting the ancient custom of dedicating the firstborn male to the service of the temple. The child is "bought back" or redeemed from this sacred obligation by his father, who gives a symbolic sum of money to the temple priest. The *Ben Zacher* is simply a party, often given by the baby's grandparents, celebrating his arrival. All of these are home ceremonies, and not part of a synagogue service.

It is striking to us that there is no special ceremony to mark the birth of a female child. There is a practice of naming girls in the synagogue, but this is a custom, not required by Law. The father goes to the synagogue on the Sabbath during the reading of the Torah (Law). A blessing is added for the baby girl which includes a naming formula. Blessings such as this are recited on many other occasions also. Thus, the naming is not a distinct ceremony and has very little impact or special flavor to it. Its importance is further diminished by the fact that mother and daughter are usually not present. It should be noted that such a practice can be done for a boy child as well.

In short, there is a great disparity between the ceremonies for greeting the birth of a son and the practices attending the birth of a daughter. This inequality, with its implied value judgment, seemed to us distasteful, unbecoming to the Jewish tradition which we value so highly. Although understandable in historical perspective, the situation seems strangely out of place today. It is also jarringly dissonant with the love we feel for our daughters, the pride we take in them, and the expectations we have for their future. There are some of the feelings which moved us to create this new ceremony for celebrating the birth of a daughter.

This is not meant to be a female version of the *Brit Mila*. We have adapted one passage—the naming formula—from the *Brit Mila*, but in all other respects we have tried to create a distinct ceremony for girls.

Concepts exist only in thought. To become part of life, a concept must be given some concrete form. Thus, every ritual of Jewish life is associated with tangible ceremonial objects, and this new ceremony is no exception. Here, a Kiddush cup (ritual wine cup) is given to the baby. We selected the Kiddush cup for several reasons. Kiddush is the blessing over wine which sanctifies almost every Jewish ritual and religious holiday. It is included in *Brit Mila*, marriage, Sabbath, and all holy days. As a constant part of family ritual, the Kiddush represents ongoing Jewish tradition as we hope our children will experience it. In addition, the cup can be used from childhood through adulthood. Finally, the giving of a Kiddush cup expresses our hope that the full range of Jewish experience will always be open to our daughter. This is not true at the present time, as much of Jewish ritual observance is customarily denied to women.

We wrote the *Brit Kedusha* in anticipation of the birth of our second child. In concentrating our efforts to create something new and exciting, almost revolutionary in terms of Jewish tradition, we sought to preserve the flavor and language of the tradition while giving it new meaning. Therefore we were careful to include such elements as a traditional psalm, the blessing over wine, and the blessing for special occasions. These are all established parts of Jewish liturgy which we have here combined in a new way.

The title of the ceremony reflects two of our people's most vital ideas. *Brit* is usually translated as "holiness," but it also encompasses the ideas of uniqueness, specialness, and spirituality. All of Judaism expresses the idea of *Kedusha*, and every Jewish act is a striving toward the goal. *Brit* means a contract, covenant, or pact between man and God. This Bible uses the word to describe the agreement between Abraham and God—as symbolized by the Circumcision ritual—and between God and the whole Jewish people—as symbolized by the giving of the Law at Sinai. The word *Brit* also represents the long chain of tradition and learning which stretches across the generations to the present day, constantly reworking and revitalizing that ancient covenant.

In their striving toward *Kedusha*, we hope that our children will add a new link to the living chain of the *Brit*.

Our ceremony was held eight days after the baby was born. Before the ceremony, we chose the cup we would give our daughter and had it engraved with her name and date of birth. Her Kiddush cup was of medium size, so that she could not only use it as a baby but also as she grows up.

On the day of the ceremony the room was arranged with places at the front for ourselves, our parents, our three-year-old daughter, and several other relatives and friends who had parts in the ceremony. The rest of the guests sat facing us. In front of our places a small table was set up, on which the new Kiddush cup and a bottle of wine were placed.

We felt that the ceremony needed a leader, and we designated certain parts in the text to be read by the leader. Ideally the leader should not be one of the parents. But when we performed the ceremony for the first time we took some of the leader's parts ourselves and distributed the rest to several close friends and relatives. In addition we wanted to demonstrate the fact that the leader need not be a rabbi. A rabbi is basically a teacher. He is the outstanding leader of the community and is regarded as more learned than the lay population in deciding questions of Jewish Law. Although his presence is not required for any liturgical ceremony of Jewish life, it is customary in most synagogues that the rabbi and/or the cantor conduct the service. We felt that our ceremony could be led instead by any knowledgeable and sensitive layperson.

The ceremony was originally written in Hebrew, the language of the Jewish liturgy. Use of the traditional Hebrew conveyed the feeling with the spirit of Jewish tradition. Since many Jews these days are unable to read or understand Hebrew, we followed each section in our liturgy with an English translation. In performing the ceremony we did each part first in Hebrew, then in English.

Brit Kedusha

The guests having assembled, the grandparents took their places at the front and the parents then entered with the baby and took their seats. One of our friends recited:

Sing out to God, all the earth,
Break forth and sing for joy.
Sing praises to God with the harp,
And with voices full of joyous melody.
With trumpets and the sound of the horn
Sing out to God.

Let the sea roar in all its fullness,
The whole world and all its inhabitants.
Let the floods clap their hands,
And the mountains sing for joy
Before God and the nations. (*Psalm 98*)

The grandparents:

We praise you, O Lord our God, who has kept us alive, and strengthened us, and permitted us to see this day. (*This is the traditional blessing said on all special or unique occasions.*)

Dana's sister, who had come from Israel, then took the baby in her arms and said:

Our God and God of our people, sustain this child along with her mother and father. Let her name be called in Israel:

Tamar Yael Debora

daughter of Ellen and Dana Charry

May the father and mother rejoice with their child, as it is written, "Let your parents be happy. Let your mother thrill with joy." (*adapted from* Brit Mila)

She then returned the child to us and we said:

Our God and God of our people—

May the life of this child be one of happiness, goodness, and wisdom.

Grant that she may seek after peace and pursue an end to strife among her fellowmen.

Strengthen us to guide our daughter in the path of our Torah and its beliefs.

Help us to lead her in the footsteps of the great leaders of Israel, whose deeds continue to shine across the ages of our people.

We praise you, O God, whose Torah links the generations one to another. *(original)*

This is a point in the ceremony where the leader may speak informally. The leader may, for example, add a personal prayer, express personal hopes for the child, or say something about the significance of the baby's name. In the case of our daughter, each of us spoke for several minutes. We explained the background of the ceremony, expressing many of the ideas set forth above in our prefatory comments. We held up the Kiddush cup for all to see, and filled it with wine. We then chanted together:

We praise you, O Lord our God, who has created the fruit of the vine. *(This is The Kiddush)*

We then stood with the baby and, placing our hands on her head, blessed her with the following traditional blessing:

May you be blessed in the city and blessed in the country,

May you be blessed as you enter and blessed as you depart.

May God bless you and keep you,

May He cause His face to shine upon you and be gracious to you.

May He lift up His face to you and grant you wholeness and peace.

In conclusion, we and our older daughter recited the blessing, and all the guests joined in:

We praise you, O Lord our God, who has kept us alive, and strengthened us, and permitted us to see this day.

We then went on to eat, drink, and celebrate. The ceremony was received with great enthusiasm. All of those present, without exception, felt that they had witnessed something beautiful and innovative. A close friend of ours commented that she found it hard to believe the ceremony was brand new, since its language and spirit fit so well into our tradition.

PART IV

Young Children

The Blossoming Soul

Artist Betsy Damon is preparing for a May Day ritual with friends and sees that her seven-year-old daughter has sponta-neously decorated herself in yards of gauzy material and flowers; Catholic author and artist Gertrud Mueller Nelson discovers her three-year-old daughter in the back yard taping strips of old fab-ric to a pole in order to make a banner "so that God will come down and dance with us;" Naomi Strichartz remembers her five-year-old son going about the house sprinkling herbs. "It's God's Day," his two-year-old sister proudly informed their mother.

From the age of about three onwards, small children seem to intuitively comprehend the essence of spirituality and commun-ion with the Divine even though they are not yet able to articu-late anything resembling theology. When they are told about God or the Divine Presence, however it is presented, young chil-dren seem to understand at once what you are talking about. Yet their most immediate concern seems to be not the unseen world, but the environment around them, for to small children the boundary between this world and the Other World is by no means as clearly defined as it is to adults.

As soon as a child can fluently articulate her thoughts and questions, her powerful and ever-present sense of wonder becomes evident. "What's that?" and "Why?" are heard every five minutes. This is the age when some explanation of God/Divine Power becomes possible, as enough language skills have developed so that a certain amount of dialogue can take place between adult and child. Some children, as Karey Solomon describes in "Children and Angels," seem to already understand what the parents are hesitantly trying to convey, as if these early lessons in heaven, death, the Other World, and sacred beings, merely confirm the knowledge the child already has. After listening to a long explanation, these children will nod and go back to their play. Some become intensely curious about the ritual practices of the parents and want to know the meaning of every spiritual symbol or gesture.

It might be a good idea to take a child of this age to a church and/or a temple during the week when her outbursts of curiosity will not disturb other worshippers. This will give her a chance to see where it is that other people worship God and can open her to all sorts of questions that might otherwise not be asked until much later. And making churches and temples known to your child will keep her from thinking of them as strange places of great mystery as she begins to meet other children who attend regular services.

Naturally, spiritual practice will not be limited to the Judeo-Christian tradition. Many adults participate in ritual circles of one kind or another: healing circles, gatherings to observe the solstices, equinoxes, and ancient sacred days in between (Candlemas, May Day, Lammas Day, and Hallows Eve), or impromptu attunements convened at the start of celebratory dinners, political actions, meetings, etc. The issue of children comes up when parents wish to include youngsters in gatherings ordinarily intended for adults.

Although we no longer expect attendants at religious services or spiritual rituals to sit rigidly while all the action of the ritual is enacted by one or two people, adult circles sometimes require a significant amount of quiet concentration and little or no movement. Children under twelve find staying still for five or ten minutes to be very difficult, and it seems unjust to demand it of them. This is one reason why it is so important to teach meditation techniques to children, for they learn that they can still themselves, for a time, at will.

There is no question that noise, running around, and interruptions can be very irritating and distracting to the quieter members of the circle. Noise is frequently a problem, for parents rapidly adapt themselves to a level of noise and crying that people who do not live with children may find intolerable. There needs to be some give and take in this matter, particularly when very young children, who can't obey when asked to be quiet, are present. One minister put a sign on his bulletin board that read, "Crying children, like promises, should be carried out." Most people agree that it is the responsibility of the parents or older siblings to control (if that's the right word) the child during a ritual. Keeping an eye on the child is important during active parts of the ritual as well—if ecstatic dancing is going on, a small child can't be allowed to wander about the room getting bumped into or stepped on. Some parents feel comfortable with allowing other adults to admonish the child as needed; excusing little Sundance's pushing and destructiveness with "He doesn't understand yet" will not make either of you very popular.

Spiritual parents are often eager to include their child in their activities as soon as possible, yet delaying bringing the child to many gatherings for the first few years of life will not necessarily stunt her spiritual growth. My brother did not go to church until he was four, and then he had us laughing hysterically with his innocent questions about "God's angels" (nuns) and "God's crackers" (the Eucharist). He went on to become an altar boy and now receives his spiritual sustenance from Zen and the wisdom of Native Americans.

When you do include your child, bear in mind that it is more to her benefit to nurture her by providing a loving, supportive environment which is safe emotionally and physically, than to expose her to a spiritual community that is unwilling or not able to accommodate children. If the adults in the class or circle are likely to become irritated and disturbed by a wriggling baby or active three-year-old than you are doing your child more of a service by not bringing her along. Remember, too, that some children go through periods during which they are intensely shy and therefore need to be shielded from too great an array of strange faces.

You can help young children feel they are part of the community by enlisting their aid in setting up the space, ringing bells, lighting candles when they're old enough, passing out food. Allow them to attend only as much of the proceedings as they can tolerate, for example, physically active parts such as dancing or yoga exercises performed in preparation for meditation, or singing and chanting. When the child needs to leave the circle, either a parent or a designated child-care person should take him or her off to a place where they can play, read, or do whatever they like together.

When there is a time set aside for each participant in the circle to speak, the children should also be asked if they wish to contribute. Often they are too shy to say anything, but if they do speak they deserve to be listened to and to be allotted no more and no less time than the adult participants.

Finally, remember that you need to appeal first to a child's senses, not her intellect: whether in the home or elsewhere, make a beautiful altar space or shrine to stimulate her sight, use songs, chants, bells, and musical instruments for sound, special clothes, jewelry, and sacred objects for the sense of touch, flowers and incense for smell, and food and drink for taste. At their best, conventional religious services introduce us to poetry, music, and art; surely we can do no less.

Young children love playing with figurines, and their innate sense of ceremony can be nurtured and stimulated with help from adults. In her article on "Shadow Boxes," Naomi Strichartz describes the pagan holiday scenes she has made with her children since they were very young. We can't always enter into the fantasy-life of children, and as they grow older they may even reject our intrusions, but we can at least pay an occasional visit.

In time more formal instruction is desired. Some adults are introducing meditation to children at quite young ages, and pre-school children often take to it readily if it is presented in a simple, low-key way. In "Call It Something Else" Karey Solomon describes simple meditation that is practiced very beautifully in one nursery school. She also told me about coming upon her daughter, not yet two, who was sitting in her room in perfect meditation pose with her eyes closed, though she had never been taught, a phenomenon that was described by Rev. Jiyu Kennett in her essay in the first section of this book. In the next section on "Older Children" we will encounter more formalized meditation training, with exercises included. At this first stage, however, the most basic suggestions suffice for three- to five-year-olds: breathing deeply and quietly, going deep within, visualizing a loved one, directing love and light towards that being.

Because it may be a while before a child is fully able to participate and enjoy religious rituals or services with the community at large, spiritual practice with young children is often centered around the home and prayer. Here the parents' example becomes all-important. Whether you say grace at dinner, pray or meditate together or singly, or conduct rituals in the home, the child will usually try to imitate and participate in what is going on. If you customarily do none of these things, the child can still be engaged spiritually through the practice of prayer.

Despite thirteen years of religious education I was never taught how to truly pray, and I was spiritually the poorer for it. In childhood most of us were taught to recite certain prayers over dinner and at bedtime and to ask God's blessing upon our loved ones. Internal prayer was not often taught to children or even put forth as an option. We learned that we could ask God or a favorite saint for some favor, from the trivial (a new doll) to the critical (the health of an ailing relative). We learned to fold our hands just so, recite the words just so, but what did it all mean?

Churches are now trying to reclaim meditative prayer, aware that they must compete with Eastern and New Age meditative techniques. Yet there is nothing very complicated or advanced in learning to pray, for prayer is nothing more than talking to God/dess throughout the day and listening for a response. A child might try talking to a guardian angel or a favorite saint such as St. Francis, and can learn to listen through meditation or by spending some time out-of-doors in silence and solitude. Prayer is not only talking to God, it is expressing love of God, by giving thanks and by seeing God in Nature and in her creatures.

Most people grow up with the impression that praying means words to be memorized, unaware that it is an important tool for psychological well-being. Reciting certain prayers or mantras becomes powerful in itself, but we need to regard prayer as a spring of living water.

In traditional Native American cultures people were allowed to go off by themselves to think over a problem and ask the spirits for help when there was a crisis, and this was encouraged from the time they were young children. The vision quest was the

Native American equivalent of going on a spiritual retreat. Generally adolescent boys were the ones who went on formal vision quests during their puberty rituals, but a vision quest might be undertaken at any time it was deemed necessary. There are stories of seven-year-olds spending three days alone in the woods in order to come to an important decision.

I used to work with a woman whose predecessor had had a nervous breakdown and ultimately quit her prestigious position to spend six months in a monastery. Every time my colleague related this story, she would roll her eyes at the part about the monastery—clearly no self-respecting professional would do something so flaky. If we call up our offices our supervisors are not likely to be pleased when we say, "I'm not going to be in for a couple of days; I need to pray and meditate and ask for guidance about my career, divorce, etc." Could we call up our child's second grade teacher and tell her that Katie isn't coming to school because she wants to spend the day in fasting and meditation on how to handle a quarrel with a friend? Our culture does not understand that you may be doing something very valuable while you are supposedly "doing nothing."

Prayer as petition is an issue some parents are not comfortable with, sensing that they are deceiving their children or giving them false hopes—though in reality children know perfectly well that bicycles don't come from God, they come from relatives (if not Santa Claus). Some people do not feel it is right to teach children to expect an outside force, such as God/gods, to solve their problems and achieve their goals for them. In the European esoteric tradition, magical work is regarded as essentially a highly concentrated form of prayer, in which the petitioner plays an active part in effecting the desired result by focusing her or his intentions into a mental image or symbolic object such as a burning candle or a bag filled with herbs. The person who is doing the magical work is expected to ask the gods/spirits/cosmic forces to realize her desire in a way that will benefit the world as a whole, not just the petitioner. Children are naturally attracted to the concrete and the symbolic, and when a child becomes capable of understanding what it means to direct one's mental energy, then prayer as petition can be taught in forms such as creative visualization, sending healing energy to an ill person, performing simple magical rituals, and/or repeating affirmations ("I work hard at school. I know how to do long division. Every day I am getting better at softball."), all in accordance with the spiritual values and traditions of the parents.

The recitation of traditional prayers—the Lord's Prayer, the 23rd Psalm, "Now I lay me down to sleep," with its archaic language and peculiar raising of the subject of dying in one's sleep—hardly comforting to the sleeper!—can easily degenerate into a tiresome ritual, like brushing one's teeth, that is performed for the appeasement of the parent, not for any benefit perceived by the child. I recall asking my mother with some annoyance why I had to say my prayers at night when she didn't. "I say them after I get into bed," she answered. "Likely story," I thought. Recently, however, I have relearned the value of ritual recitation of prayers before sleep—many people use formal meditation for the same purpose—deriving comfort in the recitation of and meditation on "The Lord Is My Shepherd," often falling asleep before reaching the end of the psalm. Much the same effect can be had by meditation, centering exercises, or bedtime stories. Whatever form is used, a settling-down time of centering or fantasy can be very beneficial. One of my fondest memories of my father is of the stories he used to tell me about Prince Darling (not to be confused with Prince Charming), complete with his maps of the princedom.

When we are about to fall asleep our minds are open to more fluid motion of thoughts. Psychically we are very vulnerable in the minutes before falling asleep, that is, susceptible to both good and ill. People who take hallucinogens report that falling asleep is the most difficult and frightening part of their drug experience, as "monsters from the id" arise seemingly from nowhere to torment the would-be sleeper. Conversely, the time just before sleep is a very effective time to recite affirmations, whether they deal with immediate concerns ("I will wake up at six") or long-range goals ("I am a confident person").

If the child seems too busy to want to go to sleep, then perhaps the parent is mentally busy as well. Strive to make yourself full of peace and concentrate on the love you feel. Bedtime is also a good time for fathers to get involved, especially since mother may have worked all day, cooked dinner, done the dishes, and needs a bit of time for centering herself. In her essay below, René Knight-Weiler describes two mothers' unusual approaches to evening prayer.

Bedtime stories are, of course, a time-honored means of calming and centering before sleep. In addition to the customary European fairy tales, parents may also relate the myths, legends, and fairy tales from other cultures. There are countless editions of fairy tales from around the world available in bookstores that carry children's books. There will naturally be certain stories the child feels drawn to and wants to hear over again; but surely telling the stories of a people whose struggles are in the news— Arabs, Koreans, and Filipinos come to mind right now—must serve to make these cultures less intimidating and fearsome to a child. A child may not be able to comprehend a sociopolitical explanation of why the streets of Belfast, Seoul, and Jerusalem are filled with soldiers and rioters, but if she hears the stories of

Ireland, Korea, or Palestine, perhaps the people of these lands will be less likely to be viewed as Them.

And don't forget that your child can tell you stories as well.

Another important kind of prayer is grace at meals. Our lives may be so hectic, when we are trying to get dinner on the table, feed the dog, keep the kids from squabbling, and listening to the evening news all at the same time, that it seems unlikely anyone would be in the mood for prayer before dinner. Yet nourishment, like rest, is one of the cornerstones of existence for all living things, and its sacrality ought to be honored at least occasionally. It brings us back to who we really are as children of the Earth.

At a cafeteria where I occasionally eat lunch, from time to time I have noticed an Asian employee of the university who works as a repairman. He sets down his tray, sits and places his hands on his thighs in classic meditation pose, and bows his head for a few seconds. What his religion is, or what words he is saying over in his mind, I do not know. But he makes a beautiful sight amid the clamor and activity of the lunchroom.

Some people are turned off by the idea of evening grace—it sounds too much like Christianity, particularly if they were brought up Jewish. If you can remember to do it, though, grace can be a gentle reminder of our sacred connection to the earth, to the Divine, and to each other. When God is imaged as Mother Earth the concept of material bounty proceeding from the Divine is more easily comprehended, for we can see plainly that food comes from our Mother the Earth.

When it comes to the words themselves, you might prefer to compose your own evening grace, extemporize, or adapt traditional blessings that carry cultural or family associations. A simple grace such as "Come Thou, Lord Jesus, and be our guest, And let this food to us be blest" can easily be altered to "Come Thou

O Goddess," or "Come Thou, Lord, Buddha," or whatever expression you feel is appropriate.

A grace for general use:
> We give thanks for our food, and remember those who
>   are hungry,
> We give thanks for our health, and remember those who
>   are ill,
> We give thanks for our family, and remember those who
>   are alone.

Some traditional blessings can scarcely be improved upon. A favorite of mine comes from my Presbyterian stepfather:

"Dear Heavenly Father, we humbly beseech thee to bless this food and our fellowship, and to enable us to enjoy the presence of that Divine Unseen Guest whose coming to earth has filled all life with new meaning and beauty."

For very young children, perhaps even more important than form and ritual is their introduction to the natural world, where God/dess manifests such a powerful presence. Surely the most direct way to allow children to recognize the Spirit is by introducing them to the beauty, power, regularities, even the terrors, of nature. As Rachel Carson wrote in her beautiful book *The Sense of Wonder*,

> If I had influence with the good fairy who is supposed to preside over the christening of all children I should ask that her gift to each child in the world be a sense of wonder so indestructible that it would last throughout life, as an unfailing antidote against the boredom and disenchantments of later years, the sterile preoccupation with things that are artificial, the alienation from the sources of our strength.[4]

This wise naturalist knew that

> There is symbolic as well as actual beauty in the migration of the birds, the ebb and flow of the tides, the folded bud ready for spring. There is something infinitely healing in the repeated refrains of nature—the assurance that dawn comes after night, and spring after the winter.[5]

In childhood we have a natural affinity for the physical environment until it is civilized out of us. The world is not simply experienced as being "out there," but is instinctively perceived as more or less a part of oneself. At the age of five or six children often experience a unity with nature, a sudden cosmological understanding that at the same time is an intensely transpersonal experience. This is not specifically an awareness of God, but a "getting under the skin of the landscape," as English writer Caroline Glyn expressed it in her novel *The Unicorn Girl*. Teaching nature-awareness is important for children—so that they can retain the sense of wonder and cultivate a passionate love for creation.

Understanding the natural world begins with the discovery of our own bodies, discovering the carpet, our caretakers' faces, anything within reach. As we grow we come to know that the wonders of nature—the universe in a leaf or stone—are never exhausted. In the 1950s many parents moved to the suburbs if they could afford to, "for the children." Being able to regularly experience the natural world is a powerful resource for children. It doesn't take much: being able to dig up worms in a patch of ground behind an apartment building will keep many two-year-olds happy for hours. Later on, discovering trees, dirt, shrubs, flowers, insects, birds, rocks, and weather become important.

Interestingly, most of the child's first books, particularly those by English authors, take place in the natural world: *Peter Rabbit, Winnie-the-Pooh, The Wind in the Willows*. In a sense young children are innately animistic, convinced that every-thing, whether natural or manufactured, is alive in some way. Eggbeaters and cars readily take on the appearance of animals, and surely real animals comprehend what we say to them. This sense that everything is alive persists for many years until science instruction persuades us that some things are lifeless and need not be treated with respect.

If you do not have access to a backyard or park, your children can still observe the natural world by studying weather phenom-ena and urban wildlife—pigeons, sparrows, and squirrels. Respect for nature can begin with teaching respect and compas-sion for those worms and insects that so fascinate little folks. We can teach that the creeping things, while entrancing, are not toys created for our pleasure, but have lifeways of their own which must be honored. At this level, nature begins in the home! Likewise, the limits of nature should be taught as well, as when we explain why we use insecticide against cockroaches or kill other forms of pests.

Another direct and very beautiful way to share nature with children is to keep a garden, as Joel Copenhagen describes in his article "A Child Plants a Seed." Gardening can be taught in a real garden plot that is the child's own, or a in community garden plot for families who live in apartments, a windowbox, from plants in a pot, or an unobtrusive special little spot in a public park, where the child can plant a few seeds and care for them. In the absence of a plot of land, beans or grapefruit or orange seeds can be sprouted when planted in a glass filled with good dirt. The glass sides of the plant's little "pot" permit the child to watch the miracle of growth—almost as good as time-lapse photography!

Give the novice gardener a head start by reserving a piece of the garden which is well-favored in soil, moisture, and sunshine. Candidates for the child's garden are seeds from dinner or the out-of-doors (petunias usually germinate well), vegetables (lettuce and radishes put up shoots quickly), or even sprouts in the refrigerator. For the most impatient young gardener, nothing beats cress—it can be eaten only ten days after it is sown.

Schooling in nature does not necessarily mean knowing the names of things—it means looking, listening, touching, smelling, even tasting. The sure turn of the Wheel of the Year, the seasons following one another in a predictable fashion, provides a fundamental resource for children to learn faith in the goodness of the cosmos.

Turning Toward the Morning

René Knight-Weiler

It would come up through the floorboards some mornings—so early and so soft that I could barely detect it. The sound rose through the floorboards as softly and glowing as the sun beginning its ascent in the predawn sky. It was, simply, part of the morning. It was the sound of Jeanne's prayers.

She lived with us for a time and I had the chance to watch her life and to store away a picture of two for the future, which is right now.

An hour (or two, or three) for devotions each day? Me?? It would be wonderful, but what mother has the time for such luxury? Jeanne did.

We with families find ourselves cherishing a hope of spiritualizing the journey and then considering it an accomplishment if we "make it through the day" without setting one foot into hell. But those forays into the land of our own demons, triggered so reliably by the normal stresses of family life, only serve to remind us of the urgent need to establish a regular time for devotion. Jeanne has always understood the urgency.

She had two children—an infant, a four-year-old. She was a single mother, and a full-time registered nurse. For a home she had only the extra room in her friend's basement. I'd have found plenty of excuses in that brief scenario to excuse just about anything. And I know with this vivid picture in my mind I'll never again be able to plead lack of time as an excuse for a lack of prayer.

Remembering Jeanne's voice in the background of the morning reminds me that there are ways of doing whatever needs to be done. Hers was this: after work, dinner, and playtime with the kids, she would go to sleep when they did. Eight o'clock. She'd rise at three a.m. Then for three hours—at a time of day when the heart is receptive, the mirror of the soul unsullied, and the mind alert but quiet, she would pray, meditate, study the sacred writings and often do some calligraphy or other artwork. Her prayers were spoken aloud by soft light, and it was to this music each day that her children would gradually waken. They may not have been active participants in this devotion, but the world they found each morning was a holy place and their sleeping beings surely drank in the beauty and love of their mother's prayers.

There is the morning—a time of rebirth, a time when the soul is attentive to the voices around it. And there is the late evening, as our children pass from one world to the next in sleep and we can clearly see the fears and struggles lifting while the angel settles serenely upon their visages. These are the times, I believe, when children are most clearly revealing and becoming their true selves. These are the important times when we parents are privileged to look through that magic window and *see* the children, and these are the times when they invite us in with whatever influences we may bring to bear on what is now an unguarded, trusting, intensely absorbing soul. Just before sleeping, just upon waking: take care with these times.

People ask me all the time: Why do I do it? How can I stand it? Doesn't it take too much time? And, Isn't this going too far? They're referring to my practice of lying down with my children until they're asleep for the night. Tine Thevenin's groundbreaking book, *The Family Bed*, has publicized many benefits of this practice, but one advantage the author failed to explore is the opportunity for shared devotions. "God must really love us to put so much good magic on us," said Denali as I lay down with her last week. That's the kind of thing this particular child only says (and always says) when the lights are out—daylight would never find her quite so admitting. And in those quiet, uncomplicated moments, she and I and God can relax and gratefully experience this tremendous love swirling around us. Every night, in a room that's completely dark but holds no fear, we talk (differently), then speak or sing our prayers, and finally she closes her eyes as I sing her to sleep with songs about beauty, and sacred verses set to melody. Though it might be nice, we don't have a meditation room in our house, we don't attend services once a week, we don't even say grace around the dinner table. But we do go to sleep together. That's our way, and it's good.

"When the children are ready for bed, let the mother read or sing them the odes of the Blessed Beauty, so that from their earliest years they will be educated by these verses of guidance."

—Baha'i Writings.

A Child Plants a Seed

Joel Copenhagen

The rhythms of nature—wind, rain, gentle breezes, storms, changing seasons—directly affect the moods of our planet. Farmers and primitive people sense this cosmic connection. A farmer prays for rain or warmth so that crops can be planted, grown and harvested. Primitive people worship the seasons and weather out of respect or fear because their survival depends on it.

The modern child in a technological society is also directly affected by climatic factors, as are his parents and, for that matter, all members of the human race. How sad it is that the vast amount of a child's impressionistic years are spent in windowless, climatically controlled, artificially illuminated buildings—in school or in front of a television set—saturated with commercial trivia, violent action or vicarious sports events.

Nature can be serene, violent, exciting, miraculous. Events happen by the second but pass unobserved before a hypnotized populace whose education has been geared toward the "scientific" approach in which all curriculum is separated into isolated subjects—often giving would-be answers to questions that have no answers. Everything must have a label. Thus the beauty and poetry of climate, growth, life and death upon this planet are dissected, distorted, and then presented in a dull, "learn-the-facts" style. Miracles are treated as names to be learned.

So much is involved in nature's wonders, and so much of it goes unappreciated or taken for granted today, hence, our present ecological mess. We are a segmented, though literate, society. We know all the sums but not the total product. We all depend on air, sun, water and the growth of plants for survival. But if we do not take a direct part in the miracle of growth this wonder is rarely sensed.

How many parents of small children have ever planted a tiny seed, then nursed it until it became a healthy plant, bearing food for the table? There is spiritual as well as physical exercise to be found in the planning and planting of a garden. A package of seeds can open a new world for the young child. Planting a seed and watching it grow entails a series of events that are spontaneous, exciting, rewarding, and truly educational. The growth of a seed, dependent on water and sunlight, into a plant capable of feeding the child who planted it, is a miracle beyond words.

We are trying to raise our son, Eddie, with these ideas in mind. We have attempted to present the world to him as the series of interrelated miracles it is. He enjoys long walks and, if we allow him to lead us, we learn a lot about the environment. He notices things we take for granted: rocks, tiny flowers, or dead weeds that have their own kind of beauty. Each walk seems to stamp its impression. Months later, he can recall what we said or did at a given tree or spot in the middle of the woods.

Being outside brings out the best in him, whether it's hot or cold, sunny or cloudy. He spends hours beside us, helping in the garden, weeding, picking up rocks, or just quietly playing—creating his own fantasies, planting sticks for trees or real seeds which, lo and behold, become real plants: peas and radishes to pick and eat.

The toys he uses the most outside are replicas of our garden tools—rakes, hoes, a wagon, shovels—and he is really learning to handle them. He's beginning to help in the actual gardening and is happiest when he feels he is making a real contribution.

As a father, I feel that I'm very fortunate in being able to spend so much time with Eddie during his very impressionable years. Each age has its lessons to teach. The father is learning from the child and the child from the father. I've been watching the world unfold through my son's eyes. They know of no violence, they see only love. Daily life need not be relegated to the latest fashion, what's new in the world, or this year's television shows with commercials shaping our lives. But people can make the choice to learn the lessons of parenthood from the observation of unfolding genius in children. If nurtured with a hopeful heart and a watchful eye, the child can keep his genius through life and the parents recapture a part of theirs.

In our small way, we are doing our best to change the world. We are trying to teach one new citizen of the universe to live in harmony with the rhythms of life.

Afterword: The Flow of Things

The seasons have come and gone. The planet has turned twenty-five times since we left the sub-tropical Miami maze to settle in the rural foothills of the Allegheny mountains. It was October, and the hills were ablaze with magnificent colors. Our new home consisted of ten acres on an isolated hilltop, where we felt our dreams could be realized in a place where the magic could be felt without the obtrusive disturbances of traffic, street lights, and banal suburbanites caught in the twentieth-century Madison Avenue pipedream.

The garden has been harvested twenty-five times: "the child is becoming a man; the man becoming a child." Our journeys in time, space, and cosmos have taught us lessons by our living and growing together in a landscape where the sounds of seasons, wildlife and growth cycles have filled the air.

At the time "A Child Plants a Seed" was written I was busy planting a thousand seedling pine trees, and Eddie and my wife Julie were planting the first peas in our first garden. Now the trees are twenty to thirty feet tall, Eddie is twenty-seven, Julie and I are twenty-five years older chronologically (but younger spiritually). The magic of gardening enchanted Eddie for about five years and will always remain a part of his earliest experiences, but growth from toddler to adolescent has taken him to new places. Over the years interests in art, animals, cartoons, comics, science fiction, history, books, and cinema have captured his imagination. His mind is creative, open, and questioning. Having received an alternative secondary education, he attended an alternative college to pursue his intellectual goals.

Julie and I continue our journey. We have chosen the paths where mountains, hills, wildlife, and magical natural spirits dominate and merge with one's being.

Eddie's own journey has begun. New cycles and phases will hopefully lead him in the direction of his dreams. His character, spirit, intelligence, and independence seem to be finely tuned and ready for whatever will follow. Whether he chooses to live in a rural or urban setting, his formative years have been spent in a place where magic, mystery, and a sense of wonder prevail.

Our goal of teaching our son to become a citizen of the universe and to live in harmony with self and planet has, we hope, been realized in his first phase of life. The house in the country, the many gardens, the walks, hikes to mountaintops and our daily life together will always remain a part of us. We have nurtured each other and been part of a microcosmic "learning place" on earth.

As Eddie entered the world on a cosmically full-mooned evening twenty-seven years ago, his facial expression was one of having experienced life, birth, death and possibly many previous existences. Wordsworth wrote:

> Our birth is but a sleep and a forgetting:
> The soul that rises with us, our life's Star,
> Hath had elsewhere its setting.

The essence of a child is nurtured if parents, teachers, and guides will attempt to tune into the rhythms of the earth as a living entity, where all life is an intricate part of the flow of things.

Call It Something Else: Meditation in a Secular Setting

Karey Solomon

At ten o'clock every morning, in a certain nursery school, a group of three and four year olds sit crosslegged and silent. Some of the their parents meditate regularly; other parents, staunch believers in a single "right" religion would be horrified at the idea of introducing their babes to such "oriental mysticism." So the children don't *meditate*: they work at "making their stars shine bright."

Closing their eyes, they visualize a light in the center of their foreheads. Sometimes they send good thoughts outwards: for world peace, for the well-being of a particular suffering individual. They sit still—or almost still—for perhaps 45 seconds. When tapped on the shoulder by the teacher, the child-of-the-day rings a bell, signalling the others to open their eyes. They stretch as though they'd been sitting still for hours: the teacher told them that their stars shine brightest when they keep from moving or fidgeting. A short grace is sung, followed by a snack. The children chatter, comparing the relative brightness of their stars before moving on to other things. Star-bright is over. No parent who hears about it or observes it is offended. The dread word *meditation* has never been uttered. And after all, everyone, especially the nursery-school teacher, needs a little quiet time.

Silence frightens a lot of people. Traditional prayers let you know where you stand: there are words learned by heart or written in a book to define your innermost thoughts. Quiet can be dark formlessness—until peopled with bogeymen and monsters. Warned by the media that bizarre cult groups may snatch and convert hapless youngsters, some parents vow early to keep their children far away from previously unconsidered beliefs. So it might be useless to argue the benefits of teaching meditation, to point to the scores of mystics and secular geniuses who have consciously employed meditative techniques to refine their thoughts. Geniuses and mystics are extraordinary people anyway—enjoyable at a distance, perhaps, but not in one's family. Those of us who practice meditation may think of it as a tool, like mathematical skills, to help us live. So like the teacher who substitutes the word "sharing" for "long division", we may need to look at the concepts and feeling we would like to convey, and transmit what's important, rather than concerning ourselves with exact names.

About all we can really teach young children about meditation is to help them creatively sit still. The sort of meditation referred to here is that act of remaining peacefully, intentionally quiet—and yet very much awake. Any adult who meditates is well aware that before one can attempt to quiet the mind, there are very real difficulties in keeping the body still. The beginner is assaulted by traitorous itches, the urge to sneeze, cramped muscles begging to be stretched, involuntary twitches, yawns and body noises. Sixty seconds of stillness may easily seem like an hour to a young person. It's no small accomplishment to achieve that.

The habit of entering the same activity at the same time each day makes the process easier. So do occasional variations such as telling a short story the child can reflect upon, or preceding the silent time with a demonstration. One such experiment used several pretty chunks of turquoise at the bottom of a bowl filled with water. While the children watched, the water was churned by the teacher's fingers, then allowed to subside. While the water was turbulent, the pebbles were not visible; when the water stilled, their beauty could be easily seen. Sometimes music may be played or a lit candle placed in the center of the circle to remind everyone of their star.

In this context, there seems to be no need for adults to further direct the children's thinking. The innate spiritual sense of the child may be trusted to express itself; at this young age, the child almost invariably reflects the beliefs of the parents.

Still, prayer and silent meditation may blend together naturally and reverently. A few years ago, the mother of one of the children was bedridden while nervously waiting out a precarious pregnancy. One of the few expressions of stress her son permitted himself was to ask the other children to send good thoughts to his mother. After the baby was born, the older brother's schoolmates felt that they each had had a share in the family's small miracle.

What if things had turned out differently? Would it have proved that prayers don't get answered? Telling the child that all prayers and good thoughts are heard, at a time when a heartfelt cry appears to have been ignored, is small comfort. Nor can we adults pretend to a higher understanding than we possess. Sometimes a child's perception of the meaning of an event may be intrinsically wiser than an adult's more reasoned one. While Western religious traditions associate prayer with specific desired results, the Eastern tradition whose adherents often worship through silent meditation strives for harmony with whatever experience life offers.

Whatever we call it, the peacefulness of the quiet time and the shared silence transmit some of this meaning to the child. If nothing else, the island of calmness and relaxation reaches into the rest of the day with a positive effect. The concentrated attention the children may learn from making their stars bright can be successfully transferred to other areas of learning. The gift is such a precious one that giving it another name cannot dim its brightness. True, a lifetime of commitment to meditation *could* begin with this sort of pleasant, unpressured introduction. But we're not talking about meditation, are we? This is about peaceful silence, concentration, and the reverence that may arise out of them. No one objects to that.

The Uses of Fantasy: Can the Magical Worldview Survive?

Anne Carson

An old joke tells of two girls walking home after Sunday school, discussing the day's lesson.

"Do you believe in the devil?" asked one.

"I don't know," said her friend, "I think it's like Santa Claus—it's probably just your father."

Caroline Glyn, who was an accomplished poet at the age of nine and a published novelist at fifteen, wrote for the British dust jacket of her third novel *The Unicorn Girl*, "I suppose most children dream of fairy countries and magic lands, but tend to drop it as they grow up; I, on the contrary, believed more firmly in them the older I grew." Ultimately she entered a contemplative religious order at twenty and spent the rest of her life as both writer and nun until her death at thirty-three. Influenced by Wordsworth, Blake, and the seventeenth-century mystic Thomas Traherne, among others, her worldview was one of Platonic idealism, the philosophy that there is another reality more "real" than our ordinary experience. She was one of those rare people who are true visionaries—whose perception of the world does not significantly alter as they grow up.

Adults tend to feel ambivalence about promoting a magical worldview among children. We feel guilty about "deceiving" our children, yet consider those parents who tell their children that there is no such thing as Santa Claus or the Tooth Fairy or the Easter Bunny hard-hearted indeed. But do fairies "exist"? What do we mean by "exist"? What is "real"? What about angels? In conventional religion angels take the place of fairies: it's all right to believe in them when you're six, but don't let anyone know you've actually seen one. Billy Graham called them "God's secret agents"—as good an explanation as any. What about demons? Is the existence of angels and demons more unlikely than spirits, fairies, and devas?

Childhood is often remembered as a lost paradise, not so much in material particulars as in terms of mindset. Many scholars believe that this subtle awareness of lost bliss is the origin of the nearly universal myths of the fall from grace or the end of the Golden Age. "Once upon a time," the myth begins, "the world was a perfect place and human beings were happy." Occurring around the age of six or seven, the loss of bliss is widely believed by developmental psychologists to be an inevitable part of cognitive maturation. Other thinkers, however, lay it at the door of conventional education and socialization. In the United States children must attend school starting with kindergarten at age five, with more formal schooling beginning at six, but most children are already in nursery school at three or four. Alarmed at the poor educational performance of a large proportion of American schoolchildren, our educational hierarchy is now proposing that formal schooling begin at an earlier age, at five years old or even four, thereby hastening the destruction of the child's natural way of thought. Yet in many tribal cultures, notably in South America and Polynesia, children are not expected to start "growing up" until they are seven: little boys do not leave their mothers before this age, when they are sent to live in the men's house (males and females in these cultures often live in separate, communal houses rather than in nuclear family groups). Indeed, in traditional cultures, what we think of as childhood is brief, for at twelve or thirteen both boys and girls are considered capable of assuming adult functions in society.

Nowadays a very large percentage of children experience separation from home at a much earlier age than seven, because their mothers must, or wish to, return to work—often with bitter feelings of being cheated out of motherhood. (It is a myth that full-time mothers are always better mothers: studies have shown that most housewives actually spend more time watching television than they spend with their children.) These days few families can afford the luxury of living on only one income for years at a time, to be repeated with each successive child, and so early separation from parents has become the experience of a majority, not a minority, of our own children. A future generation will be able to determine whether the sense of loss of innocence will be as keenly felt among children who were sent to day care from an early age.

To a certain extent the magical worldview of childhood can and ought to be encouraged to remain. While in high school I babysat for a very bright four-year-old girl—the sort of child who, when you tell her, "Your mother didn't say you could have *two* cookies," points out, "She didn't say I couldn't." When I was putting her to bed a tiny worm slithered across the edge of her blanket. "Get it off!" she cried. In a flash I ripped the blanket off, then picked it up to remake the bed. We looked for the worm; nowhere to be found. "Maybe it was a magic worm," the girl suggested. If something vanishes, it must be magic.

I had never heard of a magic worm—magic rabbits, snakes, birds, yes, but worms, never—but who was I to tell this child that there was no such thing?

"I suppose that's possible," I admitted cautiously.

Some people object to this sort of thing, arguing that to admit the existence of magic—whatever that is—is to promulgate a false view of the world. Children should only be told the truth—whatever *that* is.

The child who is really psychic—who sees visions, hears voices, experiences altered states of awareness, has precognitive powers—generally learns that in modern culture, seeing things that others don't see means that you see worse than other people, not better, unlike in shamanic cultures, or those in which spirituality plays a central role, such as mediaeval Europe. Yet even St. Hildegard of Bingen, growing up in the early twelfth century, found that the people around her did not share her visions or her precognitive powers, and she told no one but her closest friends of what she saw. The modern child learns that to speak of the paranormal is to be labeled "crazy," "naughty," "untruthful," "unable to distinguish fantasy from reality," or just plain "weird." And so kids learn to repress their visions and ultimately forget about them. It is an unusual adult who accepts and encourages the visionary child. Even then, the child still knows that visions must be kept from the outside world. Often she grows up with a keen awareness that she is special, different from the rest, and sometimes never completely learns to connect with other people and to function comfortably within society. (Of course, some people regard being unable or unwilling to function within conventional society to be not such a bad thing!) This in part explains Caroline Glyn's decision to enter the convent—afflicted with poor health, she was educated at home until she was nine, at a time (the 1950s) when home-schooling was unusual in Britain and virtually impossible to undertake in the United States. By the time she entered school she was a poet and a prize-winning artist, but she found it extremely difficult to integrate with her middle- and working-class schoolmates. This sense of being an outcast persisted as she grew up, until she decided to honor her spiritual vision by living it totally via religious vocation.

The child's visionary world can be honored by paying attention to her dreams and the stories she tells. The novelist Toni

Morrison credits her grandmother with stimulating her powers of imagination, for her grandmother played the numbers, and in the numbers game in order to pick a good number to play you look up symbols appearing in your dreams, each symbol corresponding to a number, in "dream books" available at occult shops. Every morning her grandmother would ask the little girl what she had dreamed the night before, and in this way Morrison began to learn the craft of story-telling.

Reading fairy tales and the growing body of visionary children's literature, and encouraging artistic expression all serve to strengthen a child's imagination and intellect. The Waldorf educational curriculum designed by the great German philosopher Rudolf Steiner teaches reading, writing, and arithmetic via artistic or creative expression—story-telling, painting, acting—with the intention of strengthening the intuitive functions of the right brain in the crucial early years. Conventional education is largely geared towards left-brain functioning. Mathematics, language skills, and geography are all important, of course, but we need to question why they are taught five days a week while art and music are taught only a few times a month. Educators would probably respond that as adults we need math and reading skills more often than we need art and music, and in any case only a minority have true aptitude for the arts. This may be true, but in Waldorf and other kinds of progressive educational systems art and musical expression are offered from an early age, and if a child shows little aptitude or interest in them he is allowed to opt out of studying them as his education continues, whereas in conventional education most pupils are forced to study mathematics for several years of secondary education because they "need" it for college, after which their need disappears and they never study it again.

Like "God," the spirit world takes on the coloration of the style of the times, culture, and religion that surrounds us. The spirits—the unseen forces—might be called gods, or fairies and their elven kin, or angels and demons, or spacemen, or ghosts, or forces of nature, or projections of our own psyches. When John Lilly, the pioneer in research into dolphin intelligence and isolation tanks, told of encountering spirit guides on his LSD trips, he admitted that he had no idea whether these beings were spirits, angels, extraterrestrials, beings living on another plane of existence from ours, or simply psychological delusions—and he didn't care. What they were, was irrelevant. All that mattered were the teachings he received from them.

These powers are real; but we can choose how we wish to interpret them and explain them to children. One's conscience, for instance, may be anthropomorphized into "your friend inside," or your "guardian angel." Telling stories and listening to your child's fantasies and make-believe are ways to honor the imaginative life. And relating stories of your own childhood can be almost as entertaining as fairy tales.

As a family is driving at night they pass a view of the twinkling golden lights of a distant town. "Ooh, it looks like Fairyland!" exclaims a child. "Is that Fairyland?"

"Yes, that's it," her mother smiles. For several years afterwards every time they pass a cluster of far-off lights the child says, "Look! Fairyland!" She knows it isn't Fairyland; she only wishes it were, hopes it may be, just as she hopes that one of Grandmother's Oriental carpets might be the sort that flies.

Children and Angels

Karey Solomon

Look at a bright-eyed three or four year old and it's almost impossible to think of the dark side of life. But no matter how we yearn to shelter our child from misfortune, it's in the nature of life to be eventful. Before the age of five, it's more than likely that a person or pet the child loves will die; illness, injury, feelings of fear and loss will have become identifiable experiences. Child and parents are suddenly and painfully brought to recognize that our love can't be an invisible protective bubble. The child who has nightmares, whose behavior abruptly changes, who has started a career of catching every virus in the air may be reacting to the stress of this realization. What we all seem to need at this time is the guidance and support of a Guardian Angel.

Nearly every spiritual tradition relies on a Guardian Angel to get us through life's rougher spots. Angels play a significant role in the Old and New Testaments, generally as messengers from God. In Judaic teachings, among others, one or more angels are assumed to be assigned to the child at birth. However, many occultists go further in their belief that the Guardian takes up its task at around the fourth month of pregnancy, that time when the mother is first aware of the unborn child's movements—and coincidentally, that time when we tend to say that the mother has begun to glow with a certain inner radiance. In many of the primitive religions, the child is placed under the protection of a totem or guardian deity in the form of an animal, some time after birth when the child has demonstrated its vitality. In polytheistic societies, family gods take an intimate and personal interest in individual believers.

My daughter's Guardian Angel was first identified as such during a sequence of flu and fevers the winter she was three. When she was ill and afraid of the feverish dreams that came upon her when she slept, we talked about her angel at bedtime, emphasizing that she would watch lovingly over my daughter as she slept, helping to heal her, to chase away bad dreams and bring good ones. I'm referring to the Angel as "she" because this seems to be the character in which she appeared to the child. Interestingly, from the first time, we talked about the Angel, it was clear to me that I was not imparting new information but reminding my daughter of something she already knew.

The Angel helped her meditate after I suggested that we can listen for our Angel's voice when we are quiet. After incredibly brief intervals of silence, my daughter would report with satisfaction that her Angel had spoken to her. Although I didn't ask for details of the conversation, it was often followed by a time of greater self-confidence, a sense of the ease we relax into when surrounded by a loving presence. When I had the poor judgement to inquire what the Angel looked like, I received a suitably vague answer.

Years later, when mention of the Guardian Angel had become gradually less frequent, the house was suddenly redecorated with angels: large, homely, motherly figures with just the hint of wings behind their shoulders. It was around that time that I mentioned that we call our Angel by different names as we get older. Sometimes we call it our Angel, later we may know it as our conscience, or the "still, small voice," or the muse (another sort of angel, really) that brings us pictures to paint, stories to tell, songs that are ours for a while. "I KNOW that," my daughter said impatiently, being six or so at the time, and more articulate.

We still talk about angels, though admittedly less frequently. When a child we knew died suddenly, only the thought of his

Angel sheltering his soul from pain as he made the abrupt transition from life into death enabled us to deal with the otherwise incomprehensible accident. Similarly, when others act hurtfully towards us, we attempt to visualize their Angels—often with more than a little sympathy for the hard, uphill work they have with their charges.

As our children progress towards greater independence, it does become more difficult to perceive their angelic natures during the hours of the day that their eyes are open. Only the last good-night kisses on a sleeping child's forehead remind us, some days, that the Angel is there too. Having established the presence of the Angel helps us nourish that positivity. The Guardian Angel watching over our child is helping us as well.

Shadow Boxes

Naomi Strichartz

Since my children were small, I have made shadow boxes with them to celebrate the sacred moments of the Wheel of the Year. This is for us a tangible and beautiful way to bridge the material and the spirit worlds. It helps us keep track of the passage of time that returns and returns without beginning or end.

I began by acquiring a sturdy wooden box from a liquor store and buying self-hardening clay. I encouraged my children, then five and seven, to make sacred figures for Winter Solstice. Together we made people, fairies, gnomes, deer, snakes, cauldrons, horses, wagons, cats, sheep, rabbits, and all sorts of things. Some of the figures carried tiny pots for candles or incense. Throughout the year we made figures for the other seven nature holidays as well (Candlemas or Brigid's Day—February 2; Spring Equinox; May Day; Midsummer's Day; Lammas—August 1; Autumn Equinox; Halloween). Sometimes the clay told us what it wanted to be, asked to be born, as it were. The figures were left to harden for a day or two in an area not usually frequented by our cats. Then we painted the faces and clothes with bright acrylic paint, leaving a lot of the rich brown clay uncovered. We painted a background on a piece of cardboard or heavy paper which I taped to the back of the box. We now have a collection of figures and backgrounds which are used and re-used and often replenished as the Goddess moves us.

Our backgrounds depict fairies dancing around a bonfire, sheep wandering around ancient huts, a moon hovering over a pine forest, and a busy Eastern European bazaar—booths overflowing with festive food and rich materials, and street musicians adding to the array. The boxes, like the moon, earth, and ourselves, are always growing and changing.

We do the most with clay and paints in winter, when the earth settles down for a season of dreaming. One of my favorite motifs shows three wisewomen sitting around a fire. They are talking and playing primitive instruments. One is young, one is nursing a baby, and the other is old, representing the Goddess as maiden, matron, and crone. They are wise in the world's ancient secrets. Off to a corner, partly hidden under an apple tree root, fairies are celebrating in their own way. They dance and play instruments and eat tiny cakes. I like this motif around Brigid's Day, when I seem to be called back to an earlier, simpler time.

Just as the words of a poem or chant can be magical and transforming, so can a personal symbol help connect you to the Goddess. Because I believe in the magical transforming power of art, I often make scenes depicting what I would like to become, or what I would like to see happen: my own magical vision of the world. Some of my own special symbols include: cranes, snakes, deer, crows, sheep, spiders, cats, fossils, amber, cauldrons, pumpkins, willow trees, pine trees, bonfires, primitive huts, wagon wheels, fairies, Gypsies, candles, tree roots, crystal balls, baskets, and embroidered tiny bags. You and your children can make your own.

For materials you will first need a wooden box (cardboard can serve the purpose). Use a rectangular shape sitting lengthwise. This allows more room for your scene. Building blocks can be used to create levels for the figures to stand on, so more is visible to the viewer. For the figurines use self-hardening clay. The more ambitious can fire clay to make it sturdier. We just replace broken figures as needed. To color with, use any of the following: drawing paper, charcoal, acrylic paints, magic markers, crayons, watercolors—whatever you like to use. For decorations you may use any sacred object of the season, such as roots, seeds, herbs, stones, shells, feathers, dried flowers, etc.

Generally we leave a box out to enjoy until it is time to dismantle it for the next holiday. Sometimes we feel like adding a shadow box for other festivals, Chanukah or the Chinese New Year, for example. Since these days are based on already existing nature holidays it is easy to incorporate them into our boxes. Our children enjoyed participating in making the family boxes but other children might prefer to have their own. A simple shoebox serves perfectly and can become a child's personal altar that changes with the wheel of the year. This custom can become a joyful way to celebrate with children and to teach them respect for the earth and her cycles. Let your own hands be guided by the Goddess within.

PART V

Older Children

Being in the World

In the early years children do not really distinguish the spiritual world from the earthly world. In the middle years, from seven to eleven or twelve, the spiritual and the secular begin to be separated, yet the child may have no less an intense and pervasive sense of the numinous. The vaunted "personal relationship with God" may be experienced, and though the child plies us with questions, she has not yet become critical and cynical.

As children mature they become more aware of the world outside the home, in part because of school and interaction with children from many different backgrounds. Parents are no longer the fount of all wisdom: teachers, entertainers, and grown-up characters on programs such as *Sesame Street*, *Mister Rogers' Neighborhood*, and action shows enter the picture. As children's questions become more pointed, their curiosity about the world remains, and the world of fantasy and reality may be bridged by the seemingly universal fascination with dinosaurs. (Dinosaurs are modern children's mythical beasts—people swear they're real, but who has ever seen one?)

More formal instruction in the way of the spirit is now possible, and children can begin to participate in the cultural life of adults. They compare notes with friends and may argue over what they have been taught by their parents and spiritual instructors. Jewish children may become keenly aware of anti-Semitism in their environment, while Christian children argue over points of doctrine and the nature of the "true" church. Lifestyles and family patterns are contrasted; this is the time when some families may wish to take special care with the way they describe their spirituality. Kids need to learn that not everyone may accept their family's lifestyle or beliefs, and that some people don't think that freedom of religion extends to occult forms of worship.

As children grow more sophisticated in the workings of the world, it becomes possible to demonstrate the ways that spiritual beliefs and ethics impinge on life in daily reality. The articles on nature awareness in this section reveal that after we have discovered the wonderful miracle that is the natural world, it is even more important to learn that humans are part of that world and can either work with it or destroy it.

Social action, it is said, begins with good manners. It means being aware of the needs of other people, from the individual to the global level. Children who are encouraged to participate in activities like making Christmas baskets for the poor and elderly, sending cards and drawings to older ill friends, going caroling, and baking treats for others will find it easier to grasp the concept of helping the neighbors we do not see. Children are apt to be very affected by what they see of social and political problems on the evening news and to insist upon taking direct action, like the eleven-year-old boy who became a ministering angel to the homeless of Philadelphia, bringing street people cups of coffee and blankets, starting with the blanket off his own bed.

A friend told me of another eleven-year-old boy she knew who gave up his guns and G.I. Joe of his own accord after coming to the realization that war toys glorify the military.

A fine guide to teaching children social consciousness is *Parenting for Peace and Justice* by James and Kathleen McGinnis. The McGinnises are Catholics whose commitment to social justice is as profound as their faith, and in their book they outline ways to get children to become aware of racial and sexual discrimination, economic injustice, and most importantly, to help them understand that we can make a difference by taking action, whether it is by withholding the part of our taxes that goes to support militarism, making dinner at a soup kitchen, or sharing our homes at the holidays with those who have no families. They write candidly of their successes and failures and the compromises they have made with their three children. One point they stress is that the children must be invited to participate in social/political action, not coerced, browbeaten, or bribed. As with anything else we wish to pass on to our children, social consciousness is best taught through your own example. Being an example for your children means bringing them along from an early age when you shop or work at the food co-op, cook at the soup kitchen, sort clothes for a charity drive, picket or march, help with a neighborhood clean-up.

What *do* we want for our children? Our parents, many of whom suffered during the Depression or saw family and neighbors suffer, worked so that their children might know economic security and the benefits of higher education—a "better life." To our parents a better life may have meant a higher income, a nicer place to live, material comforts they could only dream about in their own youth. Now married couples often find that the best college or a house with a yard for the kids is prohibitively expensive, and most people consider this an unfortunate trend, never stopping to ask whether a materially "better life for the children" must be pursued indefinitely, generation after generation, on the assumption that economic growth is infinite.

If you ask us whether we want a better life for our children, some of us will not be responding in terms of bicycles, ballet lessons, or Ivy League schools. The better life I envision for my daughter is not one in which she can pay for college without being in debt but one in which she can live without fear: fear of being raped, fear of bombs, fear of ending her days helpless and alone, fear of hatred being directed against her by profoundly fearful people, fear of contracting disease from her tap water. When I think, "I want her to have everything I didn't have," I think of things like self-confidence, creativity, assertiveness, stable relationships (and maybe a pony).

Love is the key: love for family, community, for those who suffer, for the Earth and all her creations.

One other thing I would like my daughter to grow up with is a sense of the feminine within the Divine. Even though we may take pains to use inclusive or non-patriarchal language in our professional or daily lives, in spiritual areas many people tend to leave their feminism at the door along with their shoes. Even people on spiritual quest tend to take for granted the masculinity of God. In circles that are supposed to be non-sectarian or multi-traditional, such as Vedanta, over and over one hears "God, he," until you might just as well go back to church. In most religious circles, whether conventional or not, God is nearly always referred to as "he," except by the most adventurous (or determined). Our children will hear plenty about "God, he" as they grow up in patriarchal society, so it is our duty to offer them an alternative and to expand their vision, just as we do in other areas of life.

Some people (usually men, I'm afraid) dismiss the issue of sexism in spiritual language as trivial. If you think gender in religious language is of little consequence, wait until you go to church and hear the priest refer to "God, in Her infinite mercy."

The male God is so deeply ingrained in our culture that even people who are willing to agree that the masculinity of God is all metaphor and the Divine Being transcends male or female will get very upset at the idea of a female God. "It's impossible! It's ridiculous! God *is* Father!" railed a physician I know who is a devout Presbyterian and a sensitive and sensible parent of three boys.

The harm that is done to the minds of children, and especially to girls, when adults teach that the Supreme Being is male cannot be underestimated. If the most perfect being in the universe is male, what does that say about being female? Does it not condemn women and girls to a sense of inferiority, to accept, however resentfully, a subordinate role on earth? Our daughters need to be told that they are strong, beautiful, and wise, if only because there are plenty of people out in the world who will tell them they are not. In how many children's adventure stories does the hero tell the heroine, "You stay here—it's too dangerous"? *I* treat my sons and daughters as equals, you say. Perhaps this is so, but the society into which we send our children does not.

Feminist teacher and healer Hallie Iglehart devised a meditation that gives strength and pride to the women who hear it while subtly pointing out the psychological effect of a monosexual authority system:

"Begin to imagine what your daily life would be like from the time you got up in the morning, throughout the work of the day, until you went to bed at night, if you lived in a world where:

• your family name were passed down from mother to daughter

• the decision makers and organizers of your community were women

• the religious leaders of your community were women

- the women in your family and community were looked up to as the wise ones, the carriers of the most important knowledge, and the keepers of the mysteries of life
- when you were sick you went to the healing women for help
- when a special event came up, the women of your community gathered together to decide what to do.

When you are finished imagining these situations, note what emotions, fantasies, and other reactions came up to you." [6]

Perhaps the female reader is sighing, "How wonderful! If only life were like that!"

And how does the male reader feel?

In Christianity God is generally imaged as Father, sometimes as blustering, threatening father, but more often as loving father. Yet, sadly, with the huge number of divorces and teenage pregnancies, not to mention delinquency in child support, a very large proportion of our children literally have no concept of what a "loving father" is, just as an only child can only wonder what it might be like to have brothers or sisters, and children of older parents wonder what it might be like to have grandparents.

Some conventional religious educators still point out to children that the Judeo-Christian God is "our Father," in the hopes that their pupils will imagine God to be like their real fathers. Obviously these educators are unaware that this is one of the many ways by which boys are educated to perceive the feminine as the alien Other, and girls taught to sense themselves as hopelessly inferior. For children who are effectively fatherless it may actually make more sense to describe God as a loving Mother.

The way you choose to use inclusive language does depend on the context of your spirituality, but in some cases there are female images or actual goddesses which can be invoked. For instance, Buddhists should not forget the beautiful, powerful, and healing image of Kwan Yin, the bodhisattva of compassion; people studying yoga can draw upon India's vast number of female deities; non-denominational circles can speak of "Our Heavenly Mother," "the Mother Power," or "Mother Earth."

Some parents who are not particularly interested in the Great Goddess or Mother Earth nonetheless are amenable to presenting God as Father *and* as Mother, creating an image of heavenly parents who are the cosmic counterparts of the child's real mother and father. If you wish to teach about the Judeo-Christian God but do not wish the child to identify God with his or her biological father, you can downplay "God the Father" and instead focus on Jesus, who is Son, Brother, and loving Friend.

If you are going to introduce the Goddess or God-as-Mother, it is best to do so at as early an age as possible. Children learn very quickly from the mass culture if not their own religious training that this person called "God" is male, and to suddenly speak of God as female is as mind-blowing to an eight-year-old as it is to an adult. Even more important than using feminine or inclusive language is including your daughter in women-only gatherings, if you participate in them. Such gatherings probably won't make much of an impact on very tiny girls, but as they grow older and become aware of themselves as different from boys (starting at age five or six), it is vital to provide them with models of female strength, sacrality, and community.

Start referring to squirrels, birds, mice, etc. as "she" either in real life or in picture books (since at least half the animal population is female, it's only fair—any child can comprehend that), and you can experiment with changing the gender in some prayers. Some of the Psalms, for example, lend themselves to changing "Lord" to "Lady," as in "The Lady is my Shepherdess, I shall not want." Don't worry about the kids growing up with the "wrong" version of prayers and songs—they will hear the standard (male) versions soon enough.

Because there are several other important topics to be introduced in this section, it has been divided into five parts—
Meditation; Healing; Nature; Rituals, Festivals and Holidays; and
Death—as the child moves outward from the Self, to the environment, and thence to the larger community.

Meditation

Anne Carson

Psychologists are just beginning to recognize that children experience stress and depression, and not just those children who must contend with divorce, crime, poverty, hunger, war, or abuse. When I was a child and heard adults describe childhood as a blissfully happy time, I wondered what on earth they were talking about. Childhood happy! With all the pressures from teachers, friends, parents, siblings, the Bomb? Ridiculous. Recently fears that the world may be destroyed by nuclear war have returned to torment youngsters who would seem to have everything, who are well cared-for and loved. A shockingly large number of children and teenagers feel that it's a waste of time planning for their future, since there isn't going to be any. In the face of this despair, meditations that relieve stress, rituals that encourage empowerment, and social action that helps transform the world (even a little part of it) can be especially beneficial for a child's mental health. There is a saying among feminists that the personal is political; we have also learned that the spiritual is therapeutic. Surely ninety percent of any religion is nothing more than applied psychology.

The groundwork for prayer and meditation lies in the child understanding what it is to have a peaceful mind. Peace of mind can be cultivated by letting the child play quietly by herself as opposed to constantly being surrounded by other people, and above all, providing her with as many books as she wants, for in many homes "quiet time" or "down time" is observed by an evening of reading as often as by meditation. A private time with a parent each day, for each child, is an important part of daily ritual. Usually "private time" takes place at bedtime, but if there are several children in the family, the private times may have to be spread out throughout the day, for example while going to the store, cleaning up the kitchen, or bringing a child home from school or lessons. Or the child can take a before- or after-dinner walk with Dad. Occasionally the spiritual can be interwoven into these times, but most often spirituality is an unspoken current.

One of the earliest results of meditation is learning how to concentrate. Increased concentration itself can also help with learning. It is well-known that contemporary mass entertainment is very destructive to a child's powers of concentration. The flashing colors, rapid shift of images, and loud, monotonous music all serve to erode children's already limited (by adult standards) attention span. Even adults find that TV news flickers by so rapidly that very little information is retained. One need only cite the example of AIDS: virtually every evening the national news programs' science correspondents report the latest developments in AIDS research, yet at least a third of Americans are shockingly ignorant about the cause and transmission of this disease. In this environment, what chance does a child have of developing effective learning habits and life skills?

A second important goal of meditation and visualization practice is that of building confidence and self-esteem, and helping the child to help herself deal with her anxieties and fears. When a child has a fear, too often adults respond by laughing at her or telling her that her fear is "irrational." A far more helpful way to deal with fear is to allow the child to meet it, talk to it, face it head on in whatever way she feels is appropriate. Guided imagery or dream work, drawing pictures of her fear and the way she wishes to overcome it, or acting out a drama in which she defeats her particular demon, are all healthy methods to give a child courage and confidence; the television program *Mister Rogers' Neighborhood* also provides excellent ways for children to confront and defeat, or at least diminish, their fears and worries.

There is nothing mystical about this process—psychologists utilize the same techniques when working with children who cannot or will not express their troubles, but instead of calling it "ritual" they call it "play therapy."

Our culture has substituted some fears for others. Traditionally the first day of school has produced great anxiety in many children—being separated from mother and having to face twenty strangers is no picnic. We may suspect that the experience of day care has eliminated much of that anxiety for some children, for the child who spends all or most of her first four or five years at home is today a rarity. Instead, our children may be more concerned about concrete dangers: kidnapping, AIDS, nuclear annihilation, crime in the school hallways or on the playground.

Here the child's concrete, rather than abstract, mode of thought, is a boon, for children can be taught to face their fears, whether they are "real" fears, such as fear of the school bully, or "imaginary" fears, like monsters under the bed, and can learn to devise concrete strategies for empowering themselves and defeating their private demons. As an example, a friend of mine spontaneously made a charm for another woman's six-year-old daughter who was having night terrors. She made a small bag of herbs for the girl and put into it a tiny crystal and a plastic figurine of a bear. She told the little girl that the bear was her very own helper, and that if any of the nightmare monsters came to get her the bear would leap up and destroy them all. And she reminded the girl that really it was she herself who was working the magic.

Being the victim of bullying by other children is another common trauma of childhood, and this bullying may not be only physical. Psychological bullying can be even more damaging to a person's sense of self-worth, the effects longer lasting than being beaten in a fight, yet rarely is it ever taken seriously by adults.

An adult in the same situation might focus on projecting love and good energy toward the opponent, but it can take considerable maturity to be able to muster up positive energy when dealing with someone who is trying to hurt you. When working with a child it might be more effective to suggest that she visualize her circle of protection, as described below, or to imagine an angel, a strong person—or even God—standing beside the child with his/her hand on the child's shoulder.

Martial arts, or a self-defense class specifically intended for kids, can create a sense of self-confidence; in fact, the first thing any martial arts student really learns, in the sense of being able to utilize it, is how to face an opponent. Your legs may be shaking, but you can still deal with someone in a calm manner. Remind the child that people who study self-defense seriously seldom ever need to use it—that has been my experience and that of my classmates in karate—because a strong and confident (not cocky) person carries herself differently from someone who already thinks of herself as a victim before anything has actually happened. A strong person has a kind of "invisible shield," as they used to say in the toothpaste commercial.

Here are instructions for visualizing a protective circle; try it with your child:

Whenever you are about to go on a magical journey, or just when you need a feeling of safety and confidence, you can create a magic circle around yourself that will help protect you. To make a protective circle, imagine a glowing ring surrounding you, an energy field that can keep out any harmful energy other people might be directing at you. The circle is very bright and may be gold, silver, blue, or white, or whatever color you like best. Instead of a circle it can be a fog that is all around you, stretching out for a few feet, so that no one can reach you. This energy field is what is called "The Force" in the *Star Wars* movies.

A protective circle can be used when dealing with someone who is bothering you or bullying you, whether it's a classmate or an adult. When someone is throwing bad energy at you, the circle acts as a kind of force field that eats up the other person's energy without letting it harm you. This is what people really mean when they say, "Don't let it get to you."

If you feel you need a companion on your magical journey, you can ask for a spirit guide to appear. This guide does not have to be a magical or mythical figure, but can be a friend, a parent, a guardian angel, a pet, even a cartoon character like She-Ra, Princess of Power. This guide will stay with you on your journey and help you if you feel nervous. Each time you go on a magical journey, do the Deep Relaxation meditation and create a protective circle around yourself.

It may take some conscious effort, but TV, radio, and stereo should be kept to a minimum, and not only by the children. In the average American family home the TV is on for seven hours a day. The issue is not simply what you are watching—not everyone who is reading this watches nothing but PBS, and I'd just as soon not reveal some of my own addictions—but that staying in front of the television for hours, reading every *New Yorker* cover to cover, or maintaining a constant stream of music all prevent us from thinking our own thoughts and accomplishing anything more involved than mending clothes or kneading bread. An occasional loud rock and roll record—whether the parent's or the child's—is not necessarily more detrimental to the soul than a classical or jazz radio station that is never turned off. We need to stimulate our children's senses, but we also need to provide them with silence.

This is not to say that some noise and a little mayhem aren't a natural and healthy part of childhood. As the powers of concentration are naturally less developed in children than in adults, so less must be required of young people. Most of us can recall some exasperated teacher in our past making the entire class sit still with our hands folded for ten minutes, not as a means of gaining self-control or inner focus, but simply as punishment for too much noise and activity. How much less exasperated a teacher (or parent) might be if centering and meditation were as regular a part of the school day as recess!

And parents need quiet time, too. Often parents who have had the luxury of spending many hours a week in meditation or psychic work find that with the arrival of children regular meditation becomes an unattainable goal. Even leaving the house once a week for a yoga class seems impossible when you have a new baby who spends a few hours a day screaming. Within six months of Catherine's birth a women's spirituality group formed in my home town. Most of the women wanted to meet once a week; I was finding it was all I could do to vacuum the house that often.

It is very easy for parents to get so caught up in the daily rush, particularly if both are working at full-time, regular jobs, that the time for quiet reflection vanishes. The practice of Zen mindfulness can be a helpful way to remain centered. Mindfulness consists of a deliberate decision to maintain absolute awareness of what one is doing at every moment, e.g. washing the dishes and thinking only of washing the dishes, rather than washing the dishes and thinking about the laundry that needs to be done, or what we're going to do tomorrow, or the cup of tea that awaits us.

The age at which formal meditation is introduced will naturally depend on the abilities and interests of the child. Transpersonal educators warn that pressuring a child to meditate or to do guided imagery simply places another burden on her to perform and to compete with her classmates in having a good vision. ("You in the red shirt—are you visualizing or just daydreaming?") We need to accept the fact that some individuals are just not very skilled in this area. Spiritual teacher Da Free John says, "Some children just don't have much activity on the astral plane."

"Provide the child with the tools through which to express [non-ordinary reality]," writes Thomas Armstrong in *The Radiant Child*, "but don't program them with exercises designed to 'evoke' the transpersonal."[7] He is among those who criticize guided imagery as *telling* the child what to visualize, and recommends that visualizations be more open in structure. For the first few years simple, low-key relaxation and centering exercises are probably sufficient, and then once the child has shown interest and aptitude for meditation, practice in guided imagery can be added. The key words here are interest and aptitude; some readers may recall the intense frustration we felt at being forced to engage in certain endeavors in school regardless of our innate ability, whether it was practicing sports, studying mathematics, or speaking foreign languages. What a shame if the spiritual quest were to be regarded as yet another tiresome pursuit dreamed up by adults. Instead of pushing a child towards doing yoga or meditation, it would be more effective to *include* her in your own spiritual pursuits.

In the suggestions on conducting a children's meditation class which follow, Dr. Deborah Rozman emphasizes the importance of maintaining an atmosphere of discipline. Her approach may seem overly strict, but her point is that in order to create a space in which any meditation, prayer, and worship can take place, the participants must possess a certain degree of self-control and awareness of others' needs. Small children learn this quickly in cultures where meditation is a part of daily life, just as in the West youngsters are taught that during religious services people are expected to sit quietly except when singing or praying aloud together. Whispering, pinching your sister, and climbing around disturb the concentration of others and are not acceptable behavior.

Following Dr. Rozman's guidelines for teaching meditation are several basic meditations which form a groundwork for visualization practice.

Buddhists who meditate seriously and regularly have found that small children, from eighteen months to the age of four or five, may not be able to comprehend meditation, but they do know what it is to have a quiet time. Thich Nhat Hanh writes that for a time a little girl was living with him, and he gave her to understand that when he sat in meditation in her room, it was time for her to go to bed quietly. One day when she was thirsty he poured her a glass of apple juice, but it was full of sediment from the bottom of the jar and she didn't want it. When she came into the house later for a drink, the sediment had settled and the juice was clear. "Was the juice meditating?" she asked the monk.

Tips on Conducting a Meditation Class

Deborah Rozman

The teacher should be in equilibrium before the class commences. Meditation for equilibrium and a humble inner request for guidance from the Higher Self, the Source within, sets the tone, not only for the teacher, but for the children as well, for it must be remembered that children respond to the vibrations of the teacher.

Moods can be created in the environment to calm the children, such as restful music, incense (the odor can carry a soothing vibration), and candlelight. Children can be asked to take their shoes off when they enter the group circle. When shoes are removed the atmosphere becomes more relaxed. The circular position is recommended as a means for sealing the group energy and focusing it into the center. Since a circle represents a continuity the energies may have less of a tendency to get distracted. All of these suggestions may be experimented with for optimal tone setting.

• Have one good, deep meditation each session.

• Have one project that is explored in depth. The class will evolve dependent upon the depth of the experiences both in the meditation and in the activity.

• Have the children lead the meditations occasionally; allow them to choose the meditation format.

• Have two reserve or alternative projects that can be used in case a change of course is needed in any session. Always have your structure for the sessions prepared; however, alternatives may be needed and when they are planned for there need be little or no break in continuity of the group energies.

• It is important to maintain spontaneity in order to avoid rigidity and optimize creativity. Here again a balance between the form and the rhythm is essential.

It is always smoother, but not always possible, to have the meditations on tape or memorized or totally spontaneous, so the teacher participates and experiences with the children. The voice should be smooth, calm and relaxing. Sometimes, and especially with younger children, it may be necessary to monitor the class during the meditation so a few disruptive children do not spoil the silence for the others. The earlier the tone is set that no distractions will be permitted during the meditation period, the easier will the discipline be and the better the growth and progress of the group.

Be sure the children are seated far enough apart so that no one is touching. Have them sit in a comfortable position (usually cross-legged on the floor) with the back straight. Explain to them that a straight back allows the energy to flow freely up and down the spine which is important for successful meditation. Have them place their hands on their thighs palms up. It may take quite a bit of reminding before the habit of a proper meditational posture is learned and becomes automatic. However, this discipline in the formative years will help to prevent sloppiness in the later years. If a child finds it is just too uncomfortable to continue to stay sitting upright, he may quietly lie down on his back without disturbing the others and continue the meditation lying down.

It is important that discipline be kept in the class sessions so that the true meaning of listening, of observing, and concentrating can be understood. The greater the concentration the greater the benefit that will be received from the classes. It is an essential part of the class to have the leader remain centered and calm yet firm. The children respond more to the leader, teacher or parent's attitude than to anything else. Teaching children should basically be done through the heart centre to generate a secure, sustaining aura of enveloping love. The reason for any discipline that is imposed should be clearly conveyed so that it is received harmlessly by the child, in order to cultivate harmlessness in the children.

Elements Meditation

Earth

1. Ground, relax, and center.

2. Imagine you are the earth, one with Mother Earth. Feel that you are deep inside the center of the earth and that the mountains and oceans and rivers are your body. Feel all of the rocks as part of you; now feel all of the soil and dirt as part of you...now feel all of the little plants as part of you and all of the big trees as part of your body; now feel all of the animals as part of you; now feel all of the people, everywhere, black and white and red and yellow as part of your body. Feel all of the earth-beings as part of you, the earth, whom you feed and shelter and give a home to, for all have the same home, the earth.

3. Discuss the earth—what does it mean to you?

4. Discuss ecology and nature's cycles.

5. Discuss earth as a school.

6. Make something out of clay.

7. Meditate: feel that all of the things that live on earth are here to learn and when they finish learning on the school of earth they will enter into the One Source which is beyond the earth but which is always with them. And they will continue learning beyond what we can even imagine. Let us go deep inside our Source.

8. Open the circle.

Air

1. Relax, ground, and center.

2. Close your eyes and feel the air around your face and around your whole body. Feel the air as it comes inside your nose

as you breathe in and as it leaves your nose as you breathe out. Air is everywhere and it is breathing you in and out, in and out. Listen to the sounds that travel to you through the air. Open your eyes and see the light of different objects around you that travel to your eyes through the air. Air is everywhere. Birds fly through air. Air fills all space. Close your eyes and see the space inside yourself. Meditate on the space and let it get bigger and bigger until you know that the space of the whole universe is inside of you.

3. Fly kites with the children or do some other project that deals with air.

4. Meditate on air. Close your eyes and in your imagination pretend you are flying through air and are going anywhere that you want to go, way up over the oceans and the mountains into space, beyond the sun, beyond the stars, beyond the beyond... Now you are coming back into the universe, you are flying back passing the stars, passing the sun and coming into earth and passing over the ocean and the mountains and into the class and into your body, and here you are.

5. Telephone, television, telegraph, radio, tape recordings, walkie talkies, etc. are all examples of vibrations moving through air. Play one of these instruments to demonstrate. Have a musical instrument, e.g. a guitar, and illustrate how the sound moves through the air from the instrument to your ears.

6. Open the circle.

Fire

1. [Begin with centering and grounding exercises, or yoga exercises.]

2. Discuss: what is fire? How do we use it? Where do we find fire? candle? fireplace? sun? stars? What does fire provide? heat? energy? light? etc. We want to experience the nature of fire today.

3. Have a candle lit and have each child one at a time, and then together, concentrate on the candle flame, just on the flame,

and go deep inside of it and become one with it. Time the duration of the child's concentration. Discuss the importance of concentration.

Have the children all look at the candle together (which is in the center of the circle) and then close their eyes and concentrate on the reflection of the candle flame inside their inner eye.

4. Fire meditation. See a flame, like the flame on a candle, inside your head. It is yellow with blue inside the yellow, and white inside the blue, just like a candle flame. Feel it get warmer and warmer—feel it spreading—now step inside the flame and know that you are a glowing light. Feel yourself glowing—first yellow—now feel the heaviness of the body and the feelings and the mind burn away in the yellow flame leaving you free. Now go deeper into the blue of the flame. Feel the blue as love, as joy. Now go deeper still, into the white until you see and now feel and know yourself to be standing inside the white center of the light of the flame which is very hot and very cold at the same time. Meditate on that.

5. Did anyone have trouble keeping their attention on the candle flame inside their head and going deep into it?

6. [Optional] Make candles as a project with the children.

7. Snack or quiet activity.

8. [End in a love circle—see below.]

Water

1. Relax, ground, and center.

2. Close your eyes and feel that you are in an ocean of blue light; feel and believe that you are a wave in that ocean and are floating up and down gently, up and down just like a wave. Now feel yourself melt and disappear into that ocean just like the wave disappears into the ocean. Ahhh, feel it relaxing you. You are now one with the ocean of blue light and there is no wave, no difference between you and the ocean. Now listen...very

quietly within…hear the sound of the ocean inside your head, and feel yourself becoming one with that sound. Now the sound is dying away and the wave is starting to come back again just like the wave in the ocean and another and another, until it washes into the shore and we open our eyes.

3. Do finger painting and movement to music, being waves in the ocean.

4. Meditate on the ocean again, feeling the ocean containing all people, all life inside of itself. Go deep into the Source as the ocean of all life, the ocean of all energy.

5. Using a fish bowl illustrate how the fish swim in water and are always in the water; they were born in water and die in water and because they are never out of water they do not know that they are in water, because they don't know anything that isn't water. To them everything is water and nothing is water. Similarly, we are living in a sea of energy that we don't recognize is energy, because we are born in it and live in it and die in it and don't know anything that isn't it.

Love Circle

One very effective and very beautiful activity/meditation to experience with the children is for all of the children to channel love and light from their hearts through their hands to each child one at a time until each child feels that love energy coming into his heart and has a direct experience of the reality of consciously directed love energy. The children do this channeling while sitting in a circle and by the time each one has had a turn there is a build-up of love energy in the circle and in the whole room that is recognizable by each child and the atmosphere is usually filled with joy and peace. The whole group is made aware of the energy they have channeled and created and are now bathing in and as a group they send this energy to whomever they feel is in need of some of it. Whenever this experience of the Presence is occurring the leader will find the group to be very easy to work with and the children very receptive to learning new skills. Sometimes this meditation can be followed by chanting Om. Remind the children to listen to each other as well as to themselves to create harmony and beautiful tones.

Deep Relaxation

Diane Mariechild

Let's see if you can relax your body just like when you are sleeping, but you will stay awake and be able to hear what I am saying. Lie down and get comfortable. Now close your eyes and begin to relax your body as I talk. Wiggle your toes and feet and then let them relax. Let them go loose and limp like Raggedy Ann or Raggedy Andy. Now let your stomach relax. Let it become very loose, like you are filled with sawdust. Now squeeze your hands together, make a fist and then let your hands relax. Now squeeze your eyes real tight and now let them relax. Your whole body is very relaxed now. You are just like a Raggedy Ann, loose and limp. Your body is filled with sawdust.

Your Friend Inside

Diane Mariechild

You see a boat and you know it is a very special boat, going to a very special place. This place is a secret island. There is no map to get to the island, but you know the way by heart. And on this island lives a very special person, your special friend. Your secret friend lives inside you and you can see your friend by going to this island. This special friend is just for you and knows you very, very well. Your friend is always there to help you and to play with you.

Your boat is sailing along now and you have almost reached the island. The boat has washed against the shore and you climb out on the island. Walk over to your friend's house and stay with your friend until you hear my voice calling you back. *(Pause about five minutes.)*

I'm calling you now, calling you back. Say good-bye to your friend, fly back to the room and open your eyes.

A Trip to the Woods

Eva D. Fugitt

Today we are going to take a short trip. We are going to use our imagination, that part of our mind that sees pictures and can create. We're going to take a trip to the woods. As you breathe quietly, imagine that you are walking down a path in the woods. It is a friendly woods, a lovely day. The sun is shining and you feel it on your skin, warm and comfortable. A gentle breeze blows on you, feeling fresh and good. The sun sparkles on the leaves of the trees. The air smells oh, so good, a woodsy scent. The earth feels firm under your feet and you rustle the leaves with your feet as you walk. As the path curves, you come to a lovely stream. It is cool and inviting.

You sit on a rock, just the right size for you, and look at the water. It is sparkling in the sun, bubbling and singing as it tumbles along. You could easily wade the stream if you wished. But you continue to sit on the rock, with your feet comfortably dangling in the cool water. You take a deep breath and simply enjoy it. The sky is blue above you. All is silent and peaceful. You watch a leaf float gently down from a tree and glide and twirl in the stream. You hear the birds singing and rejoice... You feel very good deep down inside you. There is no pressure for you to do anything. Everything is just right. You can stay there as long as you wish. *(Pause.)*

As you look around, you see a deer come out of the woods across the stream and walk to the edge of the water. It pauses and looks around. You sit very quietly, looking across at this beautiful deer. You think loving thoughts about it and silently, in your mind, you send it reassuring thoughts that everything is okay and you are its friend. It stands there, quietly returning your look and seems to know that it can trust you. It dips its head and takes a drink. Then slowly and quietly looking around, it returns into the woods.

You continue sitting there for a while, just feeling good about yourself, about the beauty of the deer, and the woods, and just good about everything. You know that you are okay.

Now, in your own time, quietly return up the path from which you came and return to the room. Be aware of your body sitting in the chair, and your feet touching the floor. Hear the sounds in the room. When you are ready, open your eyes.

[Mrs. Fugitt, an elementary school teacher, writes, "Children love this exercise. They often ask for it after coming in from a busy, frustrating, everything-gone-wrong type of lunch period. One little fourth grader came swinging into the room one day saying, "Let's go to the woods, I need a vacation!"]

Healing

Anne Carson

When she was five-and-a-half months old my daughter began pulling herself up to a standing position in her crib. "Isn't that cute," we said, reaching for the camera, "we'll have to lower the mattress so she doesn't fall out."

Two weeks later I was out meditating in a women's circle while David was home nursing a cold. He heard a tremendous crash in Catherine's room and in an instant was standing over her as she was still taking a breath for her first scream. Half-hysterical, he managed to get to the phone to call the doctor, who said calmly, "First, pick up the baby."

"But what if she has a neck injury?"

"Babies don't usually get neck injuries," she said. "Concussion is more of a problem."

"Concussion?!"

The car was with me; the phone number I had left with David was wrong so he couldn't reach me. When I arrived home he had succeeded in rocking the baby to sleep. We immediately wrapped her in a blanket and set off for the hospital, I in the back seat crying, saying the Hail Mary over and over and trying to reassure Catherine, who didn't cry but wore a shocked, frightened expression, David in front crying and driving. At the hospital the doctor on duty said she seemed all right and told us how to check for concussion. I leaned over her as she lay on the table so she could nurse, and gradually she began to brighten up. We each spent six hours that night checking to see if she was reacting normally; she held up better than we did, even after I discovered, two days later, that her collarbone was broken.

To heal is to make whole. As parents we are called upon to be healers whether or not we have previously seen ourselves in this role. It is a sacred role we must play often, even daily, for comforting a crying child is healing. When illness and injury, even if not serious, enter the child's life, no matter how well or how poorly we feel we are doing as parents, the loving, powerful healer in us must step forth and be a beacon to our child.

We may smile at the chicken soup or other family remedies that were given to us as children, but the comedian Alan King hit the nail on the head when he pointed out, "It's not the chicken soup that's good for colds—it's your *mother's* chicken soup." The soup, or the kiss on the knee, is a tangible expression of our mother's love and concern for us. In a climate of love we are able to heal faster.

When dealing with a momentary injury or a minor illness, we need only assess the situation and then let our love flow as milk to the child. A baby or toddler who has fallen will stop crying in seconds if picked up and spoken to soothingly. When a more serious, or potentially serious, situation arises, that is the time to be certain that we can center ourselves and act as if we are the tower of strength our children believe us to be.

Touch, in its mysteriously simple way, is enormously effective in healing. Although most parents get along without consciously practicing it, a knowledge of the principles of therapeutic touch should be a part of the parent's basic healing repertoire just as simple first aid is. Therapeutic touch, the art of the laying on of hands, is experiencing a revival, and not just among alternative health practitioners. Registered nurse Dolores Krieger describes the techniques of this ancient art in her handbook *The Therapeutic Touch*. Nurses caring for premature infants report that touching the tiny ones, therapeutically or otherwise, has a demonstrated beneficial effect on the babies' growth and progress. The anthropologist Ashley Montagu explored many other healing properties of touch in his book *Touching*. And decades ago psychologists recognized that infants who were brought up in institutions where there were no special attempts made to touch and play with them had a much poorer chance of survival than children in foster or adoptive homes.

Visualization, by either parent or child, is also a very powerful healing tool when used in conjunction with other medical treatment. Because of the concrete way in which we view the workings of the world as children, kids catch on to visualization very quickly. Since their attitude is so accepting, guided imagery is often surprisingly effective in alleviating pain and in the treatment of serious disease. Diane Mariechild writes in *Mother Wit* of using a ritual "pain stone"—an ordinary rock—with her sons. (Some parents may prefer to use crystals.) "When someone had a pain," she wrote, "they would put the pain stone over the place that hurt and picture the pain going into the stone. When they were finished the stone would be washed, dried and put away for the next time. Sometimes it's easier to visualize if you have a concrete object. Try the stone yourself, it works!"

The use of visualization or guided imagery with cancer patients is now very well documented in the traditional medical literature; physicians who would literally have been burned at the stake for their unorthodox regimens had they lived a few hundred years ago readily use imagery with patients who are fighting cancer. In the early eighties Phil Donahue had a show featuring young cancer victims, some of whom described the imagery they used. One of the boys spoke of imagining, each time he went into the hospital for treatment, that he was walking down a long hall lit with lamps. Each lamp was connected to a part of his body, and as he moved down the hall, he would turn off a light and thereby turn off pain in each part of his body in preparation for treatment. In 1987 an eighteen year old boy appeared on the Oprah Winfrey show to describe how he had fought cancer with visualization. At the age of nine he had been afflicted with a brain tumor, and four years later he began practicing biofeedback in addition to receiving chemotherapy. Each night before bed he visualized his brain tumor as a planet which he attacked with spaceships, à la *Star Wars*. One night he suddenly found that "Planet Meatball", as he called it, was nowhere to be found—he was completely unable to visualize it. A checkup revealed that his tumor had completely vanished, leaving only a small, non-malignant calcified mass.

When I watched this program I was stunned, for I recognized him as being one of the children who had been Phil Donahue's guests six years before.

Since one's state of mind affects physical health, both positively and negatively, very sensitive and empathetic children may develop ailments or become depressed when they are involved with other people who are under stress. In their relative helplessness, children become very concerned about the health and well-being of loved ones. Being unable to take much action in a physical sense, often the only way they can contribute to the healing of another is through prayer and visualization. Children are sometimes described as being agents of healing in and of themselves, the adult who spends time with children, who gets down on the floor with them, listens seriously to them, coming away with a lightness and joy that were not there before. How many elderly people have insisted that the grandchildren or the neighborhood kids "keep us young?"

Following is a basic healing exercise you can do anytime, whether or not your child is ill or hurt.

Sit or lie comfortably. Breathe slowly and deeply, allowing yourself to relax. As you breathe in, inhale relaxation. As you breathe out, exhale tension.

While you breathe, let the life force enter your body; release any tension, starting with your feet and working your way up your legs, torso, arms, neck, face, and mind. If you have a special place in your mind that you go to in meditation or psychic work, go there now.

See your loved one before you, smiling, whole, and beautiful. There is a golden light surrounding your child, radiating out from her soul. She is beaming and happy. The golden light is the light of love and health. It is permeating the child's body, flowing in and through her. You feel your love flowing out from your heart center to your child. She is healthy. Concentrate on how healthy your child is—don't concentrate on her injury mending or the illness abating, but see your child as if the illness were never there. She smiles at you and says, "Mommy (Daddy), I feel wonderful. I am so happy." She is healthy. Believe it.

Practice this many times.

Healing Stars: A Meditation for Children

Diane Mariechild

Lie down and close your eyes. Let your body become very loose. You are very relaxed. So relaxed you don't even move. And you are taking long deep breaths. Breathing the air in as if you were blowing up a balloon and then breathing the air out so the balloon is flat.

Your body is strong. Your body is so strong that it can take care of itself. Your mind is strong. Your mind is so strong that it keeps your body well. Good energy is all around you. Every time you breathe, you breathe in the good energy and it moves all through your body and it keeps your body well.

And now picture a big blue star over your head. A big blue star is over your head. Suddenly it bursts into thousands of tiny blue stars. A shower of stars pouring down on you. It is raining little blue sparkling stars. These tiny little stars are healing energy. When you take a deep breath, you bring the stars into your body. When you breathe out, all the little stars move through your body. All the tiny blue stars are moving through your body. You feel all warm and tingly as the stars move through your body. The blue stars are moving all through your body just like your blood does. They are moving into your toes and feet. They are moving up through your legs and hips. The blue stars are filling your stomach and your chest. You feel all warm and tingly as the tiny blue lights move along your back, your shoulders, your neck. And now the tiny blue lights are moving into your head. The tiny blue lights will move all through your body all night and when you wake up you will feel strong and well.

Nature

Anne Carson

How many children have destroyed or injured plants and animal life because they have been taught, explicitly or implicitly, that anything non-human doesn't count? Most of us had to learn the principles of ecology and stewardship of the Earth's resources as adults, and it is not always an easy shift of thought. One need only think of how difficult it is for vegetarians to persuade family and friends to stop using animals for food.

As children we are disposed to literally view the world as our plaything, and until quite recently ordinary education did not teach us differently. This attitude, though it drives us to explore, learn, and wonder, can also permit us to destroy, pollute, and kill. A child's first philosophical argument could be over whether human beings are animals. The conventional belief that "man" is separate from nature—that we were created to be masters, not caretakers, of the earth and are therefore given license to do as we please with what the father-god has given us, has left us with a legacy of acid rain, dwindling groundwater, and the extinction of a living species every day. Honoring the earth is not simply a romantic thing to do—it is our children's survival. Precisely because we, their parents, sense a strong connection to nature, a reverence for the Earth, it is vital to teach respect and love of the natural world.

Of course, thousands of children are forced to remain cooped up in cities due to economic exigencies, and this is tragic. Luckily some can take advantage of Fresh Air Funds, which bring city children out to the country so they can experience greenery and farm animals. It may not be crucial for a six-year-old to see a cow in person; what is important is for children to know that they are themselves a part of this wonderful place called Nature, not visitors to it. According to specialists in child development, children who live in urban high-rises are in danger of becoming psychologically stunted simply because they have no easy access to the out-of-doors. City playgrounds are often dangerous, and a family outing to a park can be such a major undertaking that the sight of an expanse of greenery is a rare event indeed. High-rise children may become restless and destructive and are slow to become independent because they are literally unable to "go off and play." Being able to play independently and out of sight of Mother is a necessary step in self-individuation, psychologists believe. It is sad that the limits of economics and affordable housing are producing so many young people who have little or no concern for their environment.

In this section Joseph Bharat Cornell presents the most effective ways to introduce children to the natural world and the principles of ecology. Many communities sponsor similar nature programs for children; if there are none in your area, his tips will be helpful in starting your own. Appended to his introduction are several activities that especially emphasize the interconnection of living things, with humans included as part of the natural world. His activities can be done with children as young as four, but most will probably be more appropriate for somewhat older children.

In addition to active instruction, encourage your child to pay attention to the biorhythms of the place where you live, whether it is desert, mountains, or ex-farmland, and make a point of learning something about the culture of the peoples who inhabited the land before you. Help the kids to research the Native American tribes who live(d) in your area. As a child I often imagined the Lenne Lenape roaming through suburban New Jersey.

Studying the life history of the place in which you live can begin with geology, for many localities have fascinating geological histories. A real Never-Never Land is created in the child's mind as she pictures the familiar towns and hills of her home being covered with seas or glaciers, dinosaurs or saber-toothed tigers roaming what was to become her backyard.

As children become more skilled in using tools and carrying out projects, they can take a more active role in gardening, which provides basic, low-key lessons in the miracles of life. David Price observes in "Growing with Plants" that lessons in time, biology, and co-evolution can be taught not just by adults but by Nature herself.

Growing with Plants

David Price

When I was very small, my father had a Victory Garden—and so did I. During the Second World War, when Americans had to produce enough food to sustain both the troops fighting overseas and the society they were defending, city dwellers were encouraged to plant vegetables in back yards and vacant lots. My father, who had married rather late in life, was too old to serve at the front; and since he loved gardening, he seized the opportunity to have a Victory Garden. He dug up the entire back yard (which I discovered, forty years later, was really no larger than some people's living rooms), somehow managed to get half a load of manure delivered to our residential neighborhood, and planted vegetables.

There was a little space between the sidewalk to the back door and the sidewalk to the cellar door—I don't suppose it was more than two feet by three feet—where Daddy helped me plant my own garden. This was partly in his own interest. He was a very fussy man who set himself exacting standards, and he didn't want a little kid messing in his garden. So, at least partly as a distraction, he helped me make my own garden. I planted radishes and carrots and lettuce and a potato. Then he watched with me as the days passed, sharing his own enthusiasm. Time runs slowly for a small child, and I would have forgotten my garden before it produced anything. But Daddy exclaimed when the radishes pushed up, and pointed out the tender little lettuce seedlings, the feathery carrots, and the potato bursting forth. Later, he showed me how to weed my garden and water it when the weather was dry. When we actually ate what I had grown, I was very proud.

From this experience, I learned how seeds grow. Not long afterward, I learned the limitations of keeping a plant alive in water. Some neighbors who had no children of their own used to invite me over to visit them. One spring they forced a peach branch to blossom early in a kitchen window. When they showed me that the flowers had opened, I said, "Leave it there all summer and it will grow peaches."

Mr. Muller laughed. "I don't think so," he said. "A peach branch has to be part of the tree in order to grow peaches."

I don't believe I understood that there had to be bees to do the pollinating, or that plain water would fail to supply the necessary nutrients. But I understood that a plant had to be whole in order to bear fruit, and later in my childhood I was able to be very superior when one of my friends suggested that flowers, if left in a vase, would go to seed.

My parents bought an old farmhouse in the country where we went on weekends, and where my mother and sister and I sometimes stayed in the summer, while my father went back to work in the city during the week. When I was seven or eight, I began exploring my surroundings as far away as maybe half a mile from home. Sometimes I went off in the woods and fields by myself, and I remember standing by a railroad and waving to engineers, sitting in a fence row and scratching my initials on a piece of slate, finding big red jack-in-the-pulpit seeds in a little marsh near the Jones farm, and falling through the ice on a small pond and coming home with my clothes frozen stiff. My parents must have had some anxious moments.

On other occasions I went for walks with adults, and these were times when I learned the names of things. In the spring I often walked with my mother on a little lane that went down through the woods, and she taught me the early wildflowers: spring beauties, hepaticas, adder's tongues, Dutchman's breeches, violets (blue, yellow, and white), and columbine.

There was also watercress, which we brought home for salad. Later in the year a widow from a nearby town sometimes sat for my sister and me, and she took us on walks and told us the names of the flowers beside the road: red clover, chicory, Queen Anne's lace, butter-and-eggs, and yarrow. I can't remember the woman's name—and neither can my mother—but I remember the plants she taught me.

I remember finding a pink yarrow, and Mrs. What's-Her-Name said yes, yarrow was sometimes pink, although this was quite rare. I was proud to have been so observant, and I began looking for unusual plants—paying attention to samenesses and differences. My awareness of species and their variations made it easy to understand natural selection, which I learned about when I was ten or eleven. Among the books that had accumulated on the shelves next to our fireplace I found H. G. Wells' *Outline of History*, and in the course of narrating the story of the world since the beginning of time, Mr. Wells included a simple explanation of the way biological change happens. Over the years, as my understanding became more sophisticated and I learned to pollinate plants and save seeds, I came to realize that adaptation through natural selection is at the very heart of the life process.

By the time I went to high school, my family had moved to Vermont. It was a difficult time. I turned in upon myself and worried about my identity—more preoccupied with my place in society than my place in nature. Still, in my blackest moods, the woods gave me solace. I remember playing hookey in early spring and going off into the hills, splashing through the runoff and lying on south-facing ledges, absorbing the warmth of the early sun. When the first spring flowers were still far off, miniature gardens of lichens came to life on the rocks.

In the summer between my sophomore and junior years at college, I lived in an abandoned farmhouse. I worked in a nearby town to earn money for tuition, and to save as much as possible,

I got permission to live in a house whose owner charged me no rent. It was at the end of a road that was barely passable, under the highest mountain in the area. The roof was gone off the south side, and someone had stolen the windows—frames and all. I put tar paper on the roof over the kitchen, plastic over the window, and moved in. I named my estate Mildew Mountain.

On evenings and weekends I took long walks—now exploring several miles in all directions. To give purpose to my rambles, I began to forage for wild food. My obsession began when ripe raspberries appeared in an old patch beside the house. After eating them on my breakfast cereal for several days, it occurred to me that I could take the surplus back to school in the fall, in the form of jam. I found some jars, bought sugar and paraffin, and followed the recipe on the Sure-Jell package. From raspberries I went on to cherries, blackberries, blueberries, gooseberries, highbush cranberries, and wild apples. I boiled jam or jelly on my three-burner kerosene stove every other night, and by the end of the summer I had made twenty-six different varieties.

Having mastered fruits and berries, I wanted to branch out. I often saw mushrooms in the woods, and realized that many would be edible, if I could only tell them apart. A Czech woman I knew and my sister's Hungarian mother-in-law got me started, and I soon acquired René Pomerleau's *Mushrooms of Eastern Canada and the United States*, which was, at the time, the best practical guide to edible mushrooms in the region it covered. From Pomerleau, I learned to use a botanical key, and I learned to pay attention to a plant's environment. "Under pines" or "on dead maples" was as important a characteristic as "decurrent gills" or "cap 10–15 cm."

I began to make my own observations about the kind of places where mushrooms grow—the direction of slope, the amount of humidity. I didn't understand until much later that some mushrooms have a symbiotic relationship with certain trees. But I began to sense that the likelihood of finding a particular kind of mushroom depended on a number of different conditions. In a place where everything was just right for chanterelles, you would find chanterelles. Spores are carried on the wind and settle practically everywhere. But only when they land in the right place do they grow into mushrooms.

Co-evolution has since become a popular concept. We all know that flowers need bees as much as bees need flowers, and a television program explains how the fig tree needs the wasp and the wasp needs the fig tree. Termites could not survive without the bacteria that live in their guts and digest cellulose, and the tropical sloth periodically descends from the tree whose buds it eats and deposits manure at its roots. Grass and grazing animals evolved along with each other. Lewis Thomas says that we ourselves may be the result of different life forms that moved in together.

I realize, when I cultivate my garden, that the vegetables depend on me as much as I depend on them. Members of the mustard clan, for example, like disturbed ground—where they grow quickly before they have to compete with other plants. I have found wild mustard growing in the woods, on a patch of silt left by spring runoff. But wild mustard would be a rare plant if people didn't plow fields and push dirt around with bulldozers. Mustard's civilized cousins—broccoli, cabbage, kale, cauliflower, and collards—could not survive at all without a gardener to keep down the weeds.

Rather late in life, I have been blessed with a daughter. At the age of eight months, she is already eating my carrots. When the weather warms up, I will take her outside to crawl in the grass and feel the warmth of the sun. And in a few years, when she begins to comprehend the passage of time, I will make her a little garden and teach her to plant seeds.

How to Be an Effective Nature Guide (A Few Suggestions for Good Teaching)

Joseph Bharat Cornell

Before we begin exploring nature with children, let's think for a moment about our role as teacher/guides. What are the basic rules for giving children—and ourselves—a joyous, rewarding good time?

I would like to share with you five tenets of outdoors teaching that have helped me work with children's lively energies—channeling them away from mischief, and toward more constructive, and ultimately satisfying, pursuits. Underlying these principles are basic attitudes of respect for children and reverence for nature—attitudes to which they will surely respond.

1. Teach less, and share more. Besides telling children the bare facts of nature ("This is a mountain hemlock tree."), I like to tell them about my inner feelings in the presence of that hemlock tree. I tell them about my awe and respect for the way a hemlock can survive in sub-alpine conditions—where water is scarce in summer, and mostly frozen in winter; where harsh winter winds twist and bend and kill its branches. And I tell them I always wonder how the roots of the hemlock ever manage to find enough nutrients to survive, in these solid-rock crevices.

Children respond to my observations much more freely than they respond to textbook explanations. Take the case of a hemlock tree that grew near a camp where I worked. This particular hemlock sits between two huge boulders, so it has had to send its roots down twenty-five feet to reach the rocky soil below. At the time, it was at least two hundred years old, and only eight feet tall. The children would frequently make a detour on their hikes just to empty their canteens by its roots. Several of them returned to the camp year after year, watching the tree's stubborn struggle for life in its harsh environment. In fact, as soon as they arrived at camp, they would run to see how it had fared through the dry autumn and cold winter. Their loving concern awakened in me an even sharper respect for the mountain hemlock.

I believe it is important for an adult to share his inner self with the child. Only by sharing our deeper thoughts and feeling do we communicate to, and inspire in others, a love and respect for the earth. When we share our own ideas and feelings, it encourages a child to explore, respectfully, his own feelings and perceptions. A wonderful mutual trust and friendship develops between the adult and the child.

2. *Be receptive.* Receptivity means listening, and being aware. It is one of the most richly rewarding attitudes you can cultivate while working with children. The outdoors brings out a spontaneous enthusiasm in the child that you can skillfully direct toward learning.

Be sensitive: every question, every comment, every joyful exclamation is an opportunity to communicate. Respond to the child's present mood and feelings. Expand your child's interests by teaching along the grain of his own curiosity. When you respect his thoughts, you'll find your time with him flowing easily and happily.

Be alert also to what nature is doing around you at the present moment. Something exciting or interesting is almost always happening. Your lesson plan will be written for you minute by minute if you tune in with sensitive attention.

3. *Focus the child's attention without delay.* Set the tone of the outing right at the start. Involve everyone as much as you can, by asking questions and pointing out interesting sights and sounds. Some children are not used to watching nature closely, so find things that interest them, and lead them bit by bit into the spirit

of keen observation. Let them feel that their findings are interesting to you, too.

4. *Look and experience first; talk later.* At times nature's spectacles will seize the child in rapt attention: a newly-emerged dragonfly pumping blood into tender unfolding wings, a lone deer grazing in a forest clearing. But even if those special sights are lacking, the child can have an experience of wonder by just watching quite ordinary things with close attention. Children have a marvelous capacity for absorbing themselves in whatever they're looking at. Your child will gain a far better understanding of things outside himself by becoming one with them than he will from second-hand talk. Children seldom forget a direct experience.

Don't feel badly about not knowing names. The names of plants and animals are only superficial labels for what those things really are. Just as your own essence isn't captured by your name, or even by your physical and personality traits, there is also much more to an oak tree, for example, than a name and a list of facts about it. You can gain a deeper appreciation of an oak tree by watching how the tree's mood shifts with changes in lighting at different times of day. Observe the tree from unusual perspectives. Feel and smell its bark and leaves. Quietly sit on or under its branches, and be aware of all the forms of life that live in and around the tree and depend on it.

Look. Ask questions. Guess. Have fun! As your children begin to develop an attunement with nature, your relationship with them will evolve from one of teacher and fellow-student to one of fellow-adventurer.

5. *A sense of joy should permeate the experience,* whether in the form of gaiety or calm attentiveness. Children are naturally drawn to learning if you can keep the spirit of the occasion happy and enthusiastic. Remember that your own enthusiasm is contagious, and that it is perhaps your greatest asset as a teacher.

Here are some activities to get you started on the adventures of sharing nature with children:

Meet a Tree

["Meet a Tree" teaches empathy, olfactory and tactile awareness, takes place during the day in a forest or any place where there are many trees, and can be done by children aged four and up. You will need blindfolds.]

This game is for groups of at least two. Pair off. Blindfold your partner and lead him through the forest to any tree that attracts you. (How far will depend on your partner's age and ability to orientate himself. For all but the very young children, a distance of 20-30 yards usually isn't too far.)

Help the "blind" child to explore his tree and to feel its uniqueness. I find that specific suggestions are best. For example, if you tell children to *"Feel the tree,"* they won't respond with as much interest as if you say *"Rub your cheek on the bark."* Instead of *"Explore your tree,"* be specific: *Is this tree still alive?...Can you put your arms around it?...Is the tree older than you are?...Can you find plants growing on it?...Animal signs?...Lichens? Insects?"*

When your partner is finished exploring, lead him back to where you began, but take an indirect route. (This part of the game has its fun side, with the guides leading their partners over imaginary logs and through thickets that might easily have been avoided.) Now, remove the blindfold and let the child try to find the tree with his eyes open. Suddenly, as the child searches for *his* tree, what was a forest becomes a collection of very individual trees.

A tree can be an unforgettable experience in the child's life. Many times children have come back to me a year after we played Meet a Tree, and have literally dragged me out to the forest to say, "See! Here's my tree!"

Recipe for a Forest

[This activity teaches aesthetic appreciation for the balance of nature. It can be done anywhere, but is recommended for the daytime in a forest, for children aged seven and up. You will need pencils and paper.]

Give each child an imaginary deed to one square mile of land. On this virgin plot he will be free to create his own dream-forest, complete with as many trees, animals, mountains and rivers as he desires. Let their imaginations run wild. To encourage creativity you can give the children some suggestions:

"To make your forest beautiful and radiant, you might want to add things like waterfalls and windstorms, or perpetual rainbows..."

Have them list the ingredients of their forest, then have them draw a picture of it. End by discussing with them whether their individual forests are able to maintain themselves year after year. For instance, see if they have chosen representatives of the food cycle: plant-eaters, plants, and decomposers (example: ants, mushrooms, bacteria). Don't let them forget subtle factors like soil and climate.

Webbing

[An active game that illustrates adaptation, habitat, and interdependence of life, which can be done anywhere in the daytime with three or more participants aged five and up. A ball of string is required.]

Here is a game that makes very clear the essential interrelationships among all the members of nature's community. Webbing vividly portrays how air, rocks, plants, and animals function together in a balanced web of life.

The children form a circle. The leader stands inside the circle near the edge, with a ball of string: *"Who can name a plant that* grows in this area?...Brodiaea...Good. Here, Miss Brodiaea, you hold the end of the string. Is there an animal living around here that might eat the brodiaea?...Rabbits!...Ah, a sumptuous meal. Mr. Rabbit, you take hold of the string here; you are connected to Miss Brodiaea by your dependence on her flowers for your lunch. Now, who needs Mr. Rabbit for his lunch?"

Continue connecting the children with string as their relationships to the rest of the group emerge. Bring in new elements and considerations, such as other animals, soil, water and so on, until the entire circle of children is strung together in a symbol of the web of life. You have created your own ecosystem.

To demonstrate how each individual is important to the whole community, take away by some plausible means one member of the web. For example, a fire or a logger kills a tree. When the tree falls, it tugs on the strings it holds; anyone who feels a tug in his string is in some way affected by the death of the tree. Now everyone who felt a tug from the tree gives a tug. The process continues until every individual is shown to be affected by the destruction of the tree.

Still Hunting

[This quiet activity teaches children to spot wildlife. A group is not necessary; it can be done with any child seven or older, day or night, in any natural environment.]

Still-hunting was practiced by the American Indians. A brave who wanted to still-hunt would go to a place he knew well and felt attracted to. There, in the forest or on a hillside, he would sit down and let his mind settle into a still and watchful mood. If his arrival had caused a disturbance among the creatures around him, he waited patiently until the world of nature returned to its normal, harmonious routine, Usually, his only desire in still-hunting was to observe and to learn.

When you go still-hunting, let your sitting-place choose you. You may be intuitively guided to a specific place in order to learn a certain lesson. For the first part of your stay remain motionless, not even turning your head. Be as unobtrusive as you can, letting the world around you go on as it does when you aren't there. Feel that you are a part of the natural surroundings; mentally move with the shimmering leaves, or dance with the butterfly as it darts and dodges through the air. Because you are still, curious animals may come close for a look at you. I was once approached from behind by a mysterious animal that made strange thumping noises as it moved. When the beast had come to within about seven feet, my courage flagged and I quickly turned my head. Off into the bushes fled that vicious predator, the cottontail rabbit!

Sharing private experiences with friends after a still-hunt brings a group closer together. Each still-hunter can tell about a plant or animal he has seen, and the qualities he felt it exemplified. Another good way to share still-hunting experiences is for each child to act out for the others something he saw, or a feeling he had, while sitting. The others try to tune in to the deeper mood of what he is saying. The tone of these sharing times should always be respectful and sensitive, if real communication of feelings and experience is to happen.

The Night World

[Introducing nature at night helps children to become aware of nocturnal activity and to overcome fears of the dark and the night—a perennial problem for many of us. This activity can be done anywhere in the natural world, from dusk to dark, with children aged four and up. A flashlight and red cellophane are optional.]

Barking coyotes, scratching noises, ghostly owl calls—at night, strange sounds deepen the mystery of the unknown world of the outdoors.

Many of the animals that can be heard at night are seldom seen—owls and coyotes, for example. To increase your chances of spotting them, bring a flashlight to scan open clearings for their "eye shine." Hold the light near your eyes (on your forehead or nose). If you want to see them without having them see you, put a red filter or a piece of red cellophane over your flashlight lens, since animals can't see red light.

Night hiking has other benefits besides the attraction of seeing nocturnal animals. Children are more reflective and communicative at night; I've noticed that as night falls a group of children will draw closer together for mutual support. After listening to the night sounds for a while, their conversation begins to turn to fears of the dark and of wild animals. Many times, discussion of their fears helps release them, and leaves everyone feeling relaxed and confident as we head back toward camp.

Rituals, Festivals, and Holidays

Anne Carson

Children need to know that the world is essentially predictable, that they can count on the love and support of their families, and that they are part of a larger human and natural community. Not only do we need to mark the changes of the seasons, but we need to pay special attention to the many changes, joys, and losses that come into our lives, however mundane. Each of us makes an incredible number of physical, intellectual, and social adjustments on our journey from birth to adulthood. If psychologists can state that even positive life-changes such as marriage, parenthood, or a job promotion exert tremendous stress on adults, think of how much stress occurs in the life of a child!

As each child re-enacts human evolution, it is important to recognize and honor the transitions of life, even those as lowly as moving from children's shoe sizes to adult or exchanging a crib for a bed. Gertrud Mueller Nelson, in *To Dance With God*, relates the charming story of a little boy she knew whose whole family participated in a ritual marking the end of his sleeping in a crib. He was taken to the department store to pick out his own bedspread, he gathered with his parents and siblings to formally say goodbye and thank you to the crib he had slept in since birth, and then made up his new bed with his mother's help. By means of this simple, family-based ritual he was fully prepared for what is for some children an upsetting and disorienting experience. If we could devise similar rituals for the first day of school, think of how many tears could be avoided!

Ritual and symbolic activities have played a supremely important part in human life for a hundred thousand years; in her book *Earth Wisdom* Dolores La Chappelle points out that "*the* major learning situations for both children and adults, for the vast majority of those humans who have inhabited this earth, have been the great seasonal festivals where story-telling, dance, music, and chanting combine in a total, synesthetic learning experience of the earth, the sky, the mortals, and the gods."[8] In this section are two childhood experiences of ritual, the first, Margot Adler's memories of a May Day celebration that forever after gave her a sense of the beauty of ritual, and the second, a short story about two children observing the Winter Solstice with a friendly old neighbor.

Most of us have had some exposure to religious ritual as children, either in church or synagogue. Jewish children have had the benefit of the many home observances that might be practiced by the family, Shabbas and the Seder, to name two, but traditional church services seldom contain much to engage a child's interest. In my memory, mass is a blur of the priest murmuring to himself in a foreign language, uncomfortable pews, papery wafers that stuck to the roof of your mouth, and almost no singing or responses by the congregation. At least there were usually beautiful and interesting things to look at, and at high mass I could listen for my father's voice in the choir. (If you haven't set foot in church in years, check it out: you may be surprised at the amount of creativity and activity to be found there. Things have changed!) But woe betide the child who fidgeted, whispered to her neighbor, idly chewed the back of the next pew, or worse, tried to get to the bathroom! The stern nun who watched over each class was sure to grab you by the collar and demand, "Where do you think you're going?"

Sharing with other families—holidays, child care, food— combats the unnatural isolation of the modern nuclear family. It is only in this century that the mother has been expected to be the primary if not sole caretaker of the children. In ages past, and among traditional peoples today, mothering was also done by grandmothers, aunts, older children, and servants. Now the older children are in school, live-in daycare is prohibitively expensive, and grandmothers and aunts no longer live across the street. Even with the active involvement of the new breed of father, a family ought not be expected to stand alone. We still need community.

Family-based worship is popular among people of many, many religious stripes—I use "worship" in its broadest sense, of honoring and communicating with the divine, whether it is expressed through prayer, group study, private readings, song, ritual, or meditation. Since the majority of people who are not formally affiliated with a religious or spiritual group are doing their spiritual work on their own, their children's spiritual experience will of necessity be family-based. Not that friends and relatives are excluded; on the contrary, sharing and building networks with other families becomes very important. Without a self-sustaining spiritual infrastructure, home-based resources must be utilized, just as Jewish worship came to be centered in the home after the destruction of the Temple.

A sense of familiar ritual is of utmost importance to children, in fact hardly any family does without it. There are family jokes, annual vacation visits, holiday traditions. Many adult Jews who give little thought to the Torah and the Talmud eagerly look forward to the yearly Seder and can appreciate the majesty and deep emotions of Yom Kippur. Starhawk, who is a prominent spokesperson for the Old Religion of Wicca and for feminist spirituality, still observes Passover, Chanukah, and the high holy days. And every Christmas and Easter the churches are packed.

As children's personalities develop, new issues arise: when, how, and with whom can adult worship be shared? Many women who are involved in women-only circles at which their little daughters are welcome are at a loss when it comes to including their sons. With more and more single mothers around, and especially with the growing number of lesbians who are choosing motherhood, this will become an increasingly important issue. Time was when certain lesbian-separatist musicians refused to play to anything but women-only audiences. "The presence of males is oppressive to me," complained one musician, arguing that her concerts were for women and "little boys are not women." She was hard-pressed, however, to explain how the presence of baby boys in the audience could be as oppressive as the presence of men.

The very presence of young children, as we have seen, can be problematic, but the issue is at what point a boy can be said to have developed enough male energy to become a subtly disruptive influence on a women's circle. It may seem ridiculous to worry about this, but including boys has been a very real question for some women. The more optimistic among us feel that if boys are brought up in a truly open, non-sexist manner—and we have to start remaking the world somewhere—they will absorb less of the undesirable characteristics of patriarchy. There will always be a need for women's mysteries; but on that far-off day when maleness is no longer a threat to women's autonomy, the presence of males will no longer be perceived as a threat. And surely any woman who is serious about spirituality would feel more comfortable including a boy who is sensitive and thoughtful than a teenage girl who snickers at the ritual and is more interested in her purple nail polish than in reaching the spirit within.

For mothers who are involved with female-only circles there are several ways to give sons the opportunity to share in ritual without compromising the female circle. The simplest way is to maintain contact with other families who have celebrations and observances where all are welcome and to include your son in these gatherings, while of course leading home-based rituals. There may also be any number of formal groups in your area which include males and females and which would accept the presence of an interested young boy. Probably the most accessible type of group is a class in movement, martial arts, yoga, or meditation, whether geared for adults or children. Some children take very well to adult yoga classes. Very little boys who are not quite housebroken may simply have to be left with a friend or relative while the parents attend adult gatherings.

One way to give new meaning to holidays and celebrations and to make them special family days is to serve special holiday foods, and not just at Christmas, Passover, etc. For years I have bought or prepared foods that are associated with certain holidays regardless of whether those holidays were of my ethnic or religious background, reasoning, why not enjoy hamantaschen at Purim, tzimmes at Rosh Ha-Shanah, pancakes on Shrove Tuesday? I have even fasted on Yom Kippur. Eating black-eyed peas, cornbread, and greens on Martin Luther King Day or Chinese food on Chinese New Year can be a pleasant prelude to teaching your child about the lives and struggles of the world's peoples, as well as a reminder that it is rice and beans, not meat and potatoes, that sustains the majority of the peoples of the world. Eating the way the Third World does, not only assures children of a more healthful and varied diet, it may be a more effective way to get them to identify with people in other lands than the usual dinnertime guilt-trips about the starving masses, which seem to only engender antagonism and flippant remarks from the children about sending peas to the Koreans.

If you keep a garden, try to use something from your own soil at every dinnertime, even if it is only herbs, and remind the family that your very own potatoes or very own parsley are on the table tonight. Additionally, purchase locally grown produce if possible. This makes good sense economically and healthwise, if it comes from an organic garden, but it makes good spiritual sense too, for eating food grown within a few miles of home encourages us to feel a connection with our community. Being connected to the earth becomes more than a metaphor. Surely people would be more concerned about local environmental issues if they felt a real tie to the land around them.

Some suggestions are: greens on the Spring Equinox; corn on the cob or cornbread on August 1, which is the old English Lammas Day or Harvest Day; tzimmes (sweet potatoes and carrots cooked with honey, with or without a pot roast) for Jewish New Year (Autumn Equinox); pomegranates as well as apples and candy corn for Halloween; more authentic Native American foods such as blue cornmeal at Thanksgiving.

A child who is raised as a vegetarian—there are a growing number of American children who have never tasted meat—may choose to alter her diet as she grows up and becomes influenced by friends, or simply becomes curious. A boy I know whose parents were the lone hippies in a small rural town used to beg his mother for "real food." "I'm the only kid at school who brings sprout sandwiches!" he wailed. "*Please* can I have something normal?" His mother was a wise and sympathetic woman. She sent her son to school with white bread, and has no objections to fixing him a hamburger for dinner. Her saving grace is a refusal to take herself too seriously. "Can Tommy eat what we eat?" she asks her son when he invites a friend to supper. "You know, birdfood?"

By and large a child whose diet does not include certain foods or kinds of foods—e.g. meats, snacks—will not readily acquire a taste for them, although one mother told me about a little boy she knew who so craved chewing gum, which he was forbidden, that he would peel it off the sidewalks of Boston. On the other hand, an Indian friend, who never tasted meat until he was in college, used to eat hamburgers but otherwise didn't care for beef. "You just never had a really good steak," I used to tell him. Actually, his dislike for beef was probably less indicative of his Hindu upbringing than of my lifelong indoctrination by American meat producers that beef is the most nutritious food available.

Parents often notice that the children are quite happy without sodas and junk food until they go to school or to the homes of friends whose parents have less conscious attitudes towards food. Snacks are all right in their place, but sugar-phobia has opened the door to an insidious marketing campaign promoting Nutra Sweet, in which advertisers imply that this utterly artificial chemical sweetener is better for your child than natural sugar.

My motto is, moderation in all things—including moderation. An *occasional* fall from the tofu wagon can be a special treat. Naomi Strichartz says that one of the most pleasant days off she has spent recently was with her fourteen-year-old daughter, during which they parked themselves on the sofa, watched soap operas and ate Cheez Doodles. The secret to decadence is to save it for special occasions.

Teaching about the web of life is not easy when much of our food comes in commercial packages, far from the farms on which it was raised. Some families will be able to grow at least some of their food, even if it's only tomatoes, but many will not. Being able to watch the cycle of life, harvest, and decay is a valuable experience. We learn that life feeds on life, that even if we do not kill animals for our food, or support the killing of animals by buying meat, life-forms—plants—do die in order to feed us. Khalil Gibran reminds us that though we may bite into an apple, in time our bodies will return to the earth and the plants will feed upon us. Food has its own sacrality. This is easy to forget for those of us who do not have to wonder where our next meal is coming from, who shop in stores where the shelves are never empty.

Once, as children, when my brother and I were complaining about whatever we were having for dinner, our mother indignantly informed us that her Irish grandparents would have looked at the meat, potatoes, and vegetables on our table and pronounced it a feast. Most of us don't consider ourselves wealthy, yet in comparison not just to other Americans but to our brothers and sisters worldwide, we Americans *are* wealthy. And when Jesus spoke about it being easier for a camel to pass through a needle's eye than for a rich man to enter heaven, he was speaking about us.

Too often parents try to make children feel grateful for their good fortune by stressing that all good things come from the parents. "Be grateful for the good food which your father has worked hard to provide, and your mother has worked hard to prepare." Traditionally we thank God for providing the food on the table. A grace that is more to the point might offer thanks to the earth for providing us with food, and thanks for being well-off enough to buy it.

Birthdays

However we transform the rest of our ritual lives, birthdays seem sacrosanct—it's the one day of the year when everyone is entitled to be self-centered. Still, for our children we would like to retain the specialness of the day while avoiding the old unwelcome lessons in consumerism, social climbing, and competition so often occasioned by birthday parties. Who will I invite to my party? Will Suzy like the present I bought her? Which girl has the prettiest party dress? Can I beat Donny at Musical Chairs?

There are many ways to lend a spiritual dimension to birthdays without necessarily eliminating ice cream, cake, and presents. Low-key family traditions abound. In our home my mother always hid my presents, and in the morning I would scour the living room hunting for them like Easter eggs. This went on until I was eighteen, to my mother's bemusement. The following year the tradition was broken, as I was at college when my birthday came around.

Some people believe that meditating on the moment of your birth puts you in touch with the Otherworld whence we came. For years at school I used to eye the clock at ll:30 a.m. and rest in awareness of the beginning of my existence.

Other rituals might include having the child, as soon as he or she is old enough to do so safely, light the candles on the cake, taking time to consider each year of his or her life (the early years will have to be imagined, of course). When she makes a wish before blowing the candles out, request that she also make a wish for another person or group besides herself—a wish for peace or comfort to a community devastated by a flood, for instance. Z Budapest suggests having adults invite their mothers to their birthday parties, in recognition that a child's birthday is an important day in the life of the parent as well. Almost every year when I speak to my mother on the phone on my birthday, she has said something like, "Twenty years ago today I was the happiest woman in the world...Thirty years ago today I was so happy I thought I would burst...," and she often related the story of my birth. Even though childbirth for her required surgery and weeks in the hospital, my mother always stressed her joy in having me.

Nowadays, with fully conscious childbirth and father participation, most parents have much happier and fuller stories to tell their children about the day of their birth. Often there are photographs or videotapes to show the children—my hospital roommate made a tape recording of her baby's cesarean delivery which she played for her visiting in-laws—a very moving tape for me to hear just a few hours after my own delivery. In any case, whatever the circumstances of the birth, parents can let the child know what an important and hopefully joyous event the child's arrival into their lives was.

For parents who would like to tone down the commercialism and plasticity of conventional birthday observations, The *Alternative Celebrations Catalogue* (see the list of resources at the end of this book) gives ideas for new ways to celebrate birthdays, as well as recipes for wholesome party treats. In Germany and in the Eastern Orthodox Church, the Name-day, or feast day of the saint whose name one shares, is celebrated with greater festivity than one's actual birthday. The *Joy of Cooking* contains a German recipe for a traditional (though non-health food) name-day cake, which could be tried out on the child's saint's day if her birthday falls in the high summer when it's too hot to bake.

Seasonal Festivals

Candlemas/Groundhog Day

February marks the beginning of the farmer's spring, when signs are sought that will tell when the new year's planting may be started. For generations people have searched for signs of spring at the beginning of February. In Europe they watched for badgers and hedgehogs leaving their burrows, while in the United States we look for the groundhog or woodchuck. Groundhog Day is considered as something of a joke, but it has a sacred underpinning, even if it seems no more religious than rolling Easter eggs on the White House lawn.

Candlemas was also an important holiday in the ancient Mediterranean mystery religions, when it was celebrated as the Presentation of the Divine Child and the emblem of the waxing light of the soul. It also marks the lengthening of the days, as spring approaches. To celebrate this day, we place thirteen candles around the house in honor of the returning light. One year we lit seven extra candles, in memory of the seven Challenger astronauts who had been killed a few days before.

This is also a time to do early spring-cleaning, especially if it's a snowy or rainy day. The kids can go through their clothes, toys and books and help take them to the Salvation Army or other charitable organization. Soon the season of Lent will be upon us, the time of purification and examination of conscience.

Easter/Spring

Even if you don't actually celebrate Easter, you can still observe some of the old folk practices around the time of the Spring Equinox (March 20 or 21) such as dyeing eggs (which for thousands of years have symbolized creation, rebirth, and eternity) and hunting for candy or more healthful treats. Dyed eggs can also be hung on trees, either outdoors or on a special indoor Easter Tree. In our home the day of the Spring Equinox is the day the grow-lights come up from the basement and the planting of the year's vegetables and flowers is begun. You can also have an out-of-doors family outing to hunt for signs of spring in your area—snowdrops, daffodils, crocuses, robins, cats in heat, or whatever signs fit your climate. Or you can take the family out hunting for the first wild foods, which may be wild leeks for vichyssoise or dandelions for dandelion crown salad. An old English custom is to let parsnips winter over in the garden and then dig them in March. The children may not think they like parsnips, but try them glazed with maple syrup or grated in parsnip pancakes.

This is the time of year to encourage the children to start caring for their own small section of the garden or windowbox. They can help clean up the yard in preparation for spring, or, if you have no yard of your own, go to a park and help clean up litter. Everybody brings trash bags, and the kids can keep the money earned by turning in cans and bottles.

Some people object to perpetuating the fantasy of the Easter Bunny, regarding it as simply a rip-off fostered by candy manufacturers (and it must be admitted that a chocolate cross is pretty tacky), but in truth there is something wonderful, as well as very ancient, about an unseen visitor leaving gifts. Parents can make up their own stories about Mother Nature passing by and leaving crocuses, or mothers can tell their daughters the story of Demeter and Persephone (there is a feminist version for children in *Lost Goddesses of Early Greece*, by Charlene Spretnak).

Midsummer's Eve

The first day of summer is around June 21st, but most likely the children will be more interested in the coming of summer vacation than in the cosmological fact that at this time the days begin to get shorter. Usually school is out by then or will be shortly, so a big general party can be held for the children. In Brazil, Midsummer's Day—actually St. John's Day on June 24th—is celebrated as the coming of winter to the southern hemisphere, though it has its roots in European Portuguese custom. Brazilian children dress up like country people in bouffant dresses or jeans and straw hats and cook-outs are held where roasted corn and special desserts are served. If the school year is over the Midsummer bonfire might include old school papers (use the fireplace or woodstove if a real bonfire is not permitted in your community).

Lammas

Celebrated on August 1st, this ancient festival of the bounty of the Earth barely survives in Western culture. The British still take the day off and call it a Bank Holiday, but it has disappeared in

American popular culture. All we have left is the Roman Catholic feast of the Assumption of the Virgin on August fifteenth, observed in Europe in part as a harvest festival. This is time when we celebrate abundance, and in hard times, express gratitude for what we do have. Seek out county and state fairs, or take a trip to the country.

Autumn

You may wish to have some kind of ritual or observance the day before school begins in order to say good-bye to the summer. "New Year's resolutions" can be made at this time. Around September 22nd comes the Equinox, the second of the great harvest festivals in the Wheel of the Year, falling between Lammas and Thanksgiving. This is a good time to hold a harvest dinner made up largely if not entirely of produce from the garden or local markets: potatoes, tomatoes, beans, broccoli, greens, squash, or whatever is in season in your climate. This is also the time to be aware of the turning of the year as we wind down into winter, when the flowers are ending their blooming period and are setting seeds for next year. We can consider the year's accomplishments, looking back on what we have reaped. On the mundane level, children can help with fall clean-up by raking leaves, plucking old stalks.

In classical mythology, the autumn equinox marked the time when Persephone returned to the Underworld and Demeter the grain mother sorrowfully bade farewell to her daughter. Retell their story, and just as you went outdoors to search for signs of spring, now go out and look for the autumn crocus, or gather the wild foods that are in season.

Halloween

There must be ways to reclaim the centuries-old festival of All Hallows Eve from the mayhem of ghoulishness, vandalism, and junk food this once sacred holiday has degenerated into. (I confess that Halloween at our house would be unthinkable without candy corn.) Originally, November 1st was celebrated by the Celtic tribes of Europe and the British Isles as the beginning of winter and as a rite of remembrance of the dead. Because it was a time between times, a day between days, the door between this world and the next was believed to stand ajar, and spirits and shades of those who had died were thought to roam the world for one night. The Celts, like the Jews, reckoned the beginning of a "day" at sunset, which is why the Feast of the Dead starts on October 31st.

Today, however, except for Christians who remember the dead on All Souls Day, the death-aspect of Halloween means only monsters and decomposing flesh, and children vie with one another for the most horrible-looking monster masks. This demonic interpretation of Halloween has become so prevalent that some conservative Christians are holding alternative "Hallelujah Night" parties for children, with Biblical characters encouraged and goblins and witches banned. They are, of course, unaware that modern-day witches have nothing to do with the Devil.

Vandalism has become a serious problem in many communities on Halloween and tends to be committed by adolescents and college students who are too old to go trick-or-treating and don't care about the potentially sacred aspect of the holiday. The traditional mischief-making is supposed to occur the night before All Saints' Day, that is, October 31st, but the spree of destruction often takes place instead on the eve of All Hallows Eve, October 30th, and is called in different communities Mischief Night, Cabbage Night, or Devil's Night. (No wonder religious conservatives are concerned.) The vandalism has become so serious that in the past few years the city of Detroit, which has had a dreadful problem with arson on "Devil's Night," has had to impose a curfew on young people. Then there are the parents' fears about night-time trick-or-treating and accepting food from strangers. When you think about it, it's better to keep the kids inside and organize neighborhood parties instead of allowing them to vent their most destructive, anti-social impulses on the hapless community.

Monsters and ghosts aside, there still remains something magical in the time-honored custom of dressing in disguise, and if we can steer our children away from monsters, terrorists, and Rambo, Halloween costuming can certainly be encouraged for the fantasy and creativity it inspires. I don't mind opening my door to two little witches and a frog, but a couple of Nicaraguan contras is another thing!

As for the death aspect of Halloween, the family can use this day to remember relatives and friends—even pets—who have died. My husband and I follow the Irish custom of setting extra places at the dinner table for our deceased fathers whom we invite to be with us while we have the traditional pork, apples, and colcannon (mashed potatoes mixed with chopped cabbage). A brief prayer can be said before dinner in which we ask the children to remember their grandparents or other loved ones. The parents can also use this time to tell stories about relatives now passed on. ("I wish you had known your great-aunt Evelyn—she was a real character.")

Thanksgiving

This is a profoundly spiritual holiday, the one holiday apart from New Year's that can be celebrated by everyone regardless of creed, or lack of creed. We count our blessings and begin the season of active love in the world. Now important lessons in love and sharing can be realized through community food and clothing drives or by inviting others into our homes to share the feast, whether they be elderly neighbors, students far from home, or just solitary friends. Children sometimes feel uncomfortable and resentful when a stranger is brought into their home, so extra care may be needed in explaining the importance of family and sharing, and that "family" means more than just those who are related to us by blood. In fact, scientists believe that everyone on earth ultimately is related genetically, to the extent that no one can be less than your fiftieth cousin! Therefore, every stranger really is your distant relative, and we bear responsibilities towards those of our cousins who are poor or alone.

In mindfulness of the Native American contribution to Thanksgiving and the origins of our food, an appropriate hymn or grace for dinner would be the traditional Native American song:

> The earth is our mother, we must take care of her,
> The earth is our mother, we must take care of her.
> Hey yana ho yana hey yon yon,
> Hey yana ho yana hey yon yon.
> Her sacred ground we walk upon with every step we take,
> Her sacred ground we walk upon with every step we take,
> Hey yana ho yana hey yon yon.
> Hey yana ho yana hey yon yon.

(Another version continues, "The sky is our grandfather, we must take care of him...")

Christmas/Winter Solstice

The Winter Solstice, which occurs around December 21st, signals the rebirth of the sun as it begins its northward swing, heralding longer days. Metaphysically Midwinter symbolizes the birth of the Divine Child, in whatever guise his worshippers choose to perceive him. Children may not be interested in the spiritual significance of the first day of winter, but they can recognize evergreen decorations as the emblem of life in the midst of death, and can appreciate the beauty of a new light shining in the darkness. The light of the sun may be symbolized by candles in the home (children love Swedish angel chimes) or friends singing and drumming around a bonfire.

Like European pagans who retained the old customs after the Romans and Irish missionaries imposed Christianity, many practitioners of earth religions just can't give up Christmas. Likewise, many Jews who have also come to honor the turn of the seasons in the Pagan manner would never let Passover go by without a Seder. For seven years I have made a Winter Solstice altar—even photographing it proudly the way people take pictures of the annual Christmas tree—and performed variations on the Wiccan midwinter ritual honoring death, darkness, and rebirth, yet, like any good syncretist, December 25th without tree, presents, and family would be unthinkable to me. The same is true for most Americans who are not Jewish, Moslem, or Buddhist—even for some who are.

In the Yule 1987 issue of *The Crone Papers*, a Wiccan newsletter, the editor, Grey Cat, observes, "Many people who have embraced religions featuring Yule as a serious 'holy' day feel it necessary to celebrate only Yule and except for indulging family to ignore Christmas.

"Christmas, however, is not only a religious holiday in our society. I notice that I get lots of 'Yule' cards from Pagans and Wiccans—presents as well. We may not wish to celebrate the religious holiday, but it isn't necessarily a betrayal of our beliefs to participate in the non-religious aspects of the celebration."

In the same issue a grandmother suggests that the pagan origins of Christmas customs and symbols such as the tree and mistletoe can be diplomatically explained to children without offending their more conventionally-minded parents.

Christmas, which for most Americans is already a secular rather than a religious holiday anyway, can certainly be indulged in by families who do not consider themselves Christian. For children there certainly is something powerfully magical about an unseen guest from afar coming to your house. We bake cookies and set them out with milk for the sacred visitor, and behold! the next morning the offering is gone and beneath the waiting tree lie heaps of presents seemingly from nowhere. One imagines Santa Claus himself, that wise, mysterious figure, seated by the fireplace with his legs crossed chatting for a few minutes with Mom and Dad before he has to be on his way, just like any grown-up visitor. *Our* house has been touched by the magical presence. And I remember the figurines we used to set up around the house: the old papier-mâché village with lights burning in all the houses, the crèche, Santa and his reindeer, and the mysterious Holly Man, made from styrofoam balls, pipe cleaners, and green felt leaves.

It goes without saying that many people are repelled by the consumer orgy that Christmas has become, whether they embrace an alternative lifestyle or not. At least children are generally spared the social burden of having to buy presents for relatives and business acquaintances they barely know. A non-commercialized Christmas, grounded in unselfishness, is possible with some forethought, planning, and family discussion. Regardless of one's opinions on Christ's divinity and the Resurrection, Jesus can certainly be regarded as a great teacher, and the mysteries of Christmas as beautiful lessons in love and hope.

The *Alternative Celebrations Catalogue*, which got its start as a guidebook to celebrating a non-commercialized Christmas, has many suggestions on more meaningful and socially conscious ways to observe Christmas as a day of showing love for family and our neighbors, with directions on homemade gifts and ideas on substituting charitable contributions for the usual presents. It would be wise, however, to check this out with all family members ahead of time. One family I know was not particularly thrilled to receive poems instead of gifts from an impoverished young relative. "Surely he could have afforded some two-dollar gadget!" they grumbled to one another.

Gift-giving ultimately depends on individual inclinations. Some people truly love shopping for the sensual pleasure they derive from the visual displays, the array of textures and shapes amongst the merchandise, and the fun of selecting just the right item. These people tend to begin their holiday shopping in July. We all know people who have a special talent for making creative and beautiful gifts by hand, and they have the blessings of all of us. Then there are those of us who feel uninspired when it comes to choosing gifts, regard shopping as a tiresome chore, resent the growing number of relations in our lives who all require holiday presents, and are concerned about the message that compulsory gift-giving sends to children. In defense of gift-giving, for thousands of years before the market economy was established—and among tribal peoples this is still the case—people gave presents purely as a means to maintain social ties with people who played an important part in their lives, or upon whom they might have to depend, such as the tribe in the next valley. In our own lives it is aunts, grandparents, teachers, acquaintances, upon whom we may in some way have to depend for social support. Though at Christmas and Chanukah it can appear as if we have become slaves to the mass culture, in actuality we are re-enacting a very ancient custom.

In her book *To Dance With God: Family Ritual and Community Celebration*, Gertrud Mueller Nelson describes dozens of creative and charming rituals and celebrations, many of them stemming from her German childhood, which her family has engaged in, not only at Christmastime but at all of the major liturgical holidays. You definitely do not need to be Roman Catholic to appreciate the love, creativity, and profound spirituality her family enjoys. One way her own family separates Santa Claus from the birth of Christ is to celebrate December 6th, St. Nicholas Day, as the primary day of gift-giving festivities. Other gifts are still reserved for December 25th; in fact, the gift-giving is literally spread out throughout the twelve days of Christmas, with packages marked "Do not open until St. Stephen's Day" (Dec. 26th), "Do not open until New Year's Day," and so forth.

May Day

Margot Adler

When I was a child, one of the most important ritual events that I remember was May Day, 1957. It seems like a simple event, and I am sure many of my classmates have forgotten it, but it forever changed my life.

I was fortunate to go to a wonderful grammar school in Greenwich Village called City and Country. This was a school where we ran a post office when we were eight, a general store when we were nine, and we were operating a printing press by the time we were eleven.

Each period of history came alive for us. We were ten when we came to the Middle Ages. We made parchment from animal hides and learned how to bind and illuminate books. We read about the pain of serfdom and the romance of falconry, we threw ourselves into historical novels and lived them. I read eighty books that year, and I was not unusual. It was before dawn on May Day morning in that year that my mother took me to school. I remember riding the subway at four a.m., watching countless bakers and painters begin their day.

We had learned many old medieval May carols and they were going around in my head:

A branch of May I've brought to you
And at your door it stands,
It is but a sprout, but well budded out,
The work of godly hands.

We were taken in cars to the home of the sister of one of the teachers. As dawn came, we were led to gardens filled with flowers and told to pick armfuls. When we were laden with more than we could carry, we returned to the school. It was about ten in the morning and you could hear the other classes in session. We entered the school singing and handing out our flowers. How simple and unexpected and joyous! Later, as we would every year, we danced the Maypole dance.

Singing was always an ecstatic experience in school and at camp. I think by the age of twelve I knew at least fifty rounds. When I was thirteen, and it was time to enter high school, I sneaked into the music room and took a copy of every song. Now, thirty years later, I still have all these rounds bundled up in a drawer somewhere: "Great Tom Is Cast," "Ah, Poor Bird," "When Jesus Wept the Falling Tear," "Rose Rose," "Orleans," "White Coral Bells," "Dona Nobis Pacem," "Vine and Fig Tree," "Chairs to Mend," "All Things Shall Perish," and countless others. And the strange ones that I have never heard anyone ever sing since, like:

> Seven great towns of Greece 'tis said
> Claimed Homer's birth when he was dead,
> Through which alive he baked his bread.

Or:

> Oh, Miss Smith, do be careful,
> Do not heed that wolf,
> His honey-dripping words, Miss Smith,
> Will break your tender heart.

(and then very fast):

> He says you're sweet, he says you're pretty,
> Says he'll never kiss another girl, and yet he will,
> He says he's true to you, the gay deceiver.

Years later, chants and rounds are an essential part of my religious life. Chanting and singing is still the backbone of all the workshops in women's spirituality I give. There is something about a group of people singing, perhaps at night before an open fire, or in a living room, or sitting by the side of a stream. These sounds of simple harmonies seem to bring the Gods—or God, if you will—close to us. Music brings us back to the experience of wholeness and allows us to feel our own connection with the world as alive and harmonious. Singing also connects with our dreams and visions, and it allows us to feel our always-present but often unfelt connections with all living.

By the waters of Babylon
I lay down and wept for Avalon.
We remember, we remember, we remember Avalon.

Solstice Celebration

Naomi Strichartz

[In this story Amber and Jesse are two children living in the country with their parents Sarah and Paul not far from a mysterious old woman named Rosemary, who keeps a tame crow named Calvin and is wise in the ways of the earth.]

"Why do you celebrate the solstice, Rosemary?" Amber asked, looking at the table covered with all sorts of interesting things.

"I celebrate all of the ancient festivals," Rosemary answered, "and this is one of my favorites, the longest night of the year. It is a prayer for the return of the sun."

"But the days don't get long again until spring," said Jesse, who was afraid of the dark.

"That's right," said Rosemary, "but after tonight each day is a few moments longer. Let's celebrate by making presents for you and your parents, then it will be one of your favorite holidays too. First we'll decorate a box to put the presents in. Don't worry, Calvin, there will be presents for you too," she said, because Calvin was looking anxious.

It was really fun. They pasted cloth and feathers and small stones onto the box until it was very beautiful. They tied on boughs of pine that had fallen to the ground, and dried winter berries added the perfect touch.

Then Rosemary showed them how to make her favorite face cream. First she gently simmered some herbs in olive oil and let it sit. Then she strained the oil and added a lump of bee's wax. She let Amber stir the mixture over the stove until the wax completely dissolved. Then Rosemary poured it into clean jars. Jesse said it wasn't cream, it was oil, and Rosemary smiled at him.

Slowly, in front of their eyes the fluid hardened, first around the edges, and then, like magic, the oil had completely turned into cream, smooth and molded to the sides of the jars.

They went outside into the snowy woods and collected pine cones, dried berries, seed pods and leaves. It was cold and blustery. In less than an hour they were back in front of the wood stove, their winter treasure spread out on the table. Rosemary gave them dried spices and corn to add to their collection and they all strung necklaces until there was one for everyone, including Calvin. This went on for several weekends. They covered notebooks with cloth for dreambooks and Rosemary taught them how to knit scarves and hats.

One Saturday they made figures out of clay. Rosemary made tiny Goddesses and gave them each a name. Amber made fairies and gnomes and snakes doing different things. Jesse made deer and birds and bears. Some of the figures carried little pots for holding candles or incense. Rosemary's whole table was covered with the tiny figures. Each was different from the other and had a personality all its own.

"They were all there before, hidden in the clay," Rosemary said, "we just had to find them."

The next day, the clay was dry and hard. They painted eyes, hair, feathers and claws, and gave the fairies and gnomes little green hats. But mostly they left the lovely clay color alone.

At home, Amber and Jesse finished their scarves and hats, putting them away quickly if Sarah or Paul came into the room.

Slowly, the box filled up with special things.

On the afternoon of the celebration, Amber and Jesse helped Rosemary bake Solstice cookies. They were shaped like the moon and stars and of course the sun, since they were celebrating its eventual return, on this the longest and darkest of nights.

"Do you think Sarah and Paul will be surprised?" Jesse asked.

"Oh, yes," said Amber, her eyes sparkling.

The twenty-first of December finally came. Amber and Jesse led their parents down the road to Rosemary's hut. Rosemary sat waiting for them in the room that had been exquisitely decorated for the occasion. The walls were covered with colorful cloth in different textures. Boughs of pine gave off a delicious scent and candles flickered in their clay holders. On the table the Solstice box sat bulging with handmade gifts. Calvin cawed excitedly after checking to see what was in the pot simmering on the stove. Sarah and Paul exclaimed over their gifts. There were clay figures, dreambooks, scented creams, necklaces, hats, scarves and cookies for all five of them.

And then Rosemary brought out a special box for Calvin and helped him open it. The contents glittered delightfully in the candle light. There were odd earrings, marbles, pieces of colored glass, strings of necklace made out of raisins, dried berries and nuts, and of course, cookies. Calvin cawed delightedly and nibbled at his necklace. Then he flew into the other room and came back with something shiny in his mouth. He plunked down a silver dollar on the table, and looked very proud.

"Where did you get this, Calvin?" Rosemary asked, wondering.

"Thank you, Calvin," Amber said seriously, "that is a very good present."

Calvin cawed his special caw and flapped his wings excitedly. He couldn't say any more, but his eyes shone with happiness and love.

Death

Anne Carson

While holidays like Halloween and All Souls Day can be used to address the subject of death in general, the actual event of the death of someone close, whether friend relative, or pet, is another matter. In our grandparents' day it was not uncommon for a small child to be told that a dead parent had gone away on a long trip, leaving the child to wonder what she had done to deserve to be abandoned, and to hopelessly wait for the parent's return. Children were generally banned from funerals and wakes or sent to stay with an aunt or another family, making the child feel rejected, insecure, and shunted aside. But including a child in the family visits and discussions following the death of a relative— even a not very close one—can be a valuable experience, an opportunity for him to meet relatives, to travel, and to learn family history. Often the only chance some family members have to see each other is at funerals. Including the child can be an important way to give her a sense of family and belonging, even if the relatives are distant cousins one may never see again.

For the spiritual seeker there may be no pat answer to give to the child who asks "Where do we go when we die?" There are as many ideas about death and the afterlife as there are spiritual paths. A pitfall of the concrete approach to spirituality is that we ourselves often have vague, generalized ideas about what happens when we die, whereas children want to know once and for all where we go and what happens to us, and what becomes of animals' spirits. Does the dog go to heaven? No? Why isn't the dog's soul worthy of an afterlife? If we refrain from eating animals for food because we respect their right to exist, why can't they go to heaven?

Educator Dora Chaplin related the following story in *Children and Religion*:

> I remember walking in the woods with a three-year-old when we came upon a dead thrush. She regarded it with the greatest astonishment, and informed me that the birdie was asleep. She said we had better go and get him a blanket and some orange juice for when he waked up. She was not asking me about death, and at that particular moment, I did not feel that the perfect time had come for an explanation. Later, other chances presented themselves and were utilized. She readily understood that her body was the house she lived in, that her real self—the thinking, loving part—she could not see. She had put the rather extraordinary question to me, "What could I be that will never die? Could I be a duck?" I do not know why a duck should be especially promising in the way of immortality. Then it was that we talked about the advantages of being a little girl, and she saw that the house of her body was as useless to her without her real self to live in it, as the piano, standing there with no one to play upon it.
>
> Later in a city street, as we were walking together, a flowered-covered coffin was carried out of a house as we passed by. She plied me with questions: what was inside the casket? What were they going to do with it? I answered her with the simple facts. "I see," she said, after a thoughtful little pause; "It's a going-away party," and she tripped on ahead in her usual happy way·[9]

In the following piece, Eva Fugitt relates her own experience of dealing with death. She had no ready answers for her inner-city pupils, but she allowed her intuition to guide each step and relied on her own sincerity to make the event of pet's death a comforting and edifying experience for all involved.

"Teacher! Myrtle the Turtle Is Dead!"

Eva D. Fugitt

"Teacher! Myrtle the Turtle is dead!" These words greeted me as I arrived in my fourth grade class one morning. "Oh dear," I thought, "now what do I do?"

Myrtle the Turtle was a classroom pet. Harold had brought him with pride and shared him shyly and lovingly with the class. The children had fed him, talked about him and watched him dreamily when needing to retreat for a while.

Just the day before one of the reading groups had been reading about the death of a turtle. The children in the story had a funeral for it. It had stimulated quite a discussion about pets.

Now Myrtle the Turtle was dead. The children asked if they could have a funeral.

"Yes," I heard myself answering. "We can have a funeral."

"When?"

"After lunch."

Inwardly I thought, "What if the principal comes in? How do I handle this?" I believed, though, in the importance of allowing children to experience grief, to express it and experience release and healing.

When I returned from lunch the children were already in the classroom. Some of the girls had gone home and brought flowers. Some of the boys had fashioned a small box out of paper and much tape. I saw that much talking and planning had gone on during lunch.

Edward said, "I'll be the pallbearer. I know what to do."

Edward's father had died suddenly of a heart attack in October and it was now April. He was an only child, very close to his father. Edward had been crying almost daily since then.

I was hesitant..."But... Yes," I thought, "let him experience it. Perhaps healing will come."

The children all agreed that Edward was to do it. Desks were pushed back. A table was placed in front of the room. The flowers were placed on the table. Edward went to the back of the room and announced that he would carry the coffin and the rest were to sing as he marched in. I was stunned to hear the children immediately begin chanting a funeral dirge in total rhythm. Where had they learned it?

As Edward placed the "coffin" by the flowers the children said to me, "Now you've got to say a prayer! You've got to be the minister!" "Oh my," I said to myself, "I think this is supposed to be against the law!" However, I did say a couple of sentences, giving thanks for the happiness we had had with Myrtle the Turtle. The children took it all very seriously, with occasional giggles of excitement and nervousness.

A spontaneous sharing began. The children shared about funerals they had attended, asking and giving answers to each other. One girl shared about how her cousin, a Black Panther, was killed in a shootout and how her aunt had thrown herself on the coffin. Another shared about her uncle being killed in a motorcycle accident. One shared about how a neighbor got mad and killed his wife and the family all went to the funeral. They talked about the music, about things the minister said, about the behavior of the people. I was surprised at how much the children had experienced about death. They learned that there were different types of funerals. I shared that funerals were a way people expressed their love as well as their grief. However, mostly I just sat and listened to their sharing with a minimum of direction.

Edward shared a little about his father's funeral. The class listened intently and lovingly every time a child shared. A sense of caring and acceptance for each other was present. Edward rarely cried the rest of the year. He began playing and laughing more. Something seemed to be released within him that day.

Generally children are quite curious about death. They are eager to talk about it. One day as I returned to class after attending a funeral a child asked, "Did you cry?" Another child said, "Don't ask that! It isn't nice."

I replied, "That's all right. Yes, I did cry. You know, there are many types of tears. Tears of sadness, tears of joy, tears of pain. My aunt died. I loved her very much, and I shall miss her. Mine were tears of sadness."

This triggered a lengthy and exciting discussion on death and tears. There was no judging of right or wrong, but simple sharing of feelings. The children's awareness had expanded to include acceptance of tears as a natural part of life.

PART VI

Adolescence

The Time of Letting Go

Adolescence is a period of excitement, conflict, anticipation, contradiction, drama, power, passion. We become aware of the multiplicity of our selves and become conscious of our very consciousness. We know that we have many true identities. "Show me your true face," goes the Zen koan, "the face you wore before your parents were born."

"Am I still a child?" I wondered at fourteen. "When does childhood end?" I mused at fifteen. At sixteen I knew for certain that I was a new sort of being, not a grown-up yet, perhaps, but never to be a child again. It was a time when I keenly felt the pull of both the spiritual and the secular within me. The radio played while I did my homework, I grew proficient with make-up and hair curlers, pursued boys in vain, loved the Beatles with a passion seldom experienced since.

I also wrote poetry and two novels, read all the children's books I had missed previously (*The Secret Garden*, the Narnia books), and with my friends Catherine and Jessica sagely discussed world affairs in the passionate manner of the young, cried over *Dr. Zhivago*, stayed up all night, despised the small-town goody-two-shoes mentality in our English class reading of *Our Town*, and yet was intensely affected by Thornton Wilder's question, "Is anyone ever truly aware of what it is to be alive, every minute of the day?"—"Saints, or poets, maybe." We weren't saints; therefore we must be poets.

If the first loss of the Garden's innocence comes with the socialization of schooling, adolescence brings the second loss. Altaira, the young woman in the science fiction film *Forbidden Planet*, who has grown up knowing no man but her father, is nearly torn apart by her pet tiger while she is in the arms of a male visitor, for the tiger's mistress no longer wears a child's guise. "He didn't recognize me," she mourns tearfully. "Why?"

Her first love can only respond, "Don't you know?"

In the first rush of growing up—here I refer to the girl's experience—childhood may be abandoned with a vigor. For a few years, poetry and magic remain buried in the closet along with the favorite dolls, who stare at us accusingly while they accumulate dust. Only to our closest friends will we confess the guilt we feel at neglecting our dolls, now that we are striving to turn ourselves into real Barbies (at least until we wise up). A boy has an even more difficult time retaining the miracle of childhood, for the "sensitive" boy is likely to be harassed and ridiculed by his classmates.

Faced with the sudden flood of superficiality, the clothes, the ubiquitous music, boys/girls, giggling, boasting, drawings of fast cars, and nowadays, alas, drugs and sex, parents may despair that all their efforts to instill spirituality into their children are being defeated by the mass culture. "My daughter used to love planning and participating in rituals with me," a mother lamented in *WomanSpirit* magazine, "and now she's thirteen and all she wants to do is listen to the radio." Wistfully a Pagan mother remarked to me, "My children were mine until they were twelve."

"Sometimes you can't tell about your influence," another mother observed to me. "Two days ago my sixteen-year-old son said, 'I've decided I'm no longer an atheist, I'm an agnostic.'"

One divorced mother I know discovered a novel way to handle adolescent rebellion: when her son was fourteen he wanted to live with his very conservative father in Texas. She gave her consent, and when her son returned to visit her for the summer, she was relieved to see him wearing an old Army jacket festooned with peace buttons!

It is a truism that young people will suddenly reject the ways of their parents and announce that they know their own minds and don't need to be preached at or brainwashed any further. This apparent rejection can bring great pain to the parent who is sincere in his or her spiritual beliefs. Yet in adolescence many people actually begin to explore the cosmic consciousness, though they may do so in ways that are not obviously spiritual— by keeping a journal, reading or writing poetry, composing songs, or becoming politically active. In fact it is at this time that a child's commitment to social and environmental justice can be put into action more effectively. Teenage boys, in particular, may become fascinated with science fiction, a time-honored way in which to question assumptions about the culture in which we live.

The creation of an identity becomes all-important. In adolescence girls will become extremely conscious of their self-image and will often drop names they bore in childhood: Victoria may decide to stop being Vicki and start using Tori, or a girl may adopt a new spelling of her name or an entirely new name. A boy may let it be known that he is to be called Bill from now on, not Billy.

At present our society does not provide for any genuinely sacred ritual observance of the transition from childhood to adulthood. Rather, the teenage years themselves are regarded as one long transition period, with various events taking place along the journey: the first menstrual period, the first bra, the first date, etc. Yet these are private occasions, not ones at which the blessings of God are publicly invoked in the presence of all of your friends, relations, and neighbors. Even the usual religious ceremonies of confirmation and Bar or Bat Mitzvah, while they technically mark the entrance into adulthood as far as the religious life is concerned, in reality have little or no effect on the child's daily life or position within society. In the societies that spiritual seekers tend to admire, notably tribal cultures, the tasks of life are quite simple, so that becoming an adult essentially means that now you can marry, or take your place in the council of adults, or perform heavier work, whereas in our society adulthood requires long years of training, experience, and education. No one would think of allowing a twelve- or fourteen-year-old boy to leave home and begin working to support himself or letting a fourteen- or fifteen-year-old girl marry, yet this was not at all uncommon several generations ago.

Even among tribal peoples who observe puberty rituals, young people will go through a period of wildness and adventuring, whether in daring, defiant behavior or rebellious thought. In some cultures, notably Native American and Australian, this is institutionalized in the vision quest, for boys at any rate, while in other societies the adults simply expect adolescents to sow their wild oats in whatever way is appropriate for their culture. Anthropologists who work among South American Indians notice that in some tribes the unmarried, post-pubescent girls suddenly become loud and saucy in contrast to the way adult women usually behave, while the boys may move to other villages or even journey a thousand miles away to Brasilia or Rio de Janeiro. In one village in which a friend of mine studied, some of the boys became particularly mischievous and destructive. "What can we do?" the fathers shrugged. "You just can't control them at this age."

Boys do need recognition of their emerging manhood, and not via aggressive, destructive customs such as getting drunk and exploiting women. Because male puberty is not so dramatically marked as is the female, some educators and spiritual thinkers are now working to restore the sacrality that coming into adulthood deserves, by leading young men in modern vision quests or devising other kinds of appropriate sacred rites for men to share. In his essay "Passage into Manhood," Steven Foster, who has done a great deal of work in this area, describes the need for sacred recognition of the Mother within a rite of passage for young men. He writes of the need for true spiritual recognition of manhood and offers suggestions on how to honor male puberty within the context of American society. The ritual he envisions is to take place directly after high school graduation, though it might be advisable to actually lead a boy through rites of passage at an earlier, more impressionable age, perhaps fourteen or fifteen.

In Foster's model for the rite of passage, the young initiate is guided by older men, but his relationship to the Goddess is not ignored. In many cultures, including our own, a male rite of passage often contains a ritual rejection and/or conquering of the feminine, whether it is cutting off a toddler's curls or taking a teenager to a prostitute, even though true psychic maturity cannot be attained unless both masculine and feminine are recognized and honored within the self. Ironically, in patriarchal society the boy whose destiny it is to love men has a far easier time accepting the feminine within.

Following Foster's essay, for those who want to experiment with ritual, Z Budapest reconstructs a young man's self-dedication to the Goddess from ancient Greek sources. A girl might also wish to dedicate herself to the Goddess, or the gods as she understands them, and this ritual can be adapted to that purpose.

Likewise, a girl may prefer an initiation that includes physical as well as psychological challenges, along the lines of the initiation ritual for young men. In fact, Steven Foster has led both girls and boys on wilderness vision quests. At a workshop I attended, Native American teacher OhShinnah Fastwolf described her own adolescent initiation, which included seclusion in an underground kiva and running up and down a mountain with her mouth full of water, which she had to accurately spit into holes along the mountain path as she ran. "The girls had the same initiation as the boys," she recalled, "but we had to do it twice."

In our mother's day menstruation was the Big Secret. Girls were often given no information about what was going to happen to their bodies, either from their mothers, older sisters, or doctors and nurses, and might have no idea what was wrong with them when they began to bleed. Back in 1927, my mother thought she was sick when she began to bleed, her two older sisters never having mentioned it to her. When she went to her mother, my grandmother said, "This will happen to you every month from now on. Come, I'll make you a sanitary belt." That was the extent of my mother's initiation.

In my generation our mothers may still have been embarrassed by the subject, but educators took the position that those old wives' tales, superstitions, and prejudices were to be swept away and a healthier, more rational approach should be taken to this inevitable bodily function. Menstruation was still a secret to be kept, but no longer something to be ashamed of. Now "feminine products" of a dizzying array are advertised on television, pre-menstrual syndrome is discussed on the evening news, and talk shows and women's magazines have become major sources of information on women's health and sexuality.

Menstruation was not something a mother often shared with her daughter when I was growing up. I was vaguely aware of my mother bleeding from time to time but she never told me anything about it and I never asked. By the time I was eleven and it was time for the ritual initiation into the mysteries of the blood-knowledge, she had already entered something called The Change of Life, an event which my parents regarded as exciting and interesting rather than distressing or hateful. My classmates and I—those of us who didn't have older sisters—learned about menstruation at Girl Scouts from a young male doctor.

Now, thankfully, Planned Parenthood sponsors mother-daughter retreats (as well as retreats for fathers and sons) during which a host of topics relevant to growing up can be discussed. These retreats are enormously popular, booked up two years in advance in some cities.

Some girls get angry when they hear about menstruation, this thing which will someday be imposed upon them whether they want it or not. They might well ask what is so wonderful about oceans of blood. My own reaction at eleven was, "It sounds like a goddamn nuisance." (I also swore I would never wear a bra.) Two years later I was practicing wearing sanitary napkins in anticipation of the big day. Don't be put off at your daughter's initial irritation or disgust—many women secretly feel that God must have had something else on her mind when she created women. The poet Judy Grahn has written about her own girl-hood anger at menstruation, how she felt imprisoned, tamed, defeated. If the truth be told, few of us look forward to the changes our bodies undergo throughout our lives, even if we intellectually accept the necessity and even the beauty of change and decay. Although we know that life itself is change, wilted flowers remain a sad sight; a child must be told she can no longer wear her favorite sweater because it's too small; a new mother struggles to accept the permanently altered shape of her breasts and stomach. A century ago a pubescent girl used to be described by the lovely expression "where the brook and river meet." We need to teach our daughters that change may be scary, but it is also exciting and beautiful.

It is said that women who live together in groups begin to menstruate together. It would be a wonderful, sacred thing if a young girl and her mother were to bleed together. The mother could also introduce the daughter to the sacred practice of temporary retreat at the onset of bleeding. Ironically, with more and more women not becoming mothers until they are past thirty, many girls will not get a chance to bleed with their mothers, as the mothers' blood cycles will come to an end before the daughters' begin. Such was the case in my family, since my mother went into menopause when I was ten, and as my daughter was also born when I was thirty-six, very likely it will be the same for me and Catherine.

On May 25, 1964 my bleeding began. I remember the dress I wore that day, and the excited, I've-got-a-secret grin on my face, for like pregnancy, I understood one's first period to be a secret, but a joyful one. I intended to keep it a secret from my mother forever. When my best friend told me she had gotten her period the month before, I shed tears of joy.

Menstruation may no longer be shameful, and probably few American girls are slapped by their mothers when they break the news of menarche (a custom among Mediterranean cultures), but a girl's first period is probably not something she would want her parents to go running around the neighborhood shouting about, as happens in societies in which the female puberty ritual is an important part of social and cultural life. My husband observed two such puberty rituals when he was working among the Nambiquara Indians of Brazil. A people who have survived on the fringes of several different cultural groups, including Western civilization, the Nambiquara traditionally followed a simple way of life, hunting and gardening. Compared with some other South American tribes, the ritual life of the Nambiquara is extremely sparse, but the most elaborate ritual marks the onset of female puberty.

"Miriam is bleeding!" shouts her father to the twenty or thirty other members of the village. Hastily a seclusion hut is thrown together from thatch, scrap lumber, whatever comes to hand, and Miriam is whisked inside where she will remain for a month, visited only by her mother and other women of the village. At the end of her seclusion, Miriam is led out of the hut by two men selected by her father who represent the people she might marry one day. The villagers sing as the girl emerges into their midst, feigning weakness and in a ritual attitude of bashfulness. She wears a crown of precious red feathers from the throat of the toucan and is painted with distinctive black dots.

Among many tribal peoples the moon hut is where the girl is taught the sacred and secret ways of womanhood by the older women. The only anthropologists who have worked with the Nambiquara have been men, and it would be improper for a man to ask the women what they discuss in the girl's seclusion hut, and so, for the time being, the secrets remain. No one has ever, to my knowledge, asked the Miriams what they think of the puberty ritual, but it seems to be rather like having Christmas held on your birthday: people from neighboring villages make a special visit, everyone sings and dances, dances and sings, all night long, or longer if the meat and drink hold out. The final song of the ceremony is, "Caterpillar awake, the dawn has come." Sadly, some of the Christian missionaries who have worked with the Nambiquara have been forbidding them to hold the puberty festival, the most important ritual they observe.

In simple, tribal societies, choices are few and so are corrupting temptations. There is not a vast difference between adult culture and children's culture, and so the transition from girlhood to womanhood is more easily marked by the dramatic events in a woman's maturation: first period, first experience of sexuality, marriage, motherhood. In our society, however, menstruation is merely one of several way stations on the road to adulthood: while it does happen to ten-year-olds who are still playing with dolls, it is more likely to hit a girl who has already been watching rock music videos, wearing fashionable clothes, and dancing with boys for several years. In those circumstances, menstruation is not the sudden shock that jolts a girl out of her comfortable identity that it once was. Thus the ways by which we mark this life transition may need to be more subtle and less dramatic than the rituals observed in simpler societies.

In this section I outline the elements of a menarche ritual, giving examples of liturgy and rites that have been performed at a number of ceremonies honoring first menstruation. Even if the time of menarche has already passed, a rite of honoring your daughter's coming womanhood can still be celebrated. At the end of this section Rochelle Wallace provides a very beautiful description of a coming-of-age rite she and a group of women enacted for a seventeen-year-old friend.

Parental assumptions of childish innocence are often colored by romantic, hazy memories of the way they remember their coming of age. Nowadays, however, such adolescent accouterments as pop music, MTV, and conspicuous consumption are to be found among children seven or eight years old, or even younger. Certainly the institution of the middle school, in which eleven-year-old sixth graders go to school with thirteen- and fourteen-year-old eighth graders, is partly responsible for this. Back in the sixties when middle schools began to be established, many of us fourteen-year-olds warned that exposing children of eleven to the corrupting influence of ninth-graders was a very poor idea. Over the years what is supposed to be teenage culture has slipped down the age brackets until a ten-year-old who occupies herself with fairy tales and dolls seems as rare as hen's teeth.

Perhaps most of all, the spiritual training of adolescents must be grounded in the study of ethics, rather than theology. Young people need to learn how their spiritual training can be applied to everyday problems. Even conventional Sunday schools tend to focus on moral issues during the teenage years—racism, economic justice, sexual expression, reproductive ethics, social responsibility.

For kids raised more or less according to New Age/earth religion precepts, the important task is to teach them that every action has an effect—that we do not live in a vacuum but all of our actions and political and social attitudes have consequences we must live with. Young people are rarely capable of perceiving the future or planning more than a year or two ahead—the future seldom means more than "Someday I'll go to college and then get a job and then get married and have children and then my life will be complete." For this reason adolescents are tempted to lead reckless lives, driving too fast, staying up too late, eating poorly, ignoring birth control, using drugs and alcohol, being convinced that accidents, pregnancy, or overdoses will never happen to them. A teenager finds it almost impossible to imagine being any older than, say, twenty-eight.

As for drug usage, things are of course very different than in our day. Many middle-class parents never laid eyes on drugs until they were in college—at the age of eleven or twelve we barely knew what drugs were, let alone had to struggle with classmates' pressures to experiment with them. Our own parents' and teachers' admonitions fell on deaf ears; grown-ups seemed to be

opposed to using mind-altering drugs because a) they were ille-
gal, and b) there must be something wrong with feeling that
good. At least parents who have used drugs themselves can speak
about it from a position of authority, not ignorance. We can take
our children over to our record collections and point out every
album that features a dead musician.

If we expect the Father-God of our youth to be tolerant and
understanding of our apostasy, our flirtations with atheism or
journeys into new realms of consciousness and the spiritual,
shouldn't we at least try to cultivate some tolerance of our children's foibles? Like as not they will probably remind us that they
need to make their own mistakes—not the mistakes we think
they will make, the ones we hope they will make, or the ones we
made ourselves.

To allow what is true and good in the child to unfold—to
allow the child to become the best possible Tom Wilson or Mary
Martinez—this is what is required of us. Kierkegaard wrote that
each of us arrives on earth with sealed orders from God. It is our
life's mission to discover what those sealed orders are. Our own
orders—not someone else's.

In the following essay, feminist writer Diane Mariechild and
her two sons, now in their twenties, reflect on how she brought
spirituality into their lives. Diane was at the forefront of the feminist spirituality movement in the seventies and was among the
first teachers to address the needs of children. Following her
account, seventeen-year-old Ed Copenhagen describes what has
stuck and what has fallen away in his own non-traditional spiritual upbringing.

Sharing a Spiritual Path with Adolescents

Diane Mariechild

Spiritual freedom is the freedom to develop oneself. The source of originality and creativity is the divine spark within every human being. It is this creative essence that we connect with when we embrace the spiritual dimension. My spirituality, my love of women, and my lesbianism are inseparable. The spiritual and emotional connections I have with women have empowered me to realize more of my creative potential. My lesbian feminist politics and my spiritual practice have the same goals: the revelation of our true inner beauty and the freedom from limiting thoughts and conditions.

To share a spiritual path with adolescents is quite challenging today. A few generations ago religious traditions were simply passed from generation to generation. If you were born into a Catholic family, you married into a Catholic family, and you died in a Catholic family. The lines that divided us culturally, religiously and racially were strongly enforced. Today, while fear and prejudice still operate, the races and cultures have become more intermixed. Space age travel and modern media have transformed the world into a global village.

We are moving from an age of aggression and warfare into the coming age of peace. For the peoples of the world to survive we must find a way both as individuals and as nations to celebrate our differences, resolve our conflicts and care for the planet to ensure fresh air and water for ourselves and the coming generations. The spiritual traditions which we share with our young people must have in common a foundation of non-harm and loving kindness. If we look at the volatile situation that has existed in the Middle East for thousands of years, we see major religious traditions at war with one another. We have used our different religious paths as weapons to persecute and destroy each other. The world today has many people who are not afraid to kill. We need more people who are not afraid to live fully: to be kind, to have self-respect, to share, to respect others. Spiritual structures, forms and rituals will change according to the person, the nation, the generation. It is the essence of our traditions— the love, generosity, and caretaking—that we must share with our growing children.

As a lesbian mother raising male children in the 1970s, I was often invisible. My then partner (also the mother of a young son) and I had to struggle to create new forms of family relationships. We were unable to rely on the structures, support systems and beliefs of the dominant culture, yet we were often able to identify and resolve questions that are taken for granted by many heterosexuals. Our lack of safe assumptions encouraged our freedom to investigate and create new forms, rituals and ways of being. Our children were not limited to one idea, form, or lifestyle. They had access to greater choices while they were growing up.

When I was an adolescent in the fifties, I received two strong messages: "Do unto others as you would have others do unto you" and "Actions speak louder than words." These simple maxims formed the philosophy by which my parents lived. In turn, they also became the foundation of the philosophy I shared with my sons. The form through which they were expressed looked very different.

My father, coming from generations of staunch German-Dutch Baptists, and my mother, a first-generation Italian Catholic, both left the churches of their childhood and together joined the local Lutheran Church. Here we attended Sunday School, sang in the choir and participated in many social activities. My parents had a very active faith, filled with generosity and caretaking. However, for my children, there was no corner church to join, no weekly catechism class to attend. My spirituality took the form of a daily meditation practice and frequent women's circles. I created an altar in my room with crystals and statues of goddesses. Once a month I gathered with my women friends to celebrate the full or new moons or the passing of the seasons. Through ritual we celebrated and affirmed the power of being women, our innate connections with nature, our ability to change, heal and transform.

Since my children were boys, they could not participate in woman-only rituals. What of my spiritual tradition did I pass to my sons? How did they feel growing up with women's rituals and meditation? In a recent conversation, we talked about their experience.

"I didn't always feel the affirmation and strength of maleness, being around so much woman-centered ritual," Mike volunteered. "The positive side of having a lesbian mother and being around so many women was that ultimately you do acquire some of their qualities."

While the form of my religious expression was created from my body, mind and spirit, the heart of the ritual was universal. What Jake and Mike could absorb was the sense of freedom to explore one's deepest truth. "Ritual is making physical what you feel or think. Art does the same thing, "commented Jake, a recent art school graduate. "The first year in the Icons and Images class we went out on the beach with Joan [their instructor]. She gave us each a rock, something of the Earth, and told us to keep it until we graduated, and then come back and return it to the Earth. I did that."

In sharing a spiritual path with adolescents our love, warmth and kindness is most important. We want to create a space where dialogue can occur. "You expressed very strongly what you believed and yet you always told us to find out for ourselves, to basically do what we felt in our own hearts was right," Mike said.

My spiritual practices have been important doorways to my heart and I trust that my sons will find their special doors. Jake remembered my encouraging him in his karate practice. "You told me that karate was a meditation: the breathing, the focus of the mind, the awareness of movement. In karate you were connected inside yourself and aware of what was happening all around you. You had to keep balanced."

Today my sons, who are now 23 and 20, are not outwardly interested in spirituality. They don't practice rituals, chant or meditate. Jake said, "I don't physically express my spirituality. I don't often do rituals. I haven't searched for a spiritual teacher to show me the way. I believe spirituality is something that comes from inside me. I grew up with it."

"You have to get away from your family to reflect on what it was like. When you're a kid you accept everything your mother says," Mike considers. "You didn't specifically say do it this way or meditate. I learned about spirituality because of who you were and what you did. It is something that is a part of me."

Jake agreed, "I didn't notice the messages coming in until I ran into something that contradicted them." For Jake, growing up, some of the differences centered around more freedom to choose clothing and hair styles as well as having more privacy in his own room. "Other parents would either clean their kid's room or tell them how it should be cleaned. My space was respected. I know I didn't always respect other people's things. I remember taking tools and not returning them."

Mike, too, remembered the hassles he encountered when he didn't respect other people's possessions. At the same time everyone knew the importance of sharing. Throughout the years there was often at least one other child, not a family member, living with us. Along with the permanent guests were the friends who often stayed the night or the week-end. "I remember once when I was around eleven or twelve and my friend and I were having a huge argument," recalled Mike. "You had us both come inside and sit at the kitchen table. Then you handed us a small piece of cedar and said we could only talk if we were holding the cedar. At first it was weird, then it worked. We were laughing. We really listened to each other and the fight was resolved."

To share a spiritual path with adolescents we must be disciplined in our own spiritual practice. This practice, more than the ritual of our choice, is the way we live. Are we kind and respectful? Do we create clear boundaries? It is that kindness and clarity that creates the space where truth can emerge. Without gentleness there is no room, therefore no growth, no freedom.

Freedom to develop oneself includes the freedom to be a sexual being. Sexuality is an emotionally charged issue for many people. Adolescence is a particularly sensitive time. Bodies are changing, desires are emerging. The freedom to love a partner of our choice, to express our sexuality whether woman to man, woman to woman or man to man is precious. To learn what is appropriate behavior is challenging in this changing world. There is enormous pressure to follow a heterosexual lifestyle, and the interactions between women and men are not free from power struggles and gender role expectations. As parents not always comfortable with our own sexuality and having our own prejudices, it can be confusing. Children are very sensitive; they absorb far more of being, our actions, than the words we say.

"I don't think it's just what you say, I think it is certain attitudes that you absorb. You always talked about being respectful to women and I think that is pretty important," Mike observed. "I don't think Jake and I are typical males, because of the way we were raised. I think no matter how you are raised it is difficult to be totally comfortable with your sexuality. We were raised to think that sex is good, something to be enjoyed, as long as people are not getting hurt by it."

Jake added, "When I got older I felt embarrassed about being thin. At home the body was portrayed as something to be valued, like the way you had some pictures [of nudes] in the house." While Jake did not remember any specific negative messages he received at home about the body or sexuality, he realized that at some point messages from outside the home had become stronger. "I knew I was more idealistic and romantic about sex, not that I thought you had to be married, or even in love, but I would never go out with someone just for sex. There had to be friendship and respect."

Parenting is a special commitment. To parent adolescents is demanding. To share our spiritual truths with young adults we can offer our open-mindedness and ability to be non-attached. There are so many distractions in the world today, and so much needless suffering. We can begin to transform this pain in simple ways by listening, and sharing who we are, and what is important to us, through kindness and caring about ourselves and others.

The spiritual path is a means to open the heart. The rituals and practices are only guides to the truth. They are not the truth. How do we share a spiritual path with young people? Mike says, "What my brother Jake taught me is this: learn to think before you speak and think about how your actions will affect those you care about. That's the simplest way I can define ethics."

One Kid's View

A Conversation with Ed Copenhagen

Recently I spoke with seventeen-year-old Ed Copenhagen, the son of Joel Copenhagen, whose article "A Child Plants a Seed" appeared in the section on "The Blossoming Soul." I had watched Ed mature from a quiet sixth-grader who helped out in the university library where his parents worked, to a soft-spoken, intellectually voracious teenager working part-time in bookstores and in animal shelters, writing a hundred-page term paper on Charlie Chaplin that made me long to see the films, applying all over the country to colleges. His parents, Joel and Julie, are deeply spiritual people whom I had long admired, finding the breadth of their interests impressive. The natural world, music, gardening, Ram Dass, Thoreau, Meher Baba—the list goes on and on. In fact it was Julie who introduced me to the writings of Thich Nhat Hanh.

While one teenager is a pretty small sample, I decided to take my chances and find out what if anything their son had retained from his parents' spiritual but not easily definable worldview. I well remember how full of life and ideas I was at seventeen—in some ways I was much like Ed, though my world, in the sixties, was very different. What follows is not necessarily "what today's young people think," but what one teenaged boy thought on one particular day. We spoke in the autumn of his senior year in high school.

I started out by asking, "How do you define your spirituality?"

He surprised me by promptly replying, "Jewish, at least by culture," although he had never gone to Hebrew school or been Bar Mitzvahed, and in fact when he was ten years old he had horrified his grandmother when he innocently asked, "What's a rabbi?"

"When I get to college I want to find out more about Judaism and Jewish history," he continued. "I'm also interested in the new Catholic reform movements. There's something very spiritual about cathedrals—the high ceilings, the echoes..."

"How would you describe your parents' spirituality? No easy task, I'm sure."

"I really can't describe my parents' spirituality because they don't actually talk about it. My father uses the teachings of Krishnamurti and reads Buddhist thought, my mother is influenced by Thoreau and the Transcendentalists. Sometimes I get into arguments with my father because I have a stronger faith in science than he does—he tends to use what I call tribal explanations for unexplained occurrences in the world. Sometimes when we all go hiking in the mountains my parents will see a face in a rock, and where I think it's an interesting occurrence, they see it as something cosmically significant."

"Having grown up in the country, on ten acres of woods fifteen miles from town, do you have any special feelings about nature?"

"I admire nature and know that everything originates *from* nature, but I wouldn't say I feel close to it, even though I've grown up in the country. My parents sense that more than I do—they're really into organic gardening and planting trees. To my parents, organic gardening is spiritual, but to me it's just a biologically sound idea. We just use different words for the same thing."

"Did you have any kind of spiritual upbringing? Did your parents teach you things?"

"They never taught me formally, but they used to read to me at bedtime about every other night. And we had a saying, 'Goodbye, good night, I love you.' That was how we said good night.

"I went to public school in a very conservative rural town until sixth grade, when I began going to the Alternative Community

School. For a while in second grade we were observing two minutes of silence in class every day, since we couldn't have formal prayer. At the time I didn't understand what it was for—I thought it was just two minutes to be quiet."

I remarked that school prayer was declared unconstitutional by the Supreme Court when I was twelve, and that at the time I thought it was much ado about nothing, adults arguing over our heads. "Do you think prayer should be allowed in school?"

Ed replied, "You don't need school to pray—prayer belongs in the home or the church. Two minutes of silence is one thing, but if the teacher is leading a formal prayer you'll always end up offending someone. Meditation classes would be more appropriate in college because then you can choose to do it. Like prayer, meditation should be a private thing, not something the school forces on you."

"Would you call yourself a religious or spiritual person, basically?"

"Reading books about propaganda have made me see the negative aspects of religion and probably explains my reluctance to call myself religious. But I'm interested in science fiction, especially books by Ursula LeGuin and Theodore Sturgeon, because it attempts to provide answers for things we all wonder about."

"Do you have any concept of God?"

"God as such is not very important to me, though I know that creation has to start somewhere. If there is a God it's neither sex and probably doesn't look like a human at all! Western religion makes God the most important thing in the world, as opposed to Hinduism and Buddhism where God is within everyone. That makes more sense to me."

"Are there any spiritual people or teachers who have influenced you?"

"I've been influenced by Gandhi and the Iroquois; most of the people I admire are historical figures rather than religious ones."

"Do you ever read the Bible? What do you think of it?"

"I have a hard time seeing the Bible as true—I think just the ideas are true. In tenth grade our Death and Dying class went to a synagogue where the rabbi talked about all the dead getting up from their graves when the Messiah returns, and even he said he didn't exactly believe that literally. And on another day Father Curran spoke in front of the class. [Charles Curran, whose liberal views on sexuality and moral issues caused him to be suspended as a professor of theology at the Catholic University of America, was a visiting professor at Cornell University in 1987-88.] He said that he doesn't take the Pope's words literally and that in religion you have to read behind the words. And when I watched the PBS series on Joseph Campbell [*The Power of Myth*], I realized that you can't interpret sacred scriptures as they are but have to see the meaning behind things."

"If you have children, what kind of spiritual upbringing would you want to give them, if any?"

"If I have children I would raise them in an open-minded way similar to the way I was raised—let them read books on different religions to give them a background in religion. If you don't do *anything*, they might choose something reactionary. My parents gave me so much choice that sometimes I felt left out, especially when I was thirteen and didn't have a Bar Mitzvah. Before seventh grade, when I was still going to public school, I wanted to be like everyone else and I was really mad that my friends were having Bar Mitzvahs and I wasn't given that opportunity. I still think about it sometimes—Joseph Campbell made me understand the importance of marking transitions in life."

"It's never too late," I assured him, "Henny Youngman was Bar Mitzvahed when he was seventy."

Celebrating the Driver's License

Anne Carson

Most people pass their driver's test while still in high school, though many get their license much later. Perhaps even more effectively than all the tragic films and the lectures given by the State Police, the importance of the driver's sense of self-reliance and responsibility can be emphasized by a ceremony held at home. The following ritual can be performed by anyone who gets her or his driver's license, regardless of age.

Time: The evening of the successful driver's test.
Setting: At home with the immediate family, perhaps sitting around the dining room table; close friends may also attend.

Parent: Today we are celebrating our daughter/son getting her/his driver's license. Everyone who can drive a car feels a new sense of freedom, mobility, and independence and these feelings are especially important to a young person who is taking the first steps towards leaving her parents' protection.

Child: With new privileges come new responsibilities. Being able to drive a car is a tremendous gift that literally opens new horizons for me. But like all powerful forces, if misused it can bring about tragedy. Cars have transformed society in the twentieth century; they are also the number one killer of people under forty-five.

[Here the family may remember and bless relatives, friends, or neighbors who have been killed or injured in traffic accidents, and may add a prayer for any recent victims read about in the news.]

Parent: It is not enough to be physically capable of operating an automobile; we have to keep our minds alert and clear.

[A contract between parents and child is produced. Similar contracts are promoted by the national organization SADD, Students Against Drunk Driving.]

Child: I promise not to drive when I am not in control of myself, either physically or emotionally. I promise that if I am away from home and am unable to drive safely or to be driven by a safe driver, I will call home for a ride, no matter what time it is.

Parent: And we promise that if we get that call we will come get you or make arrangements to get you safely home. We promise that we will not ask questions until we are home and can talk. And since we cannot ask of our child what we are not capable of doing ourselves, we pledge that if one of us is out and unable to drive, we will call home or take a cab.

[Parents and child sign the contract. The parents may wish to give the child a gift such as a new key chain or a new wallet for the license.]

Parent: We ask the divine powers to bless our child and her new independence, and to give her the wisdom to know her own limits, the courage to say no, and the knowledge that her family loves her.

Passage Into Manhood

Steven Foster

Modern American males possess few meaningful, ceremonial means of formally marking their passage from boyhood into manhood. What our culture does provide (high school "commencement", driver's license, the armed services, higher education, voting rights, drinking rights, employment, the age of 21, possible marriage and fatherhood) can hardly be said to comprise a coherent rite of passage. Now that nearly 50% of American marriages end in divorce, the father and mother must prepare their manchild for adulthood separately, in different homes, often with contradictory values. Sometimes the influence of the father on the upbringing of his son is negligible or nil. Sometimes the sexual passage, perhaps the single most important adult initiation, is ignored, avoided, or distorted by the parents. The young man is left to piece together the meaning of his sexuality with his peers and such cultural "aids" as the mass media.

In attempting to remedy this by designing a meaningful rite of passage into manhood, we must be aware that a modern passage rite does not contain the full social force of a traditional one. At the present time our culture does not validate or focus on such rites. For a modern passage ceremony to gain the full power of an ancient one, the very drift of our culture toward secular materialism would have to be diverted. The young would have to grow up knowing, even as little tads, that they were getting ready for their rite of passage into manhood. But given the reality of our culture, we can only start with what we have and work to create the best model possible under the circumstances.

The Components of an Adequate Model

Before describing a model rite in detail, I will mention a few key elements whose importance must be understood. The basic dynamic of a rite of passage is described by an anthropological formula that underlies all passage ceremonies. First depicted by Arnold van Gennep, this formula divides such rites into three phases: an end (severance from childhood), a middle (threshold) and a beginning (incorporation into manhood). In other words, a rite of passage begins with an ending and ends with a beginning.

The Heart of the Experience—The liminal (or threshold) phase, the central experience of the rite, is always performed in a secluded, wild zone, away from the encroachments of other humans. Within the sacred threshold enclosure, the boy becomes acquainted with his real Mother, symbolized by that part of himself known as the goddess. Through her, he senses his true place on earth and his true place in his body. She will show him the image of his own fear of death reflected in the natural world around him. The candidate's power place on Mother Earth will serve as both a womb and a tomb, a place of birth for the man and a place of death for the boy, in the mystery of the natural world. There he will learn the challenge of being a man, a son of the Mother, and a brother to all the things on the earth. He will emerge from the split husk of his childhood with the goddess at his right shoulder. The ritual birth of a man must take place here, in the wilderworld of his true home. It has always been so, and will always be. The boy must learn that his Mother cares for and rewards those who care for and respect her. He cannot learn this sitting in an enclosed room. He must leave the comfortable placenta of boyhood and enter the all-powerful world of the goddess. She visits with him in the winds; she shakes him in her fist of thunder. She blinds him with her lightning eyes. But mostly she blesses him with the birth of herself within him as his own eternal, internal guide.

Taboo and Trial—A rite of passage always includes one or more ordeals or trials. The boy's experience of the trial is the formal confirmation of his readiness to take on the role of manhood. Though threshold trial models are many and diverse, certain taboos or means of being tried are common to most. One is the trial of aloneness or solitude. The boy is denied the support and comfort of others and is left alone in a wild place for extended periods of time. With no one to go to, he is forced to deal with outward circumstances by discovering inner resources of strength and resolve. Without other human eyes to judge him, the candidate watches himself "be". Apart from the accouterments of his boyhood life, he learns what is essential to him— and what is not. The closed door of his heart opens to the beauty and mystery of the natural world around him. He becomes aware of and communicates with his natural relations, the other creature children of his Mother. Another restriction almost universally practiced is the prohibition of food. Among ceremonial tools, fasting is one of the oldest and finest. The candidate's psyche is opened to orchestration by the elements and rhythms of the natural world. Sunrise is his meat and noon is his wine. Although his physical strength wanes, another kind of strength gathers within him: the silent immovable strength of the great mountains. Without ballast in his belly, he orients himself to the harmony and proportion of his Mother, compensating for loss of strength by applying the muscle of spirit. The goddess rushes into the breach and teaches him about surrender. A man who does not know the power of surrender does not possess true power.

Male Midwives—One of the most important components in any model of an adequate rite of male passage is the presence of older men, or elders, who supervise and enrich the progress of the young men through the ceremonial birth canal. The older men help the younger men to bring themselves forth. They are not there to answer questions, but to ask them. They work to enable their charges to give birth to answers of their own, to know themselves. The midwives are exclusively male, because the time has come for the boys to become men, to live in, to respect, and to accept the men's world. A father must not be the principal midwife to his son, as the past often shadows them with too many habits for the father to be an effective teacher or the son an attentive learner.

Discipline and Work—The classic archetypal male is unaccustomed to self-indulgence. He has learned to accept hardship as his lot. He does not brag of his harsh life nor does he secretly hope his woman will pity him. This is the man's way. Any passage rite for men must include components of hard work and self-discipline. The candidates must be expected to be part of the group, to pull their own weight. Hence, the young men facing adulthood must be gathered together within a communal order where each has his work and does it, as part of the preparation for the passage. They must be expected to accept the discipline that communal living brings and to seek the joy that comes with the exercising of self-control and the intimate knowledge of the meaning of work.

Sexual Instruction—Sexual instruction and advice on marriage is traditionally a part of ceremonies of passage into manhood. The importance of a young man coming to understand and accept the power of his own sexuality cannot be underestimated. Any ceremony of passage into adulthood must take into account the young man's sexual growth and relationships with women (or men, if he is gay or bisexual). Open, honest, *adult* sexual education would seem necessary and appropriate. Supervised by wise, qualified male elders, such education might also include older women who can present the issue from the feminine point of view. Without the woman's input, the candidate's sexual education would only be half complete.

Giving Birth to the Goddess—All young men require an official introduction to the intuitive, psychic, and mysterious darkness of their inner beings. They need to learn how to surrender, how to listen closely to an inner voice, how to clarify their values, how to pray, how to seek vision, and how to prophesy. All young men must ask themselves such questions as: "To whom do I pray?" "Who are my sacred ancestors?" "What is my life story?" "Why was I born?" "Why will I die?" "Who are the true heroes and teachers of my life?" "What gifts have I been blessed with?" "Who are my people?" Above all, young men must confront and ponder the meaning of death. Time spent with death will make an inward space in them, and the goddess will be born and live within this death space. Her presence will enrich his appreciation of life and enable him to face the justice of his own death.

A Model for a Modern Rite of Passage

Applying these elements and more, I have created a model for a modern male rite of passage. What follows is a somewhat detailed description of that model.

The boys who are candidates for passage into manhood formally begin the severance phase one week after their graduation from high school. They leave their childhood homes and families behind and assemble with older men, elders and midwives of the community, at a retreat in a secluded, natural place. There they remain for nearly one month, or one cycle of the moon, during which time they enact the rite of passage into manhood. During the month in which they are gathered together, the young men are not allowed to leave. The area is sealed off and consecrated for the purpose of the rite. No drugs, alcohol, or nonparticipants are allowed.

Severance: The End of Boyhood—The severance phase lasts approximately 20 days. It ends when each initiate crosses the threshold and undertakes the ordeal of the second phase. During the time of preparation, the candidates and the older men live together in large tents or yurts in groups of 25 (20 candidates, 5 midwives). All work and cooking are be shared on a communal basis among the men. Each group is led through a disciplined routine of daily activities and classes by the five elders appointed for that purpose.

Throughout the ceremony, from end to beginning, each midwife is responsible for the welfare of four candidates. His role is to facilitate their passage through the three phases of the ceremony, to personify the Mentor function to them, to aid them in giving birth to the goddess. He acts as a surrogate uncle, teacher, counselor, wilderness guide, vocational guidance counselor, personal friend, or superior officer, according to what is needed at the moment. The curriculum for each group includes the following:

• Activities related to the natural environment and self-orientation within it: solo or group medicine walks, night hikes, environmental awareness studies, "survival" activities, and individual seclusion in a natural place at least once a day.

• Activities related to the use of the intuitive or "feeling" faculties: instruction in self-hypnosis, meditation, communication with other species, listening to the "inner voice", praying, and other "goddess" processes.

• Physical education with emphasis on cooperation, leadership, self-discipline, and consensus democracy: ropes and obstacle courses, relay races, and other activities involving group problem solving.

• Sexual education, from the mechanics of "how to" and contraception to broader issues of relationship, including marriage and fatherhood: films, other audio-visual aids, and frank discussions of ethics and manners involving women elders as co-facilitators.

• Spiritual education with emphasis on individual religious expression: personal values, ethics and morality, storytelling, myths, discussions regarding death, after-life, life destiny, and personal ancestry.

• Preparation on an individual basis for incorporation as a man: the setting of goals and priorities, vocational counseling, clarification of personal ambitions regarding profession, and other concrete particulars involving life on the physical plane as a man.

• Ceremonies of togetherness and preparation: saunas, sweatlodges, communal bathing, or activities involving self-purification.

• Activities relating to preparation for the threshold trial itself.

On the eve of the threshold trial, all the candidates and midwives assemble together, and a celebration of the end of boyhood is held. At that time, each candidate is given an opportunity to symbolically enact his severance from childhood. Then the individual groups of 20 reassemble with their midwives and embark on their several journeys to remote, secluded areas where the threshold trial will be enacted. The following morning, the trial begins.

Threshold: Passage Through the Goddess—Each candidate is removed from human contact. With just the barest essentials requisite to his survival, he lives alone in a wild, natural place for four days and nights. Though water will be provided during this time, he otherwise ingests neither food nor any other kind of sustenance, relying on the beneficence of Mother Earth to protect, nurture, and teach him. Depending on the advice of midwives, he may or may not undertake certain ceremonial activities during his time alone to heighten his receptivity to Nature, the goddess, and the spirits and deities he worships. But the basic elements of trial—aloneness, fasting, and exposure—must be preserved in as pure a state as possible.

The threshold trial must be designed with an eye to harmony and balance. The idea is not to make the candidate suffer unduly for the sake of a "vision". What really matters is whether or not each candidate stands ready, with a pure heart, to receive impressions from his experience. Within the limitation of his fast and his environment, each candidate should feel free to express himself as he desires, to investigate the many dimensions of his being as reflected by the natural setting. He may spend his time walking, sitting, meditating, sleeping, dreaming, praying, crying for a vision, writing in a journal, talking with the stones or the wind. Regardless of what he does, he will learn to yield, to be patient, to watch himself, to look within, to listen to the voice of the goddess.

The allegorical nature of the trial must be clear to each candidate. He is enacting a story with a mortal/immortal meaning whose main protagonist is both human and divine. The protagonist lives out the plot of the story in an environment having two levels of meaning. The goddess is both nature and his own anima. Fear is both a monster and an opportunity. A dream is both dream and divine visitation. Absence from the company of others is also presence with their spirits. Signs or messages appear in this natural/sacred world, carrying the same double meanings. An animal is both an animal and a spirit. A mountain is both a mountain and a god. A star is both a star and an angel.

A mosquito is both a nuisance and a messenger. A sunrise is both a sunrise and a birth.

The midwives should employ effective means to insure the safety of their charges while they are alone. A system of daily checks called the "buddy system", whereby their safety is ascertained (without their solitude being intruded upon) can be effectively used. Provision must also be made for the early return of candidates to basecamp, should they become ill, suffer accident, or otherwise be unable to continue their lonely vigils. The early return of a candidate, for whatever reason, must not be accounted shameful or a failure. Rather, he should be encouraged to come to an understanding of why he returned and what he learned from such an action. He must then be given another opportunity the following year to confirm his readiness by completing the passage.

Incorporation: The Birth of a Man—The incorporation of a boy into manhood is not without its difficulties. Birthing is accompanied by powerful contractions and much inner conflict. The new man meets and takes on the consequences of his boyhood life; he finds out whether or not he learned his lessons well. His return from the threshold is a delicate matter not to be treated lightly by the male elders. Now he is back in the "secular" world of his everyday body, and his life as a man stretches before him.

The confusion and bewilderment of the incorporation phase (especially in its initial stages) can be mitigated by the elders' careful, ceremonial attention to the re-entry process. Each candidate's spirit must be brought back into his body and aided to reside there solidly. Each candidate must be debriefed and helped to see the meaning of his threshold experience. Each must be formally welcomed and recognized as a man, brought into the group of men, and given a symbolic gift by the midwives. Then a sauna, sweatlodge, or bathing ceremony can be held, at which time the dust of the threshold world can be flushed from the new men's bodies and prayers said in thanksgiving for their well-being. After the ablutions might come new clothes befitting a man, a feast of thanksgiving, and a time of giving. Afterwards, a council of elders may be convened and the young men brought in one by one to answer the elders' questions regarding their threshold experience. The elders can offer comments and suggestions regarding each young man's future course, personal gifts, life story, etc., in a positive, supportive, manner. Within the first two days of their re-entry, the young men must also be given a good deal of time to be alone, to rest, and to reflect on their encounter with the goddess.

On the third day after their return, the separate groups reassemble for a mutual celebration of their brotherhood, to formally mark the conclusion of the rite of passage. Soon after, the gathering packs up and returns to the community. There, a final celebration of commencement into manhood is held for the new men and all those who had a hand in their childhood growth. The parents can be singled out for special honors for their untiring efforts on behalf of their sons and the community at large.

Beginning a New Life

When the ceremonies and congratulations are over, the new men enter the mainstream of adult male life. They live apart, independent of home, working for their bread, attending college, enlisting in the armed services, getting married, etc. They do not return to their boyhood living situations unless, for unusual reasons, they cannot do otherwise. If they must return to their old homes, they must henceforth be treated as adults, and adult behavior and attitudes must be expected from them. As the new men grow older and themselves become fathers, they will return to participate as midwives in the births of other men.

Within a week or two of the rite's conclusion, most of the candidates will experience a predictable depression, a period of integration when the enormity of the step taken becomes apparent. The new man may feel like forgetting about this manhood nonsense and wish fervently he could be back home in his childhood nest. Such feelings should not be seen as a setback, but as a challenge. For most new men, this depression strengthens their ability and resolve to live as men. Within a few weeks of their return, each group of candidates might plan a reunion meeting with their midwives to discuss progress in their new lives. Further support meetings might be scheduled by those in the group who feel a need for them. The emphasis in such meetings would be not on problem solving but on sharing, friendship, and brotherhood. As time passes, the new men should be weaned away from the glory and hoopla of the rite of passage ceremony and cleave to the goddess and to their "people", those who, as men, they are committed to serve with the give-away of their lives:

> *Now you belong to your greater mother. And you return to her womb to emerge once again, as a man who knows himself not as an individual but a unit of his tribe and a part of all life which ever surrounds him.*
>
> —Frank Waters,
> *The Man Who Killed the Deer*

Rite of Self-Dedication for Young Men

Z Budapest

[This ritual is for young men who wish to dedicate themselves to the two great archetypes of the forces of the nature, the Mother Goddess and the God of the Woods, often called Pan. In ancient Greece the Young God was known as the Kouros (plural "Kouretes"), which simply means "Youth."—Ed.]

Time: New Moon

Take a white candle and carve your name on it with something sharp, a rose thorn is traditional, but a clean nail, or personal pen will do. Take some aluminum foil and make a safe place on it for the white candle and the blessing incense. Pick a lovely flower that you see the force manifest in, and place it in the middle, representing the force.

Now anoint your candle with Protection oil [myrrh or rosemary oil will do], moving your hands always upward from the middle and not forgetting to anoint the two ends as well. Light blessing incense on the charcoal and when the air is filled with the smell and your mind cleared from fear say:

Appear, appear, whatso your shape or name
Oh mountain bull, snake of a hundred heads!
Lion of the Burning Flame! Oh force, Pan, beast, mystery,
   come!

Light your white candle now, saying:

Blessed be, thou creature of fire!

Watch the flame a while then say:

Happy am I, on the weary sea
Who has fled the tempest and won haven.
Happy, whoso has risen free

Above his striving! Happy I, with the Mother's blessing!
Take oil and anoint your forehead:

Blessed be my mind, to think of life!

Anoint your lips: Blessed be my lips, to speak of life!
Anoint your breast: Blessed be my breast, formed in strength
and beauty!
Anoint your genitals: Blessed be my genitals, to stimulate life!
Anoint your feet: Blessed be my feet, to walk in your path!

When you have performed this, let the candle finish all the
way down; you can burn more incense if you like, or you can save
it for other spells. Go home, it is done. Now you are a Kouros.

It is best to perform this in the woods or outside if you can
wrest some privacy for yourself.

Menarche

Anne Carson

> "On this day I proclaim an ancient mystery,
> Because all women live in consanguinity."
> —"Menstruation Ritual,"
> by Catherine Madsen

Rituals honoring first menstruation are found all over the world and are among the most ancient in human history, perhaps second only to death rites, yet they have been non-existent in Western culture until the advent of the women's spirituality movement. In generations past, a girl's sixteenth birthday was an unofficial coming into adulthood—she could now wear long skirts, put her hair up in a bun like grown up women, and might be given gifts of family jewelry. She was also considered marriageable. In tribal cultures the response to a girl's first blood is "Wonderful! Now you can marry and have children!" In an industrial society, on the other hand, marriage and children are expected to remain in the future for a decade or more after menstruation begins, and the mother's first thought is likely to be, "Oh, no! I hope she doesn't get pregnant!"

Twelve or thirteen is too young, realistically, to formally bestow upon your daughter the family jewelry that Grandmother has been setting aside for her. Perhaps instead the girl could be given permission to have her ears pierced, although so many prepubescent girls already have pierced ears that this may seem to your daughter to be a rather arbitrary privilege. Still, having pierced ears does require a certain amount of responsibility, not just in keeping track of earrings, but in taking care of the holes themselves, making sure that no infections occur. Menstruation, ear piercing, tattoos, all demand a responsible attitude toward one's body.

Many of today's mothers who have come to appreciate the sacred aspect of women's moon-times wish to honor their daughters in ways they were never honored themselves. For some time now women have been holding impromptu menarche ceremonies, each ritual being personalized and tailored to the interests and wishes of the mother and daughter, sometimes more to one than the other. There is no set liturgy or pattern, though the use of the color red is common: red clothes, red flowers, red ribbons, wine and juice, even red foods. The ceremony is joyous and heartfelt, and very likely the older women present derive more satisfaction from the ritual than the young girl, who may still be wrapped up in the culture of secrecy and giggles.

Mothers who have performed such rituals usually stress talking it over with the girl first, even though this implicitly gives her permission to be too embarrassed to want a ceremony. Unlike weddings, or the debutante and Sweet Sixteen parties of a generation ago, as yet we have no models for this kind of rite of passage. By the time a girl reaches womanhood she has had so many opportunities to observe weddings, either in real life or on television and film, or in books, that she is able to formulate some opinion of what she would like at her own wedding—or to decide that she will never go through such a charade. However she feels about weddings, she does have some idea of what to expect, as does a girl growing up in a tribal society in which every maiden is honored at first menstruation. Surely African girls daydream about the dances to be performed in their honor.

Over the last decade accounts of menstruation rituals have been published in a number of feminist periodicals and books; some of the proceedings below are gleaned from several of these, including Rosemary Ruether's *Women-Church*, but there is no set pattern—each ritual is unique, and perhaps that is as it should be. Here your daughter's input will be valuable. Start mentioning the possibility of a ritual or some sort of ceremony as soon as she learns about menstruation, which may be several years before it actually occurs. She may feel some embarrassment at having such a personal thing celebrated among women she may not know well, but she will ever after know that the rhythm of her body is a mirror of the sacred.

The Rite of First Blood

The proceedings should be women-only, but they do not necessarily need to be kept a secret from the girl's father and brothers—in feminist culture the ritual is a special ceremony held in the girl's honor, not, in all honesty, initiation into a secret society.

Grandmothers, aunts, and post-pubescent cousins may be invited, along with special friends of the mother and daughter. Inclusion of a guest should rest with the daughter.

Before the ceremony, the girl has a ritual bath, either communally with the other women as a swim or in a sweat lodge, or privately, with many lotions, bath gel, after-bath products made available as a means of loving and honoring the body. The message here is, "Your body is beautiful; it is not your enemy."

For the ritual the girl is adorned with a wreath of red flowers, whatever is in season, but rosebuds are a good choice. Other flowers may be included and their folkloric meanings explained, e.g. carnation pinks symbolizing women's love, white lilac for innocence, cinquefoil for maternal love.

The girl begins by saying, "Praised be Our Great Mother who has this day made me a woman. Praised be Our Great Mother who has made me in her image."

The mother takes juice or wine: "This is the mystery of our blood: we bleed yet remain whole."

Songs may be sung or played: "Menstruation Ritual" by Catherine Madsen, "Celebration for a Menarche" by Ruth Mountaingrove, "Testimony" by Ferron.

And since menstruation does have its drawbacks, you might wish to include a few humorous songs by feminist singers or monologues by feminist comediennes.

Each woman presents a gift with an accompanying explanation, as:

I give you a mirror that you may always see your beauty.
I give you a bracelet that you may know all life is one.
I give you an apple that you may be nourished.
I give you a journal that you may be alone with your
  thoughts.

A special gift from the mother may be given, such as a scarf or non-precious jewelry belonging to the girl's grandmother. With new status comes new responsibility: Gertrud Mueller Nelson gives her children a new privilege as well as a new duty on each birthday. For example, the girl could be given a clothing allowance or few if any restrictions on what she wears (some daughters hear "You're not going to wear *that*, are you?" long after they reach adulthood), along with instruction in and responsibility for laundering her own clothes.

In Rosemary Ruether's *Women-Church*, at a certain point in the ritual a baby or baby doll is given to the young woman, with these words: "You are now able to become a mother. But you are not yet ready to take responsibility for caring for another human life, a life that will be weak and dependent on you to feed it, wash it, clothe it, and teach it how to walk and talk and grow. You must be in control of this wonderful life-making power of your body: do not use it until you are ready to take responsibility for caring for another life; choose to use it when you decide that you are ready to become a mother. You are the decision maker."

Some mothers may wish to stress the *choice* that is involved in becoming a mother, for even in American culture, with all its freedoms and options, girls are still taught that motherhood is a necessary and inevitable part of adulthood, and most especially womanhood, thus casting scorn upon the women who cannot become mothers as well as upon those who choose not to. Girls should be taught that knowing how to care for a baby is an important life-skill but is not an inevitable part of their future.

In some spiritual traditions the parents bestow a secret, sacred name upon the child at birth or at its naming/dedication ceremony, to be revealed at the puberty ritual. In others, notably the Roman Catholic rite of confirmation, it is up to the girl or boy to select an additional name at the time of the ritual, a name to be kept in abeyance as a kind of alternate persona, a name with special spiritual significance.

The older women present may wish to have a time of sharing of experiences and knowledge about menstruation and the care of the body. The girl probably has heard the basics in school, but most likely her educators will not have provided holistic, feminist remedies for the discomforts of menstruation. Now is the time for women's wisdom to be shared.

For relief of cramps these two simple breathing exercises can be done. All the women present can breathe together:

1) This exercise can be done lying down, sitting, or standing: inhale deeply and slowly, expanding the stomach muscles— really force them out so you can see your stomach rise. Exhale slowly and strongly, silently if you wish or with a strong breathing sound, and as you do so draw the stomach muscles in. If you know some yoga, mool bund or root lock can be applied at the same time: draw in the navel and perineal muscles strongly.

2) For backache: crouch on the floor or bed on your knees with your head down and arms over your head. Breathe deeply and as you do so, arch your back like a cat's. Exhale and relax.

I have been doing these exercises since 1964 and have missed no more than three days of school or work due to cramps.

Raspberry leaf tea may be served, and while drinking it the women can share other remedies for monthly discomforts, such as ginger tea (1/4 teaspoon powdered ginger per cup of hot water), or taking 4-5 calcium tablets a day starting a week before the period is due. Assure your daughter that she does not have to suffer in silence.

The last part of the ritual may be begun indoors and then moved outside, or may be done in a large space outdoors: beginning with the daughter and then the mother, a ball of red yarn is passed around, each woman wrapping it around her wrist until all are connected by the thread in a single line. A woman says, "We are all your sisters in blood. The red river flows through all women, whatever their age, wherever they live, no matter who they are."

Still connected by the thread, the women begin running. If there are women present for whom running is difficult, you may start by walking, with these women at the end of the line. As you proceed, the woman at the end of the line snips the yarn with a small scissors, which she passes to the woman in front of her. Each woman cuts the yarn until the mother and daughter are running together. Finally the mother cuts the cord and the daughter runs on alone.

A party follows with food and merriment.

Initiation Into Womanhood

Rochelle Wallace

At the crossroads, ten women of the Svaha Lodge gather under a starry sky. We stand in ceremonial dress, each uniquely adorned in symbols of our personal journey on the spiritual dance of life. We have prepared ourselves for this female rite of passage, and we wait, alert and expectant. The signal will come from Judy, whose 17-year-old Scandinavian exchange student, Mette, has asked us for an initiation, a rite of passage, into womanhood.

Ceremonies are not new to us: we've incorporated ritual into our women's group to celebrate collective and personal transitions and transformations. But this one is special: I can see it in my sisters' faces. This is a rite of passage not only for our collective daughter, but for ourselves and, in some unexplainable way, for the women of the world. It is the initiation we yearn for in a time that is past: it is the healing for the deep, collective wound that cries for balm.

I think about that other way of experiencing time, the way that is not linear but circular. What we do tonight can release us from our angst of the past by moving the unconscious in ways that we will never know. But we do know that ceremony heals and empowers us, and we are ready now.

Some of us nervously giggle in anticipation: can you believe we're doing this? Yes, I can believe it, we nod to each other, knowing how crazy this would appear to some, yet knowing in our hearts how fundamentally sane it is. The drumming starts softly, ta-DA, ta-DA, a muffled heartbeat of the universe, and we begin a chant that one of us has written for the rite:

> *We bring our daughter*
> *We bring our daughter*
> *Our woman way*

Our woman way

Slowly, we begin walking down the rural road toward Judy's home, imagining the drumming and chanting subtly slipping into Mette's unconscious before she is alerted to our presence. Soon we are at the door; Judy, as Mette's symbolic mother, and Judith and Linda, her handmaidens for the evening, enter. Chanting, they move toward her room. She is sitting on her bed, and her blue eyes are wide; she has known only that the ceremony would take place within these last two days. Her eyes tell the three women that she wonders, now, what she has gotten herself into. But this is no wallflower, this young woman from a far-off place. Judy asks, "Mette, are you ready to embrace your womanhood?" Mette answers, "Yes."

The ceremonial blanket is wrapped around her shoulders, red diamonds on grey wool representing the red of menses, the red of the Mother's blood, the red of passion. Linda and Judith lead her from the room; they will be by her side throughout the evening, as helpers, as sisters, as midwives. The four join us at the door, still chanting, and we begin the gentle up-hill climb. I recall the Native American tradition of praying as if life depended on it ("Because it *does*," one Huichol shaman told me), of praying in the name of the wider community. Here is our daughter, and we know the weight of what we do. Dear Mette, we do this for you, for ourselves, for the world, I think as I chant. We do this sacred act that you, that we, that all people may live.

We climb into the van, a snug circle with Mette in the middle, and chant our way down the road about a mile to the Lodge. Leaving the outer world behind, we take off our shoes and enter this special, sacred place that has held us and nurtured us so gently over the last few years. Tonight, the room is filled with the scent of our earth's sacred herbs, of burning sage and cedar. Votives offer their warm glow to the rough wood walls, and branches of cherry blossoms form a lacy canopy of promise in the entrance. As we move into our customary circle, we breathe in the beauty of the room and of each other, and smile.

Judy steps to the center to open the ceremony with a blessing, a statement of our sacred intent. Though we often interweave masculine and feminine, tonight she calls upon the female powers of the four directions, the sky, the earth, and the moon. She lights some sage inside a large seashell—or tries to—and we giggle as it goes out; lighting the sage, and keeping it lit, has become a standing joke: who's got the magical touch this time? But finally it flames, then smolders as she blows out the flame. The smoke, the breath of the Great Spirit, the breath of life, rises as if it is indeed a spirit. Slowly, she walks around the circle with the shell of sage and a large feather, smudging each woman. Sage of the earth, bird of the air, embers of the fire, shell of the water: the elements join us. Some of us simply breathe the smoke: others gently fan it over our bodies in this ancient ritual of purification. We feel ourselves begin to move to a deeper level of reality. In this eclectic group of women, we mix traditions readily: Native American, Goddess, Christianity and more. By now we are rarely surprised at how well they work together. But tonight's rituals have been chosen with Mette in mind; some, we have created specifically for her; others have evolved as our experience has grown. We've done this intellectual work by preparing the evening in detail, always focusing on making it a positive but challenging experience for the young woman whom we're beginning to know and love. But I wonder how she will receive these goings on; might we unintentionally offend her? Frighten her? Judy has prepared her as best she can by sharing some of the things we do, but now it's time to let go, and simply do it with as great a love as we can find.

We sit on the floor and begin a series of culturally and religiously diverse chants and songs as we continue our deepening, accompanying ourselves with drums, rattles, bells and tambourines. We sing each chant for several minutes, aiming for that seven-minute length when the brain's neo-cortex lets go and the primal connections begin. I become aware of voices deepening and gaining power as the ancient parts of ourselves begin to stir. Now the sound comes from the solar plexus, the belly, not the throat. We are singing with our souls; we are singing women of Mother Earth; we are singing women of power and strength.

> Wise woman, woman wise
> Embers burning in your eyes
> Wise woman, woman wise
> Embers burning in ancient eyes.

When the chanting subsides, Judy asks Mette the initiatory questions: "As a woman, what do you wish to receive from this world? As a woman, what will you contribute to it?" She has prepared an answer which she speaks from her heart, and it touches us deeply. We respond with "amen," "ho," "blessed be," "may it always be so." Linda asks Mette for her giveaway, and she teaches us a lullaby in Danish. Suddenly I am struck by the paradox: we are birthing this woman, birthing her from childhood into womanhood. And she has provided the birthing song.

I recall the beauty of a story Linda's husband Rick told of their youngest son's unexpectedly quick birth at home: he spoke of how three-year-old Cody was distraught at Linda's cries of pain until Rick said, "Cody, there is no need to worry. Mama is singing Jesse into the world!" And Cody was satisfied and at peace. It was a birth our women's group shared, for we followed the ambulance to the birthing center to greet minutes-old Jesse, and held Linda in our arms as the midwife tended to her.

I look around the circle at the faces of these dear women, recalling the countless births, deaths, and rebirths we've shared: the birth of children, the birth of our selves; the death of one of our sisters, the death of our selves; the rebirth of Self. The distinction between literal and symbolic death and birth has blurred. Where, I wonder, is that clear delineation between literal and symbolic, of which I felt so certain not too many years ago? In this realm of a deeper reality, does it even exist? I am not so certain of anything now, except mystery, and grace, and the fact that we are indeed ceremonial beings, native beings, storied beings.

Linda's voice brings me back to the ceremony. "We wish Mette to enter womanhood with dreams," she says. "What are our dreams for her?" She invites Mette into the center of the circle, as we make ourselves comfortable around her. Linda uses her gift of storytelling to guide us on a meditative journey; once at our inner destination, we let images rise from the unconscious to tell us of our dreams for Mette. When we finish, we do not speak, but chant quietly as Carol and Sue leave to prepare the sweatlodge.

> *We are women who dream*
> *We are women who dare*
> *We are women who act*
> *We are women who care*

Ten minutes later, we walk the winding path, partly lit with candles, down the hill through the firs, bare feet on the damp, cool earth. "Eyes on the bottoms of our feet! Eyes on the bottoms of our feet!" I recall hearing from that celebrated ritualist Elizabeth Cogburn. How my feet can see when I let them!

The blazing fire that heats the rocks crackles and dances. The candle-lit outbuilding is cold, and we shiver in the silence as we fold our clothes and wrap ourselves in towels. Mette's handmaidens take her clothes and fold them gently, laying them in a basket with great care. They wrap the ceremonial blanket around her as if they were mothers tenderly swaddling their child. We begin to walk to the sweatlodge, with Mette nestled in the middle of the line. The grass is cold and wet; the fire illuminates the blankets covering the low dome of the sweatlodge. Struck by the variety of patterns on the blankets we've brought to help keep the heat in the lodge, I realize that they are as diverse as we are: age, religion, past experiences, careers, family, beliefs—we are all so different. Yet like the blankets, we come together to create a holy place of meaning, of living, of weaving our lives together like some kind of patchwork tapestry that warms us all.

We gather in front of the east-facing entrance to the sweatlodge, where I explain the practical aspects of the sweatlodge as minimally as I can. Then I say, "Prepare yourselves to enter this most female of holy places: the womb of Mother Earth. Here, we invoke the spirits, and the spirits come. Here we cleanse ourselves, we die and are reborn. Here, we pray, we sing, we stretch ourselves to endure the heat, dark and steam. Here, we offer our support and our dreams for Mette, and in doing so, we re-member, we re-vision our own entry into womanhood."

Sue steps forward to offer water to the four directions, the sky and the earth, pouring some upon the earth, asking that it purify us in this special sweat. She raises it to the new moon, the perfect symbol of new womanhood, in homage.

We enter the low door on our knees, moving counter-clockwise, the direction of the feminine in many cultures. The dim, earthy lodge is already hot from the pile of glowing rocks fire-tenders Carol and Sue have placed in the center hole, the navel of the Great Mother. Mette enters last, her handmaidens at each side. She sits by the door, the coolest place, though hot by any standard once the steam begins. Linda eases down the door canvas and blanket; suddenly all traces of reflected firelight are gone. The rocks no longer glow, and it is incredibly dark in this womb of our rebirth. We are about to take another step into the primal depths. Here, we return to our source, in the Great Mother, Mother Earth.

I check with Mette, then everyone else, to see how they're doing. Mette sounds good; I realize her experience with Scandinavian saunas has been helpful. Disembodied voices answer "okay," "fine," "good." There is a transitional silence, and I begin the sweat with a prayer: "Great Spirit, Mother Earth, Great Goddess, Mother/Father God, Eternal Mystery, Christ Spirit, Creator, Redeemer, Sustainer: by all names, by all aspects, we call you, the One True Thing, to be with us here tonight. Oh, Great Spirit, hear our voices: we speak in earnest; we speak from our hearts. Behold us, your daughters. Behold Mette, your daughter for whom we pray and sing tonight. Bring us your female power! Help us to own it, to love it, to share it. Help us to be loving channels for your spirit. We ask this, oh Great Feminine Face of God, that we and all people may live."

Carol pours water across the rocks; it sizzles and hisses as an unseen cloud of steam rises and moves outward toward us, blasting us with a wall of heat. We begin easy, but even so the heat takes our breath; there are groans as we adjust to our amniotic fluid. I find my voice and begin the Sumash Indian chant which calls the spirits to the sweatlodge, feeling the sound vibrate through me and around me as the others join in. I signal the end of the eight rounds with my rattle and begin the chant of the White Buffalo Woman, the female aspect of the Great Spirit in the Sioux Tradition.

For me, these Native sounds resonate with meaning and images; for others, English Christian hymns, Black spirituals, Hindu or Buddhist chants, '60s song refrains speak more meaningfully. After the opening chants, the women periodically offer songs from their own spiritual journeys. These are gifts, I think to myself, gifts to the Great Spirit in gratitude for blessings seen and unseen, known and unknown. These are gifts for Mette, too, given from our hearts and souls.

More water dances unseen on the rocks; as the heat grows, the sweat begins to pour off our bodies. We pass around water to drink, offering it with care and love to the woman next to us. Mette indicates that she's okay; one of our sisters who has difficulty with heat scrunches down to the ground to breathe cooler air. Although we know we can leave at any time, we all intend to stay. A few of us have been in excruciatingly hot sweats, and we know that the visions often come after the point at which we think we can no longer bear the heat and steam. But the intention tonight is to challenge us gently.

"What are our dreams for Mette?" I ask as the water comes full circle. We begin to share, one by one, describing the images that came to us as we journeyed in the Svaha Lodge. The dreams are rich, beautiful, touching, and sometimes funny. These are woman images, thick with meaning for us. Some of us cry at their poignancy, for they come from our souls and they speak of what we want for ourselves as well.

We begin to chant: "We are the flow, we are the ebb; we are the weaver, we are the web." I cannot see my sisters' faces, but their voices tell everything; I have never loved them more than now, though our love has been powerful, our bonding deep. Here we sit in this holy place, not even clothes to make us separate, marking our place on the spiral journey. Oh this sweet microcosm of our world! How deep and abiding is our weaving on this web of life.

We sing a favorite song, one which speaks of our hopes and dreams for ourselves, for Mette, and for each other:

By my life, be I spirit
By my heart, be I woman
By my eyes, be I open
By my hands, be I whole
By your life, be you spirit

By your heart, be you woman
By your eyes, be you open
By your hands, be you whole
By our lives, be we spirit
By our hearts, be we women
By our eyes, be we open
By our hands, be we whole*

As more water hisses on the rocks, I open the sweat to spontaneous prayers. They come from around the circle; prayers coming from open womanhearts. "Mother/Father God, may this be so for Mette." "Wakantanka, may this be so for us." "Jesus, hear our prayers." The intimacy of shared dreams speaks in our prayers. "Heart's desire, Thy will be done."

Somewhere in that inner place of knowing, we intuitively sense that Mette the child has moved into womanhood. Starting quietly, then building, we chant:

Strong woman, wise woman
Earth woman, sky woman

A final pouring of water on our sacred rocks, and we begin the last round of the sweat. "We welcome you to womanhood, Mette," I say, "now that you are a woman, you are our sister, and we offer you our stories." We begin to share our wisdom lesson of womanhood, and how we learned it. Wisdom from pain, wisdom from joy. "Wise woman, wise woman, embers burning in ancient eyes."

We sing Mette's lullaby, now our lullaby, as we draw the birthing sweat to a close, and finish with a group prayer of gratitude. Each prayer is different, each prayer is offered simultaneously, prayers naming children, husbands, lovers, friends, regions, countries, as we ask for blessings of our Mother/Father God for our interconnected web of life. The counterpoint of female voices is itself a benediction of sacred sound.

"Sisters, we are being birthed into the world as new women," I say. "Let us leave the womb." We crawl our on our knees and try to stand on the wobbly legs of newborns. We reach for jugs of ice cold water to wash the sweat away. The icy water is a shock, like a first breath in a new world. I fall to the ground, arms outstretched, to embrace the belly of Mother Earth. Later, we stand around the fire that burns like the fire inside us now. Great Spirit, we give deep and enduring thanks.

When the time is right, we return to the outbuilding to dress; Judith and Linda offer Mette beautiful new silk undergarments, then wrap her again in the ceremonial blanket. We walk up the hill to Svaha Lodge, where we dress her in her ceremonial costume, a gift to her from the women. She is adorned with symbols of life, symbols of womanhood, jewelry of feathers, beads, shells. We laugh and sing and talk, filled with joy at her joy, her beauty, her big, wide, open grin. Dee has brought food and drink; we begin singing and telling our stories.

We end the evening with a circle, arm in arm. I wonder how much time has passed; it feels like days, like years, like lifetimes, like minutes. We chant:

We are the old people
We are the new people
We are the same people
Deeper than before

The mysterious healing power of ceremony strikes me to the heart as tears flow down our faces: We have midwifed not only her, but ourselves and Everywoman.

Our daughter is a woman now, and our lives are different for it. Mette has gone through the rite of passage: the rite we never had, never held in our memory, and now do.

---

* From "Testimony" by Ferron

PART VII

Sharing Your Spirituality with Your Family

In her questioning and questing, the parent may seem like more of an adolescent than the child, and we are often called upon to explain and defend our beliefs and way of life. Children start out by accepting what is taught to them of religion, so most of the parent's apologia will be to the family of origin. If you have been following a non-traditional spiritual path for some time, you may have already encountered the reactions of your family. Their response may intensify when you plan to bring up your child more or less along the same lines. If you are able to explain your religious practices or spiritual beliefs to your parents—not always an easy task if you do not identify yourself as belonging to a particular group—the reaction might range from approval ("That's very interesting—I never thought of things that way before") to tolerance ("We all pray to the same God anyway") to ridicule ("Don't tell me you're one of those Shirley MacLaine flakes!") or outright rejection and horror ("Dear Lord, you've lost your soul to the Devil!" "We're saying a novena for your conversion") or complete uncomprehension ("Does that mean you don't believe in God?")

It is wise to tread carefully when revealing your spirituality to your family. Some families, of course, are more open-minded than others, for example if your parents are already vegetarians or Quakers they most likely will be more open to non-traditional paths as long as they see that you are serious about yours. Often the key is found in the character of their own spiritual practice— whether their faith is profound enough so that they can respect the beliefs of another seriously spiritual person, or conversely, if they attend church or temple largely for social or cultural reasons. It may not be any easier a task if your parents have never bothered much with religion or have been openly hostile to it— be ready for disgust or sneers ("You're rejecting reason—for this I sent you to college?") Readers who were brought up as Jews may face more intense pressure from parents or grandparents to preserve the family religion. One couple I know (he is Jewish and she is not) agreed to have a formal circumcision ceremony for their son, not because they practice any form of Judaism but because it meant so much to the husband's parents, who had escaped from a concentration camp during World War II and for whom keeping Judaism alive was very important.

By the time you have become parents yourselves you will know how much of your lifestyle and interior life you can confide to your own parents. For some, complete openness is possible; for others, it will be best to evade the subject altogether for the sake of family harmony. For most, a middle ground of tact and compromise will suffice. Just as people who have chosen not to be parents have to contend with their parents' disappointment when they realize that there will be no grandchildren—that one of their dreams will never be fulfilled—we cannot insist that our parents accept without dismay that there will be no baptisms, no bar mitzvahs, no First Communion parties in their future.

I never assumed I would raise my own children as Catholics, partly because I never expected to marry one, and in fact did not. For the first few years that I was dating, almost every other boyfriend I had was Jewish, so I began to think of ways to accommodate both faiths (actually, I was usually more interested in

Judaism than they were). By the time I finally became a mother, it was obvious that christening my child was out of the question—it would be hypocritical to enroll my infant in a religion neither my husband nor I was practicing. We hadn't informed my mother of this, however, so after the baby's birth she arrived at our house with the christening clothes. Whenever she mentioned baptism I mumbled and changed the subject. When at last she realized the baby was not going to be baptized, she became not angry but very concerned, as if we were doing something unusual, like home-schooling or bringing up our daughter as a vegetarian.

"What can I do?" she asked her local priest in desperation.

"You can do *nothing*," he said firmly.

Even if your family can perceive that you do have a spiritual life, it may be difficult for them to accept that it takes a form quite different from what they are familiar with. This is not so surprising if you are involved with one of the so-called "new religions," but Westerners also get nervous when a friend or family member becomes a member of an Asian religion—usually one of the Buddhist traditions, Sufism, or the Sikh religion. People who follow the devotional practices of any institutionalized religion naturally tend to adopt the customs of the people in whose lands the religion developed, with respect to such practices as setting up a home altar or shrine, chanting, burning incense, reciting certain prayers, or modifying diet or dress.

In the course of finding your spiritual identity, you or your partner may have taken a new name, or you might like to give your child a special name in honor of a spiritual teacher who has been an inspiration, the name of a favorite goddess, or a name from the natural world, in the tradition of Native Americans, but bear in mind that choosing a name from a different culture may make some friends and relatives uncomfortable. New grandparents who might otherwise smile (or sigh) at names like Forest or

Harmony may become genuinely alarmed at having a grand-child named Shiva, Devi, or Tsultrim. You might point out that you once had a Hebrew name, or chose an additional name for yourself at confirmation, and that you now wish to have a name that reflects your current spiritual commitment. And you can remind your relatives of the similarity between naming a child for a goddess or spiritual teacher and naming it for a saint or a deceased grandparent. Fortunately, unusual names are in vogue nowadays (so much so that some formerly unusual names are now quite common), so your family may not, in fact, be partic-ularly jarred by a new baby named Alta or Jamal.

If your relatives and friends look askance at your ritual prac-tices, it might be helpful to remind them that the transmission of culture works both ways—that Christian missionaries aren't the only spiritual directors who effect changes in their students' lifestyles. Americans and Europeans have always been pleased when converts from other cultures forsake flowing robes in favor of suits and dresses, wear their hair in Western styles or give their children English first names, but they seldom realize that cultural conversion can work in the opposite direction.

Pointing out parallels between your own spirituality and the religion you were born into is another non-threatening way to allay fears of an unknown culture and an unfamiliar philosophy. It also demonstrates that you have a solid understanding of your parents' religion, that you are not speaking in ignorance. Similarities between Buddhist and Christian philosophy, for example, are so numerous that there is currently a considerable amount of Buddhist-Christian dialogue, and some of the many recent books published on this subject may be of use to you.

Tact is of the essence when dealing with family members who still adhere to the religion of your childhood. Statements like, "I hated going to temple; it was boring and stupid," or

"Christianity has been responsible for more deaths than World War II," are not going to foster good relations at the Thanksgiving table. These things may be true! but if you are seeking acceptance of your own spirituality from your family, you must extend consideration to others. It doesn't hurt to describe your spirituality in the language of conventional religion. Stating that at times you become possessed by a spirit may be perfectly comprehensible to someone who understands shamanism or Afro-Caribbean religion, but it is apt to make a conservative Christian very nervous unless you describe it in terms of being filled with the Spirit as the prophets were inspired by God, or that "becoming the Goddess" is akin to becoming Christlike, as the priest represents Christ at the Last Supper.

It is also very important to reassure your family that your children are not being dragged into some cult against their will and that they are free to accept the religion of their grandparents. This latter prospect might not make us particularly pleased, but let us attempt to treat our children as we would have our parents treat us. If you wish, you might even suggest to your family that they are free to give your child books about mainstream religion, for cultural as well as spiritual enrichment. Bible stories, the life of a favorite saint or religious hero/heroine, the history of your parents' denomination, or some version of "A Child's New Testament" are all possibilities. However, you should make it clear to your relatives that the text and illustrations must not be prejudicial towards other religions. Most people would not deliberately give a child material that is anti-Semitic or racist, yet authors and illustrators of children's books about the Old Testament routinely and unthinkingly portray the polytheistic Canaanites, Babylonians, and Egyptians as inherently wicked and depraved peoples, completely obscuring their rich cultural and religious systems. It can be a challenge to find children's texts that are not judgmental towards non-Judeo-Christians, but with the hundreds of religious books for children available, it is not impossible.

If you are able to emphasize the loving, life-affirming aspects of your spiritual path—honoring Creation, prayer and meditation, maintaining a sense of joy and a powerful awareness of the Divine Presence—your family may worry less about the state of your children's souls.

Try using the language of diplomacy: say *ceremony* rather than "ritual". (This way I can tell my aunt that we had a blessing ceremony for our infant daughter under the auspices of a Dutch Reformed minister, leaving out the invocation to the four elements, the sprinkling of cornmeal, and the bestowal of a spirit name.) Say *prayer* rather than "magick" or "spell." What is prayer after all but a petition to the Divine or conversations with God? "I'll remember you in my prayers" is more easily understood than "I'll send you healing energy" or "I'll do healing magic for you."

When asked, "What church do you belong to?" you might respond, "We don't go to church, we worship at home." If you tend to frown and look at the ceiling when asked what your religion is, this might be the best response. If you actually identify yourself as belonging to a particular religion or spiritual philosophy, the question is easier to answer. "We worship God as manifest in creation" is more acceptable to a Christian than "We worship nature." If you do identify yourself as Neo-Pagan, unless you are going to be very up front with your family, using the word "pagan" tends to make people think that you are a) an atheist, b) a flake, c) joking. People who know nothing of Neo-Paganism, earth religion, or the Craft may better comprehend what you're up to if you compare your path to that of Native Americans or even the Druids. In any case, make it clear that you are serious about spirituality, that being "religious" is more than going to church or temple, and that if you don't attend services you are not perforce irreligious (many people have a hard time grasping this possibility). And know that you are not alone: I have known ordinary, church-going parents who became dreadfully upset when their children converted to Catholicism or became born-again Christians.

We must keep the door open: open that others may enter, and open that they may leave. Sometimes adolescence or young adulthood is the time when people adopt a spiritual path their parents think is repellent, whether it is fundamentalism or following this or that self-proclaimed guru. Much has been written on the reasons young people join so-called cults—and in reality what is meant by "cult" is any minority religion that inspires the practitioner to make radical changes in his or her lifestyle and which sets itself in opposition to the religion practiced by the family of origin. Possibly your family calls the religion you practice a cult, or would if they knew about it, since name-calling is a very convenient way of avoiding dialogue.

Instead of wringing our hands we ought to be asking what cults offer young people that the religion of their parents does not. Very often it is the experience of religious ecstasy, especially if their previous church experience has been sober, tame, and well-behaved. (It is doubtful that many Pentecostalists grew up in families who regularly made novenas, the Stations of the Cross, and the Nine First Fridays at St. Philomena's Church.) Often these young people are at an emotionally vulnerable point in their lives, when a sense of community is desperately longed for. Perhaps as they were growing up their family never got involved with the church or synagogue beyond regular services and Sunday school—or perhaps the primary focus of church attendance was social and not spiritual. If the children see their parents voluntarily and eagerly coming together with other adults for spiritual activities they may perhaps grow up with a stronger sense of community than the average semi-religious Christian or cultural Jew.

Joining a rigid religious group that tells its members what to do and how to do it is frequently the result of being in effect brought up with no religion—the result of parents saying lightly, "We'll let Susan decide for herself when she's older. We don't want to influence her." And when Susan becomes a Bible-thumping Christian who speaks in tongues and hates gay people, or gives away all her savings to a guru who rides in a limousine, the parents are furious and ask, "Where did we go wrong?"

Sometimes the opposite can happen: the child becomes deeply involved with the religion that the parent was raised in and rejected, to the utter dismay of the parents who had believed that the old religion was finished with. There are young adults who have become devout Catholics, and young Jews who refuse to dine at their parents' home because the kitchen is not kosher. This is what theologian Harvey Cox calls "the third generation phenomenon; that is, the children whose parents were trying to distance themselves from their ancestral religious traditions, whose grandparents were still to some extent involved in it. And now you see the grandchildren, who are often young adults, reclaiming it."[10] Once again, what is called for is a spirit of welcoming and tolerance.

Some thoughts on dealing with one's partner: sometimes one person has no interest in religion or spiritual matters and is even antagonistic to them. Traditionally, it is the mother who is spiritual while the father is either uninterested or believes himself to be above such foolishness. A few generations ago the rule of thumb was that one should have one's mother's religion and one's father's politics, but of all matters in which there may be a difference of opinion, spirituality is the one that can produce the most pain and the greatest rift between people, even between those who love each other. Here I address parents who follow different paths, and couples in which only one partner is interested in spirituality at all. One hopes that the non-spiritual partner will respect the other parent's interests and goals and not ridicule them at every turn. If they are not of one mind on the subject, the parents must agree to disagree, for it is not merely confusing, but destructive to a child to see her parents sneering at one another's endeavors. Likewise, the spiritual parent must try to respect the non-religious parent's wishes to be left alone. More than one marriage has broken up when one partner converted to another religion or found a new spiritual path and then hounded and badgered the other, until the beleaguered spouse was forced to preserve her or his autonomy by ending the relationship. I know of a successful marriage of nearly twenty years' duration that came to an end when the husband became a Buddhist and took up chanting. The wife had no objection either to the Buddhism or the chanting, but became alienated by the husband's insistence that This Was It, The Answer To Everything, and by his persistent attempts to convert her. She could no longer live in what was now an antagonistic relationship, and they were forced to separate.

I use the Tarot as a psychic/psychological symbol system, and have introduced my daughter to the Waite and Motherpeace decks. (At this point she is still operating under Sir Francis Bacon's dictum that some books are to be tasted.) My husband David, on the other hand, is not interested in the Tarot but prefers the I Ching, which he uses, with full ritual, for only the most serious decisions. When we were looking for a house and had to choose between two strong possibilities, we combined the two systems: he consulted the I Ching, I read the Tarot, and we compared our findings. (The hexagram for the house we finally purchased, number 14 [Ta Yü], "Great Possessions," now hangs on the living room wall.) This is an instance in which the differing belief systems of the parents were successfully combined. It is important that each partner respect the other's methods, for children are very sensitive to parents' attitudes and prejudices, and it is the mixed signals, not the differences in belief, that damages the child's worldview.

When parents belong to religions that insist on being The Eternal Truth for All—notably the monotheistic religions—any difference in faith and practice can become a serious point of contention, the assumption being that nonconformity will somehow confuse and harm the children. Even twenty years ago mixed Jewish-Christian couples were prohibited from adopting children. There was also a case about twenty years ago in which the husband was an atheist and the wife a pantheist. They were refused adoption of a child because, the judge contended, they would be denying the child his constitutional right to have a religion.

The contemporary seeker, on the other hand, recognizes that Truth is mutable and the Self evolves. We do not need to be ashamed of or embarrassed by former spiritual paths or lack of same, like born-again Christians who boast about how sinful they were before they found the Light (more damned than thou). Rather, we realize that with age and experience our needs and interests change, and that two people can have a harmonious relationship without sharing an identical set of beliefs. If the child wants to know, not unreasonably, why Daddy meditates and Mommy does not, or Mommy prays to Christ and Daddy does not, it can simply be explained that different people have different tastes, just as Mommy works in one occupation and Daddy another, and one parent takes tea with milk and sugar while the other doesn't.

As with dealing with other family members, a sense of humor and willingness not to take oneself too seriously are a must. I once remarked to David, "It's just as well you're such a rigid-minded rationalist. If you were as flaky as I am, little Catherine would be insufferable!" Sometimes all it takes are rituals in which playfulness and release of inhibitions are encouraged, in which it is safe to make a fool of oneself. Often this safety is the very definition of family. In any case, the best, time-honored way to convert is by example—by being a light that shines love and wisdom.

A child can bring even the happiest couple closer together, to heights of joy never dreamed of. A baby can also subtly drive a wedge between partners, the never-ending demands of a new infant leaving a parent—usually the mother—emotionally drained, as if she were given only a certain allotment of caring, with none left over for spouse, older children, or pets. Those of us who promised to stick together for better or worse must remember our promise. But admittedly, harmony in the home, providing a safe, emotionally secure, and loving environment for our children, is not always easy to maintain. Even a small baby can react with agitation and crying in response to tension between parents.

We must maintain awareness that how we interact with each other has a profound effect upon our children and the way they come to perceive the world, their relationships with other people, and the meaning of being male or female. Many parents think that if they have secure jobs, live in pleasant surroundings, take the kids to Little League and ballet lessons, and don't hit anybody that their mission as parents has been fulfilled. Sometimes we need only to look back upon our own families to become aware of how far a family relationship can fall from the ideal: we remember, not the pony we never got, but perhaps the lack of physical affection between our parents, or the snide remarks about in-laws, the failure of a father to help a working mother with the chores, or the father with no means of expressing his feelings about his work.

What is needed is twofold: awareness and compassion. Awareness of the moment, of our breath and the flow of life, awareness of our effect upon those around us; compassion for others' needs and compassion for our very fallible selves. We are on earth precisely because we are not perfect but are seeking to perfect ourselves and the world. Our instructions are to take a great boulder and polish it down to the pure point of light at its core. In sculpting the souls of our children, we continue to create our Selves.

"Your children are not your children," wrote Khalil Gibran in *The Prophet.* "They are the sons and daughters of Life's longing for itself...You are the bows from which your children as living arrows are sent forth."

Parenting is a journey that starts before a child's life begins and ends only with the death of the mother or father. Like life itself it is a journey whose destination is only dimly glimpsed and seldom turns out to be what we imagined.

With few exceptions, each contributor to this book has come to practice a spirituality quite different from the one he or she experienced in childhood, and some know that their quest is not yet over. Hence we bid our children to share in our spirituality, and teach them according to our beliefs, bearing in mind that their life paths will lead them into landscapes we have never seen. Patience, compassion, an open heart and mind—these are the qualities we must strive to maintain in ourselves.

May our children know that whatever road they take, they do not walk alone. May they have courage, and have strong minds to think with, and strong hearts to love with, strong hands to work with, and strong feet to travel with, and may they always come safely home to their own.

Notes

1. Thomas Armstrong, *The Radiant Child* (Wheaton, Ill.: Theosophical Publishing House, 1985), p. 133.

2. Examples of powerful birthing images might include Monica Sjoo's "God Giving Birth," reproduced in her book *The Ancient Religion of the Great Cosmic Mother of All* (Trondheim, Norway: Rainbow Press, 1981; revised as *The Great Cosmic Mother* and published by Harper and Row, 1987), the butterfly-yoni plates in Judy Chicago's *Dinner Party* (Garden City, N.Y.: Anchor Books, 1979), or her book *The Birth Project* (Garden City, N.Y.: Doubleday, 1985), though some women may feel the images in the latter book are too intense. Another excellent source of powerful female imagery is the "Art as Activism" issue of *Woman of Power* magazine (no. 3, 1987).

3. Starhawk, *Truth or Dare: Encounters with Power, Authority, and Magic* (San Francisco: Harper & Row, 1987), p. 297.

4. Rachel Carson, *The Sense of Wonder* (New York: Harper and Row, 1965), pp. 42-43.

5. Ibid, pp. 89-90.

6. Hallie Iglehart, *Womanspirit: A Guide to Women's Wisdom* (San Francisco: Harper & Row, 1981), p. 14.

7. Thomas Armstrong, *The Radiant Child*, pp. 130-131.

8. Dolores La Chappelle, *Earth Wisdom* (Los Angeles: Guild of Tutors Press, 1978), p. 130.

9. Dora Chaplin, *Children and Religion* (New York: Scribner's, 1948), pp. 67-68.

10. Harvey Cox, "PW Interviews," *Publishers Weekly*, Oct. 7, 1988, p. 97.

Selected Resources

Books and Periodicals

The Alternative Celebrations Catalogue, comp. by Milo Shannon-Thornberry. New York: The Pilgrim Press, 1982.

Armstrong, Thomas. *The Radiant Child.* Wheaton, Ill.: Theosophical Publishing House, 1985.

Berends, Polly Berrien. *Whole Child/Whole Parent.* New York: Harper's Magazine Press, 1975.

Betwixt & Between: Patterns of Masculine and Feminine Initiation. Ed. Louise Carus Mahdi, Steven Foster, and Meredith Little. La Salle, Ill.: Open Court, 1987.

Browder, Sue. *The New Age Baby Name Book.* New York: Workman, 1987.

Budapest, Z. *The Holy Book of Women's Mysteries.* Berkeley, CA: Wingbow Press, 1989.

Burmyn, Lynne, and Christina Baldwin. *Sun Signs for Kids: an Astrological Guide for Parents.* New York: Fawcett, 1988.

Carson, Rachel. *The Sense of Wonder.* New York: Harper and Row, 1965.

Church, Dawson. *Communing with the Spirit of Your Unborn Child: a Practical Guide to Intimate Communication with Your Unborn or Infant Child.* San Leandro, Calif.: Aslan Publishing, 1988.

Cloud, Kate, et al. *Watermelons Not War!: a Support Book for Parenting in the Nuclear Age.* Philadelphia: New Society Publishers, 1984.

Cohen, Kenneth K. *Imagine That! a Child's Guide to Yoga.* Illus. Joan Hyme. Santa Barbara: Santa Barbara Books, 1983.

Colmer, Michael. *The Stars and Your Baby: a Plain Guide to Astrological Parenthood.* Pode, England: Javelin, 1987.

Condon, Camy, and James McGinnis. *Helping Kids Care: Harmony-Building Activities for Home, Church and School.* Bloomington, Ind.: Meyer-Stone Books, 1988.

Corda, Murshida Vera. *Cradle of Heaven: Spiritual and Psychological Dimensions of Conception, Pregnancy, and Birth.* Lebanon Springs, N.Y.: Omega Press.

Cornell, Joseph Bharat. *Sharing Nature with Children: a Parents' and Teachers' Nature-Awareness Guidebook.* Nevada City, Calif: Ananda Publications, 1979.

Da Free John. *Look at the Sunlight on the Water: Educating Children for a Life of Self-Transcending Love and Happiness.* Clearlake, Calif: Dawn Horse Press, 1983.

Dillon, Mary, with Shinan Barclay. *Flowering Woman— Moontime for Kory: a Story of a Girl's Rite of Passage into Womanhood.* Illus. Elizabeth Manley. Sunlight Productions, Box 1300, Sedona, Ariz. 86336.

Ecumenical Task Force on Christian Education for World Peace. *Try This: Family Adventures Toward Shalom.* Nashville: Discipleship Resources, 1979.

Foster, Steven, with Meredith Little. *The Book of the Vision Quest: Personal Transformation in the Wilderness.* Spokane: Bear Tribe Publishers, 1980; Englewood Cliffs, N.J.: Prentice-Hall, 1987.

Fugitt, Eva D. *"He Hit Me Back First!": Creative Visualization Activities for Parenting and Teaching.* Rolling Hills Estates, Calif.: Jalmar Press, 1983.

Glas, Norbert, M.D. *Conception, Birth, and Early Childhood.* Hudson, N.Y.: Anthroposophic Press, 1983.

Glyn, Caroline. *The Unicorn Girl.* London: Victor Gollancz, 1966; New York: Coward-McCann, 1967.

Gross, Joy, and Karen Freifeld. *Raising Your Family Naturally.* Secaucus, N.J.: Lyle Stuart, Inc., 1988.

Halpern, Joshua. *Children of the Dawn: Visions of the New Family.* Box 5, Bodega, Calif. 94922: Only With Love Publications, 1986.

Hendricks, Gay. *The Family Centering Book: Awareness Activities the Whole Family Can Do Together.* Englewood Cliffs, N.J.: Prentice-Hall, 1979.

Hollander, Annette. *How to Help Your Child Have a Spiritual Life.* New York: Addison-Wesley Publishers, 1980.

James, Walene. *Handbook for Educating in the New Age: Based on the Edgar Cayce Readings.* Virginia Beach: A.R.E Press, 1977.

Jenkins, Peggy D. *Joyful Child: New Age Activities to Enhance Children's Joy.* New York: Dodd, Mead, 1988.

Johnson, Carolyn M. *Discovering Nature with Young People: an Annotated Bibliography and Selection Guide.* Westport, Conn.: Greenwood Press, 1987.

Kolkmeyer, Alexandra. *The Clear Red Stone: a Myth and the Meaning of Menstruation.* In Sight Press, 535 Cordova Rd., Suite 228, Santa Fe, New Mexico 87501.

Krieger, Dolores, Ph.D., R.N. *The Therapeutic Touch: How to Use Your Hands to Help or Heal.* Englewood Cliffs, N.J.: Prentice-Hall, 1979.

La Chappelle, Dolores. *Earth Wisdom.* Los Angeles: Guild of Tutors Press, 1978.

_____, and Janet Bourque. *Earth Festivals: Seasonal Celebrations for Everyone Young and Old.* Silverton, Col.: Finn Hill Arts, 1976.

Langford, Cricket. *Meditation for Little People.* Illus. by David Bethards, age 9. Marina Del Rey, Calif.: DeVorss & Co., 1975.

Lenz, Friedel. *Celebrating the Festivals with Children.* Hudson, N.Y.: Anthroposophic Press, 1986.

Mariechild, Diane. *Mother Wit: a Guide to Healing and Psychic Development.* Rev. edition. Freedom, CA : The Crossing Press, 1988.

McGinnis, James and Kathleen. *Parenting for Peace and Justice.* Maryknoll, N.Y.: Orbis Books, 1981.

Milicevic, Barbara. *Your Spiritual Child.* Marina Del Rey, Calif.: DeVorss, 1984.

Mothering Magazine. Box 8410, Santa Fe, NM 87504.

Murdock, Maureen. *Spinning Inward: Using Guided Imagery with Children.* Rev. ed. Boston: Shambhala Books, 1987.

Nelson, Gertrud Mueller. *To Dance With God: Family Ritual and Community Celebration.* New York: Paulist Press, 1986.

Nhat Hanh, Thich. *Being Peace.* Berkeley, Calif.: Parallax Press, 1987.

_____. *The Sun My Heart: from Mindfulness to Insight Contemplation.* Berkeley: Parallax Press, 1988.

Pearce, Joseph Chilton. *Magical Child: Rediscovering Nature's Plan for Our Children.* New York: Bantam, 1980.

Peifer, Jane Hoober. *Good Thoughts at Bedtime.* Scottdale, Pa.: Herald Press, 1985.

Perkins, Lee and Jim. *Healthier and Happier Children Through Bedtime Meditations and Stories* [book and cassette]. Virginia Beach: Association for Research Enlightenment, 1975.

Peterson, James W. *The Secret Life of Kids: an Exploration into Their Psychic Senses.* Wheaton, Ill.: Theosophical Publishing House, 1987.

Rozman, Deborah. *Meditating With Children: the Art of Concentrating and Centering.* Millbrae, Calif.: University of the Trees Press, 1976; cassette available from UTP Audio, Box 66, Boulder Creek, Calif., 95006.

_____. *Meditation for Children.* Millbrae, Calif.: Celestial Arts, 1976.

Ruether, Rosemary Radford. *Women-Church: Theology and Practice of Feminist Liturgical Communities.* San Francisco: Harper & Row, 1985.

Salter, Joan. *The Incarnating Child*. Stroud, Eng.: Hawthorn, 1987.

Smith, Judy Gattis. *Developing a Child's Spiritual Growth Through Sight, Sound, Taste, Touch and Smell*. Nashville: Abingdon Press, 1983.

Spiritual Community Guide: the New Consciousness Sourcebook [annual]. Box 1080, San Rafael, Calif. 94902. (Includes a listing of schools, pre-school through higher education.)

Spiritual Mothering Journal. Quarterly. 18350 Ross Ave., Sandy, OR 97055.

Stein, Robin. *Your Child's Numerology*. London: Futura, 1987.

Steiner, Rudolf. *The Education of the Child in the Light of Anthroposophy*. New York: Anthroposophical Press, 1965.

Strichartz, Naomi Richardson. *The Wisewoman*. Cranehill Press, 708 Comfort Road, Spencer, N.Y. 14883, 1986.

_____. *The Wisewoman's Sacred Wheel of the Year*. Spencer, N.Y.: Cranehill Press, 1988.

Tanous, Alex, and Katherine Fair Donnelly. *Understanding and Developing Your Child's Natural Psychic Abilities*. New York: Simon and Schuster/Fireside, 1988.

Thevenin, Tine. *The Family Bed: an Age Old Concept in Childrearing*. Minneapolis: Thevenin, 1976; Wayne, N.J.: Avery Pub. Group, 1987.

A Theosophical Guide for Parents. Ojai, Calif.: Parents Theosophical Research Group, 1981.

Vissell, Barry and Joyce. *Models of Love: the Parent-Child Journey*. Aptos, Calif: Ramira Publishing, 1986.

Records and Tapes

Abrahamse, Adele. *Through the Months in Song.* Cassette and songbook (Del Songs C-1).

Ballingham, Pamela. *Earth Mother Lullabies, vol. 1 and 2.* Cassettes (Earth Mother C-1 and C-2). Songs from many cultures, including Mesopotamian.

Carr, Rachel. *See and Be.* LP (Caedmon 1684) or cassette (Caedmon C-1684). Yoga and movement to music.

Ferron. *Testimony.* LP (Lucy 003) or cassette (Lucy C-003).

Madsen, Catherine, with the Greater Lansing Spinsters' Guild. *The Patience of Love* (Wormwood 001).

Mariechild, Diane, with Shuli Goodman. *Motherwit for Children.* Cassette (Aquila C-6).

Rea, Toria. *Starseed Stories.* Music by Anne Williams. Cassette (Medicine Song C-2).

Robinson, Kathleen. *A Child's Guide to Relaxation.* Cassette (Sonic Images C-1)

Sutphen, Trenna. *Exploring Your Senses.* Cassette (One to Grow On C-12009). Trenna has made a number of other story-tapes that teach children lessons in growing up such as honesty, accepting others, and accepting oneself.

Tickle Tune Typhoon. *Hug the Earth.* LP (Tickle Tune Typhoon 002) or cassette (Tickle Tune Typhoon C-002). Songs about ecology and nature.

Wilken, Arden. *Music for Children.* Cassette (New World C-407). New Age music, for day and night-time.

Sources for Songs:

For the Water Meditation on p. 174: two musical pieces set to the sound of waves are "Pisces" by Kay Gardner, on *Emerging* (Urania WWE 83), and "Tiamat" by Jana Runnalls on *Ancestral Dream* (Stroppy Cow C-1).

In the Menarche ritual: "Menstruation Ritual" by Catherine Madsen is on *The Patience of Love* (Wormwood 001); "Celebration for a Menarche" by Ruth Mountaingrove appears in the Spring 1977 issue of *WomanSpirit*; "Testimony" is on the album of the same name by Ferron (Lucy 003).

These tapes and records are available from Ladyslipper Distributors, Box 3130, Durham, N.C. 27705, or at women's bookstores.

Updated Resources

Books

Adler, Margot. "Vibrant, Juicy, Contemporary: why I am a U.U. Pagan," *World: the journal of the Unitarian Universalist Association*, Nov./Dec. 1996, p. 14-18.

Berends, Polly Berrien. *Gently Lead, or, How to Teach Your Children About God While Finding Out for Yourself.* New York: HarperCollins, 1991.

Carroll, David. *Spiritual Parenting.* New York: Paragon House, 1990.

Carson, Anne. *Goddesses and Wise Women: the literature of feminist spirituality, 1980-1992.* Freedom, CA: The Crossing Press, 1992. (Includes a section on alternative spiritual books for children.)

Childre, Doc Lew. *A Parenting Manual: heart hope for the family.* Boulder Creek, CA: Planetary Publications, 1996.

Chopra, Deepak. *The Seven Spiritual Laws for Parents: guiding your children to success and fulfillment.* New York: Harmony Books, 1997.

Coles, Robert. *The Spiritual Life of Children.* Boston: Houghton Mifflin, 1990.

Cornell, Joseph Bharat. *Sharing Nature With Children*. 20th anniversary edition, revised and expanded. Nevada City, CA: DAWN Publications, 1998.

Cortese, Saundra. *The Souls of Our Children: Lessons of love and guidance*. SF: HarperSanFrancisco, 1997.

Eastoak, Sandy, ed. *Dharma Family Treasures: sharing mindfulness with children*. Rev. edition. Berkeley: North Atlantic Books, 1997. (Buddhist)

Fay, Martha. *Do Children Need Religion? How parents today are thinking about the big questions*. New York: Pantheon, 1993.

Fitzpatrick, Jean Grasso. *Something More: Nurturing your child's spiritual growth*. New York: Viking, 1991.

Fuchs-Kreimer, Nancy. *Parenting as a Spiritual Journey: Deepening ordinary and extraordinary events into sacred occasions*. Woodstock, VT: Jewish Lights Pub., 1998 (first published as *Our Share of Night, Our Share of Morning*, by HarperSanFrancisco, 1996)

Gosline, Andrea Alban, et al., eds. *Mother's Nature: timeless wisdom for the journey into motherhood*. Berkeley, CA: Conari Press, 1999.

Hebblethwaite, Margaret. *Motherhood and God*. London: Chapman, 1984. (A candid reflection on a feminist Catholic mother's spiritual life.)

Hughes, K. Wind, and Linda Wolf. *Daughter of the Moon, Sisters of the Sun: Young women and mentors on the transition to womanhood*. Gabriola Island, BC ; Stony Point, CT: New Society Publishers, 1997. (Profiles and interviews with teenage girls and leading feminists, including Starhawk and Angela Davis.)

Johnson, Cait, and Maura D. Shaw. *Nurturing the Great Mother: A handbook of earth-honoring activities for parents and children*; foreword by Diane Mariechild. Rochester, VT: Destiny Books, 1995.

Kabat-Zinn, Myla and Jon. *Everyday Blessings: The inner work of mindful parenting.* New York: Hyperion, 1997

Linthorst, Ann Tremaine. *Mothering as a Spiritual Journey: Learning to let God nuture your children and yourself along with them.* New York: Crossroad, 1993.

McClure, Vimala. *The Tao of Motherhood.* Novato, CA: New World Library, 1997.

McGinnis, James and Kathleen. *Parenting for Peace and Justice: Ten years later.* Maryknoll, NY: Orbis Books, 1990.

Moore, Walker. *You Want to Pierce What? Getting a grip on today's family.* Tulsa: Albury, 1997; London: Marshall Pickering, 1998.

Natural Childhood: The first practical and holistic guide for parents of the developing child. John Thomson, general editor. New York: Simon and Schuster, 1994.

Noble, Vicki. *Down is Up for Aaron Eagle: A mother's spiritual journey with Down syndrome.* SF: HarperSanFrancisco, 1993. (Parenting a handicapped child, by a feminist healer, teacher, and creator of the Motherpeace Tarot deck.)

O'Gaea, Ashleen. *The Family Wicca Book: The Craft for parents & children.* St. Paul: Llewellyn, 1993. (Sensible advice and observations, with many rituals and activities.)

Parish, Ruth Ann. *Your Baby's First Year: Spiritual reflections on infant development.* Wheaton, Ill.: H. Shaw publishers, 1997. (Christian perspective.)

Prather, Hugh and Gayle. *Spiritual Parenting: A guide to understanding and nurturing the heart of your child.* New York: Harmony Books, 1996.

Rosman, Steven M. *Spiritual Parenting: A sourcebook for parents and teachers.* Wheaton, Ill.: Theosophical Publishing House, 1994.

Rozman, Deborah. *Meditating With Children: The art of concentrating and centering: a workbook on new educational methods using meditation.* Revised edition. Boulder Creek, CA: Planetary Publications, 1994.

Spangler, David. *Parent as Mystic, Mystic as Parent.* New York: Riverhead Books, 1998.

Starhawk, Diane Baker, and Anne Hill. *Circle Round: Raising children in Goddess traditions.* New York: Bantam Books, 1998.

Taylor, JoAnne. *Innocent Wisdom: Children as spiritual guides.* New York: Pilgrim Press, 1989.

Van Leeuwen, M., and J. Moeskops. *The Nature Corner: Celebrating the year's cycle with a seasonal tableau.* Edinburgh: Floris, 1990. (Instructions on creating little scenes illustrating the Wheel of the Year, based on the principles of Waldorf education; available in the U.S. via distributors of Waldorf/Anthroposophic literature.)

Yob, Iris M. *Keys to Interfaith Parenting.* Hauppage, NY: Barron's Educational Series, 1998.

Periodicals

The Compleat Mother: the magazine of pregnancy, birth and breastfeeding. Quarterly, 1985—. Kitchen Table Press, R.R.2, Orangeville, Ont. L9W 2Y9

New Moon: the magazine for girls and their dreams. Bimonthly, 1993—. Box 3587, Duluth, MN 55803.

New Moon Network (companion newsletter for parents of *New Moon* readers). 1993—.

Contributors

MARGOT ADLER is a reporter for National Public Radio, a priestess of Gardnerian Wicca, an active Unitarian, and the author of *Drawing Down the Moon: Witches, Druids, Goddesses-Worshippers and Other Pagans in America Today* (Beacon Press, 1986) and a memoir, *Heretic's heart: a journey through spirit & revolution* (Beacon Press, 1997.) At the age of 44 she became the delighted mother of a son.

AMBER K is a Wiccan High Priestess associated with Our Lady of the Woods, the Covenant of the Goddess, and the Re-formed Congregation of the Goddess, she has authored two books for Pagan children, *Pagan Kids' Activity Book* (Moonstone Publications, 1986), and, with Muriel Mizach Shemesh, *The Picture Book of Goddesses* (Nine Candles Publications, 1988; both books available from Our Lady of the Woods, Box 93, Mt. Horeb, WI 53572). Her latest book is *Covencraft: Witchcraft for three or more* (Llewellyn, 1998).

Z BUDAPEST is one of the founders of the feminist witchcraft movement. She is a priestess of the Dianic tradition, the mother of two grown sons, and lives in Oakland, California. Her rituals are from *The Holy Book of Women's Mysteries* (Wingbow Press, 1989). Her latest book is *Summoning the Fates.*

ED COPENHAGEN graduated from the Alternative Community School in Ithaca, N.Y. and Hampshire College, and works as a librarian.

JOEL COPENHAGEN has an M.A. in educational counseling and works at the Cornell University Libraries; for five years he was a full-time father to his son Ed. He writes that he has learned "spirituality through the Native American religions, Taoists, American Transcendentalists, and a sense of clarity from the insights of Krishnamurti." His focus is "love of mountains, music, trees and sun."

JOSEPH BHARAT CORNELL is a nature educator whose handbook *Sharing Nature with Children* has sold hundred of thousands of copies worldwide. His books have been translated into Spanish, German, and Chinese.

STEPHANIE DEMETRAKOPOULOS (now Stephanie Gauper) is professor of women's studies at Western Michigan University. She has published many articles on literature, women, and spirituality.

GAIL FAIRFIELD has been parenting almost all of her life, as the eldest of four children, as an elementary school teacher, and as the co-parent of a daughter. She is the author of *Choice Centered Tarot* (Newcastle Publishing Co., 1985), *Choice Centered Astrology* (Samuel Weiser, 1998), and *Inspiration Tarot: a guidebook to understanding and creating your own Tarot deck* (Weiser, 1991). She is a professional astrologer in Indiana.

STEVEN FOSTER has been working with modern rites of passage and vision quests for many years. With his wife Meredith Little he has directed the School of Lost Borders in Big Pine, California, where teenagers and adults are led through wilderness quests based on shamanic and other ancient traditions. He is the author of *The Book of the Vision Quest, The Sacred Mountain, The Roaring of the Sacred River, Wilderness Vision Questing and the Four Shields of Human Nature,* and other books. He and Meredith have three children.

EVA D. FUGITT is an educator whose work is based on the psychological and educational techniques of Psychosynthesis. She taught in the inner-city schools in Los Angeles, using exercises and meditations that allowed troubled children to find the wise teacher within.

REV. JIYU KENNETT, ROSHI was abbess of the Shasta Abbey in Mt. Shasta, California. Born in England, she received her Buddhist training in Japan. Her books include *The Wild, White Goose: the Diary of a Zen Trainee* (Mt. Shasta: Shasta Abbey, 1977-78) and *Zen Is Eternal Life* (Emeryville, Cal.: Dharma Publishers, 1976), and she was profiled in *Meetings with Remarkable Women: Buddhist Teachers in America*, by Leonore Friedman (Boston: Shambhala Publications, 1987). Kennett Roshi died in 1996.

RENÉ KNIGHT-WEILER is co-editor of *Spiritual Mothering Journal*. A practitioner of the Baha'i faith, she lives in Washington State with her husband Bill and three children.

DIANE MARIECHILD is a feminist teacher and counselor and the mother of two grown sons. She is the author of *Mother Wit: a Feminist Guide to Psychic Development* (rev. edition 1988), which is both a cornerstone of the feminist spirituality movement and one of the most popular New Age titles, as well as *The Inner Dance: a Guide to Spiritual and Psychic Unfolding* (The Crossing Press, 1987), and *Open Mind: Women's Daily Inspiration for Becoming Mindful* (HarperSanFrancisco, 1995).

THICH NHAT HANH is a Zen master, teacher, and poet who was one of the leaders of the Buddhist peace movement during the Vietnam War, a candidate for the Nobel Peace Prize, and a friend of Thomas Merton and Daniel Berrigan. He now lives in France. He has written many books on Buddhist meditation and the struggles of the Vietnamese people, including *Being Peace, The Miracle of Mindfulness, A Guide to Walking Meditation,* and *The Sun My Heart.* English translations of his works are available from Parallax Press of Berkeley, California.

DAVID PRICE spent his childhood in Irvington, New Jersey and his teenage years in Vermont. He was an anthropologist, editor, and author. David lived with his wife Anne Carson in Ithaca, New York. He passed away in April of 1999.

DEBORAH ROZMAN, PhD, is a psychologist who has taught meditation to children for many years. She is contributing editor to *A Parenting Manual: heart hope for the family,* by Doc Lew Childre, and co-founder of the non-profit HeartMath Institute.

JOHN-AMBARISA MENDELL SHIELDS, a PhD candidate in clinical psychology at the California School of Professional Psychology in Alameda, has been a member of the International Society for Krishna Consciousness and a consultant to their Board of Education for children.

KAREY SOLOMON is a journalist, a needlework designer, and the mother of a college-student daughter, Janna. She is completing a book about parenting, told in part from the perspective of children raised in alternative spiritual traditions.

NAOMI RICHARDSON STRICHARTZ, formerly a dancer with the Ballet Russe de Monte Carlo, is a writer, dance teacher, and sculptor who lives in Danby, New York. She is the mother of a grown daughter and son.

ROCHELLE WALLACE lives near Seattle, She described the Svaha Lodge, which conducted the initiation ritual recounted in her article, as "an eclectic, non-structured spiritual community that explores ways to empower the individual for the benefit of the planet."

About the Author

Anne Carson was born in New York City in 1950 and grew up in Tenafly, New Jersey. A Catholic before coming to feminist spirituality, she has master's degrees in mediaeval history and library science. She lives with her daughter Catherine in Ithaca, New York, where she is a librarian at Cornell University. She is the author of two annotated bibliographies on women and religion—*Feminist Spirituality and the Feminine Divine* (The Crossing Press, 1986) and *Goddesses and Wise Women* (The Crossing Press, 1992), has completed a biography of the writer Caroline Glyn, and contributes articles and book reviews to feminist periodicals. She is an oblate of the Order of St. Benedict and performs with Mirage, a troupe of belly dancers.

Index

BOOKS BY THE CROSSING PRESS

Changing the World One Relationship at a Time: *Focused listening for Mutual Support and Empowerment*
By Sheryl Karas

Could you use some support so that you can go after the life of your dreams? Changing the World One Relationship at a Time will provide you with the information, skills, and practice you need to arrive at a more joyous life.

$10.95 • Paper • ISBN 0-89594-945-8

Clear Mind, Open Heart: *Healing Yourself, Your Relationships and the Planet*
By Eddie and Debbie Shapiro

The Shapiros offer an uplifting, inspiring, and deeply sensitive approach to healing through spiritual awareness. Includes practical exercises and techniques to help us all in making our own journey.

$16.95 • Paper • ISBN 0-89594-917-2

Fundamentals of Tibetan Buddhism
By Rebecca McClen Novick

This book explores the history, philosophy, and practice of Tibetan Buddhism. Novick's concise history and explanation of Buddhism teachings help us understand Tibetan Buddhism as a way of experiencing the world, more than as a religion or philosophy.

$10.95 • ISBN 0-89594-953-9

Fundamentals of Jewish Mysticism and Kabbalah
By Ron H. Feldman

The Hebrew word *Kabbalah* means "that which is received" and refers to a broad range of Jewish mystical traditions and texts which have come down to us over the centuries. This book will open a door for you into the hidden courtyard of the Kabbalah, and those of you who enter will find a community with whom you can practice and learn.

$10.95 • ISBN 1-58091-049-1

Healthy Parents, Better Babies: *A Couple's Guide to Natural Preconception*
Francesca Naish and Janette Roberts

This book is an easy-to-follow guide to optimal health for both perspective parents. It will give you important information while it's still time to make a difference in your baby's health.

$18.95 • ISBN 0-89594-955-5

BOOKS BY THE CROSSING PRESS

It's Not Fair!

By Dominique Jolin

"It's not fair!" a little girl complains to her father, who listens patiently and in the end points out the one thing she has that no one else has-him! Sure to make both children and parents smile.

$12.95 • ISBN 0-89594-780-3

Peace Within the Stillness: *Relaxation & Meditation for True Happiness*

By Eddie and Debbie Shapiro

Meditation teachers Eddie and Debbie Shapiro teach a simple, ancient practice which will enable you to release even deeper levels of inner stress and tension. Once you truly relax, you will enter the quiet mind and experience the profound, joyful, and healing energy of meditation.

$14.95 • Paper • ISBN 0-89594-926-1

Shamanism as a Spiritual Practice for Daily Life

By Tom Cowan

This inspirational book blends elements of shamanism with inherited traditions and contemporary religious commitments. "An inspiring spiritual call."-Booklist

$16.95 • Paper • ISBN 0-89594-838-9

Walk When the Moon is Full

By Frances Hamerstrom; Illustrations by Robert Katona

"An unusual offering for parents in search of ways to share nature with their children. Careful black-and-white drawings match the hushed mood of the moonlit walks."-Booklist

$6.95 • Paper • ISBN 0-912278-84-6

To receive a current catalog from The Crossing Press please call toll-free, 800.777.1048.
www.crossingpress.com